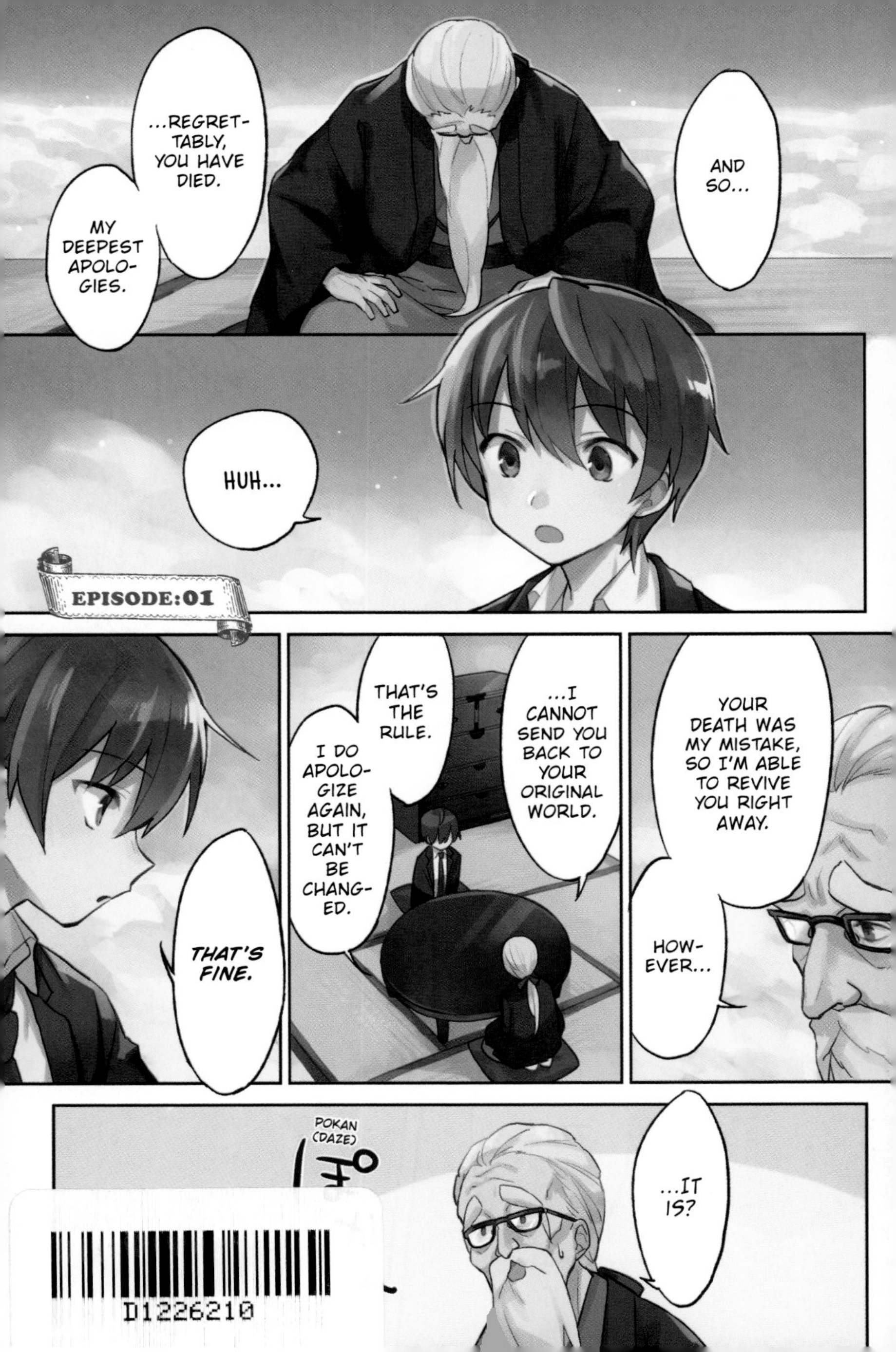
AND SO...
...REGRET-TABLY, YOU HAVE DIED.
MY DEEPEST APOLO-GIES.
HUH...
EPISODE:01
YOUR DEATH WAS MY MISTAKE, SO I'M ABLE TO REVIVE YOU RIGHT AWAY.
HOW-EVER...
...I CANNOT SEND YOU BACK TO YOUR ORIGINAL WORLD.
THAT'S THE RULE.
I DO APOLO-GIZE AGAIN, BUT IT CAN'T BE CHANG-ED.
THAT'S FINE.
...IT IS?
POKAN (DAZE)

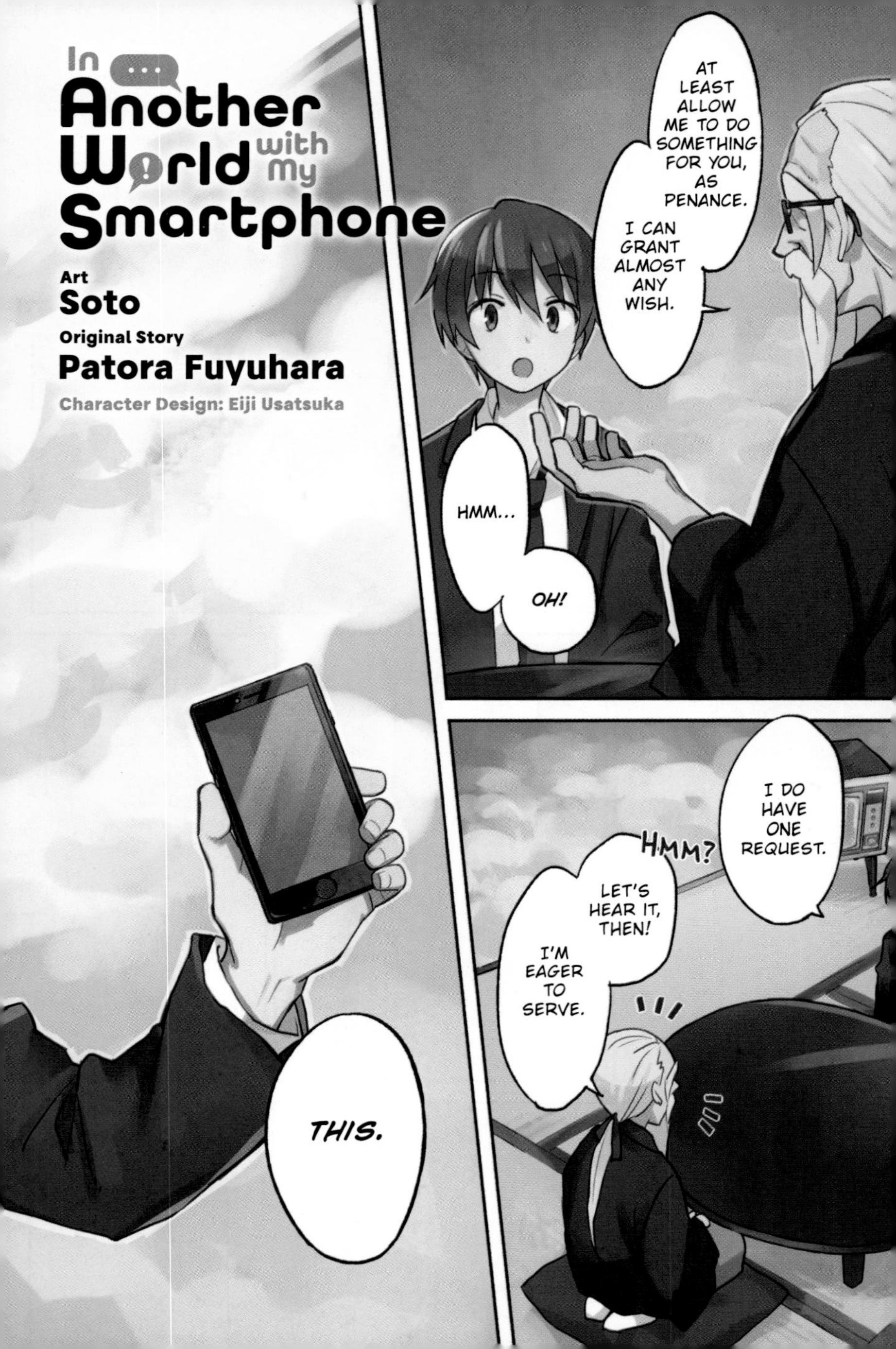
AT LEAST ALLOW ME TO DO SOMETHING FOR YOU, AS PENANCE.
I CAN GRANT ALMOST ANY WISH.
HMM...
OH!
I DO HAVE ONE REQUEST.
HMM?
LET'S HEAR IT, THEN!
I'M EAGER TO SERVE.
In Another World with My Smartphone
Art
Soto
Original Story
Patora Fuyuhara
Character Design: Eiji Usatsuka
THIS.

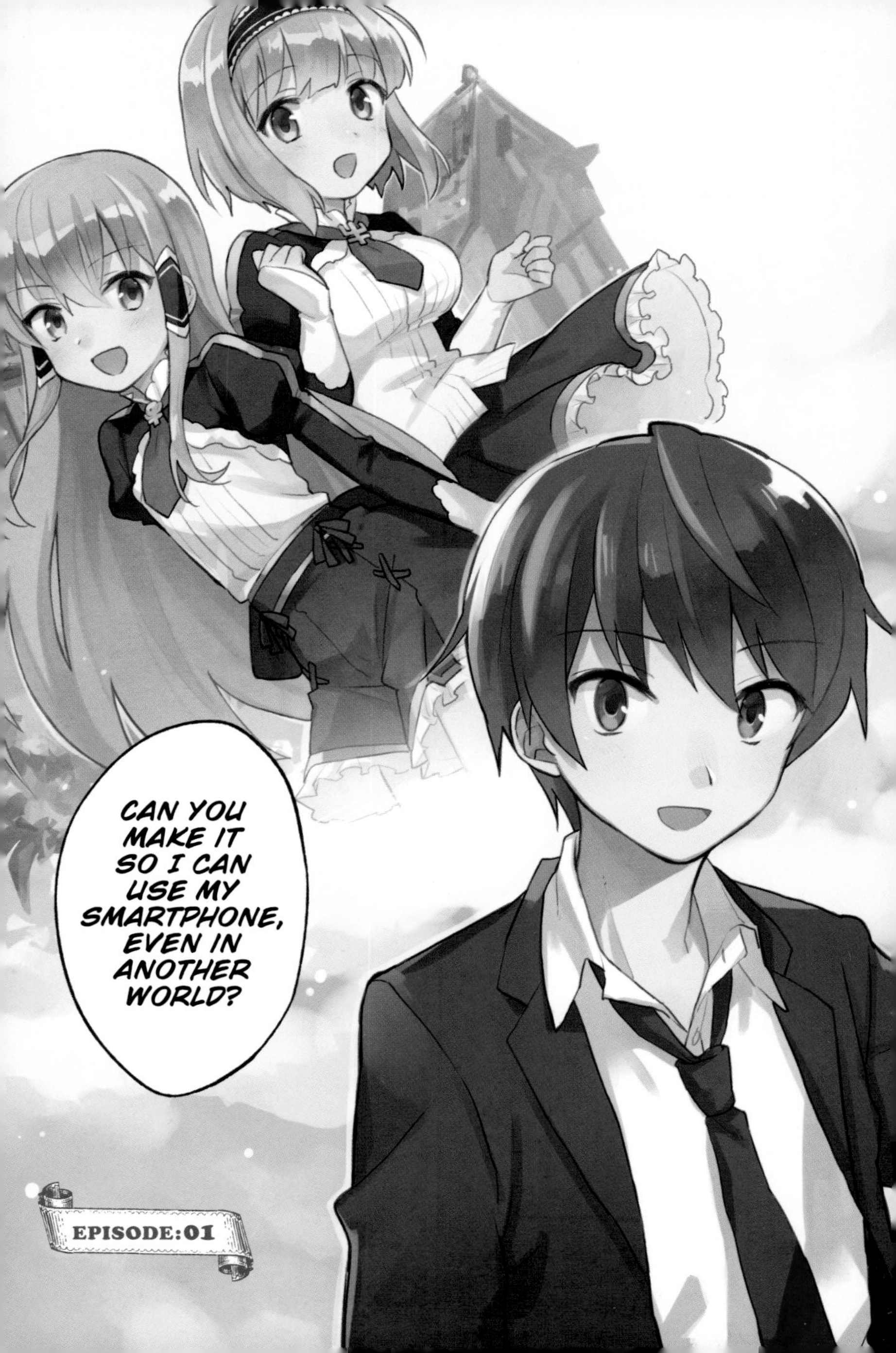
CAN YOU MAKE IT SO I CAN USE MY SMARTPHONE, EVEN IN ANOTHER WORLD?
EPISODE:01

In Another World
With My Smartphone

Vol.1

«contents»

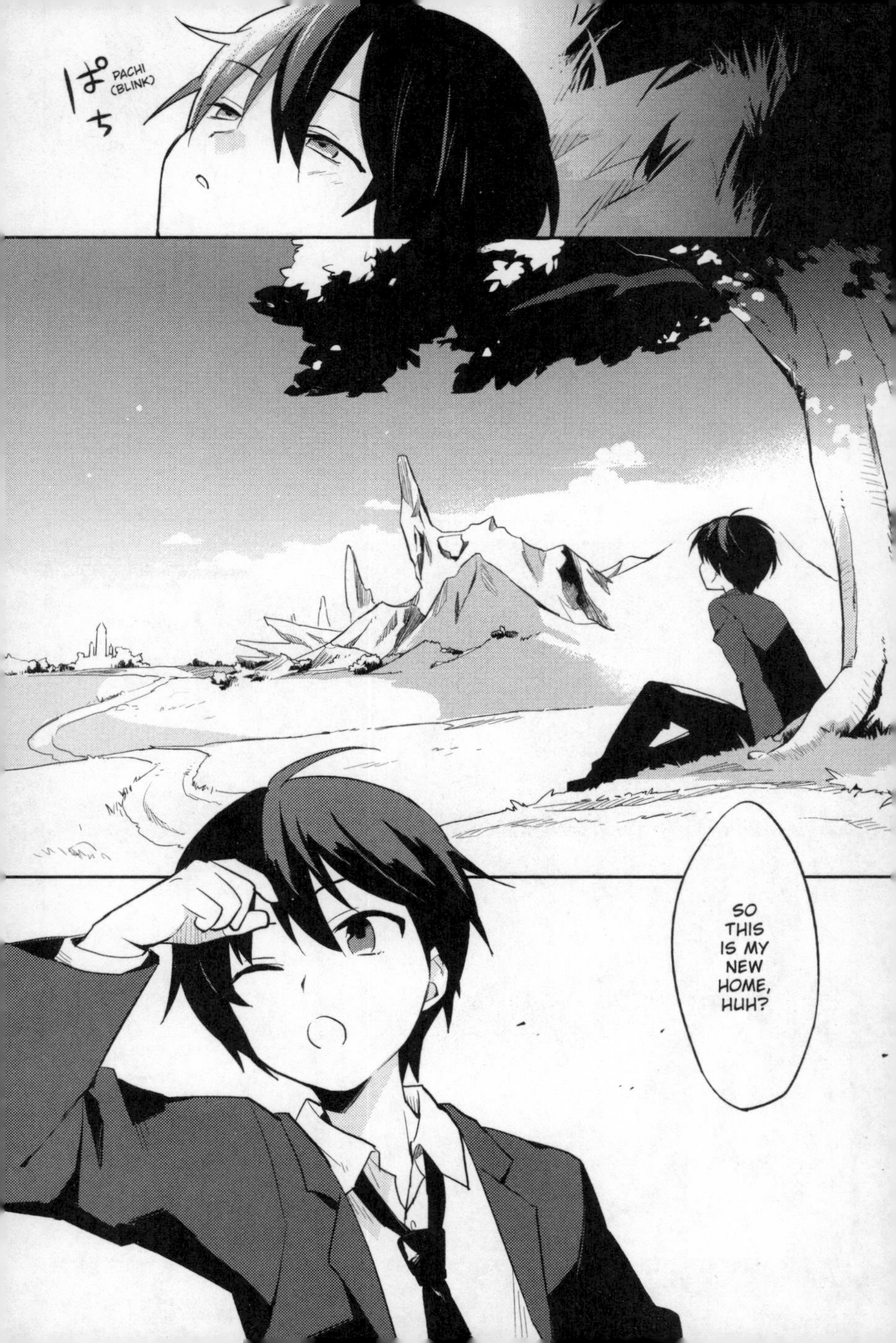
ぱち
PACHI (BLINK)
SO THIS IS MY NEW HOME, HUH?

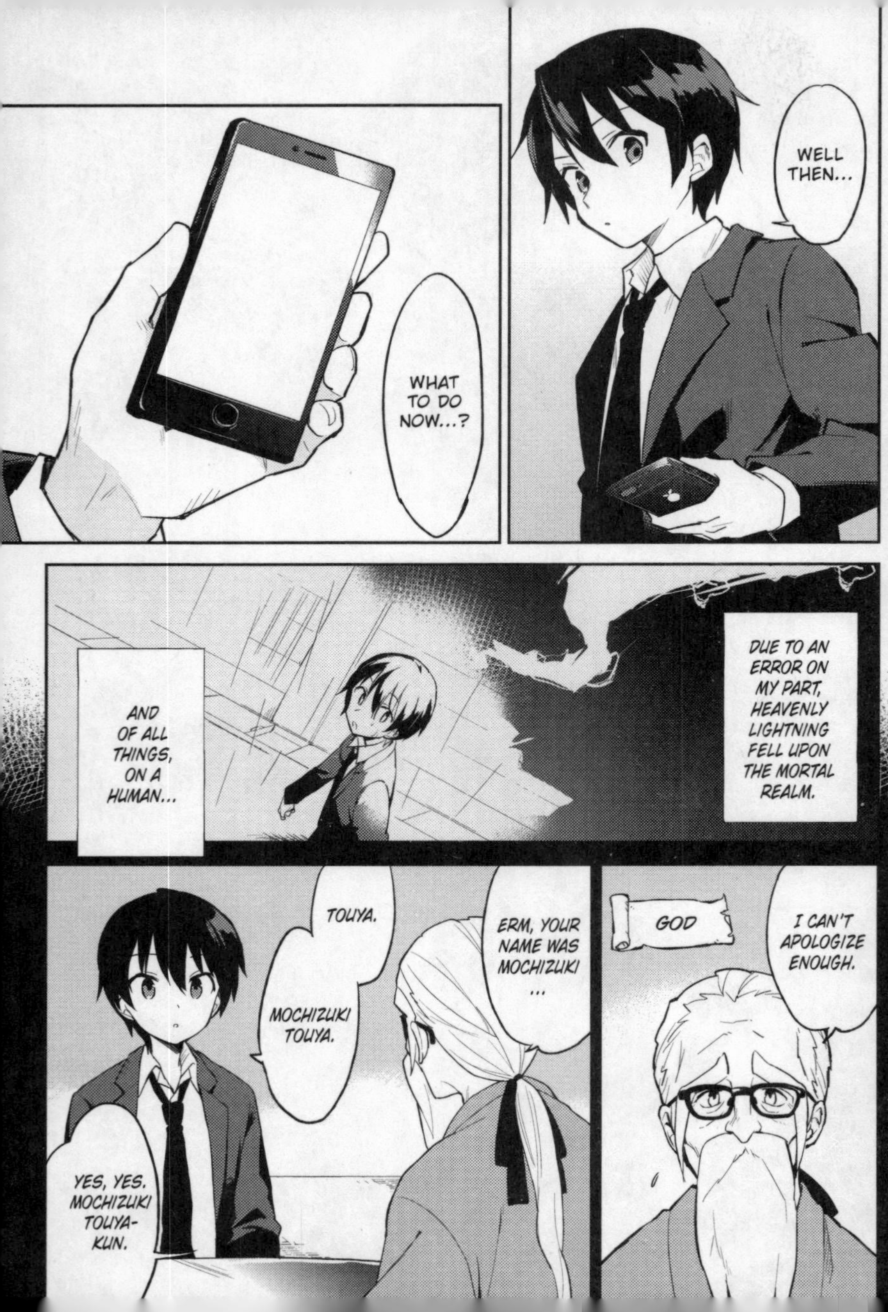
WELL THEN...
WHAT TO DO NOW...?
DUE TO AN ERROR ON MY PART, HEAVENLY LIGHTNING FELL UPON THE MORTAL REALM.
AND OF ALL THINGS, ON A HUMAN...
I CAN'T APOLOGIZE ENOUGH.
GOD
ERM, YOUR NAME WAS MOCHIZUKI ...
TOUYA.
MOCHIZUKI TOUYA.
YES, YES. MOCHIZUKI TOUYA-KUN.

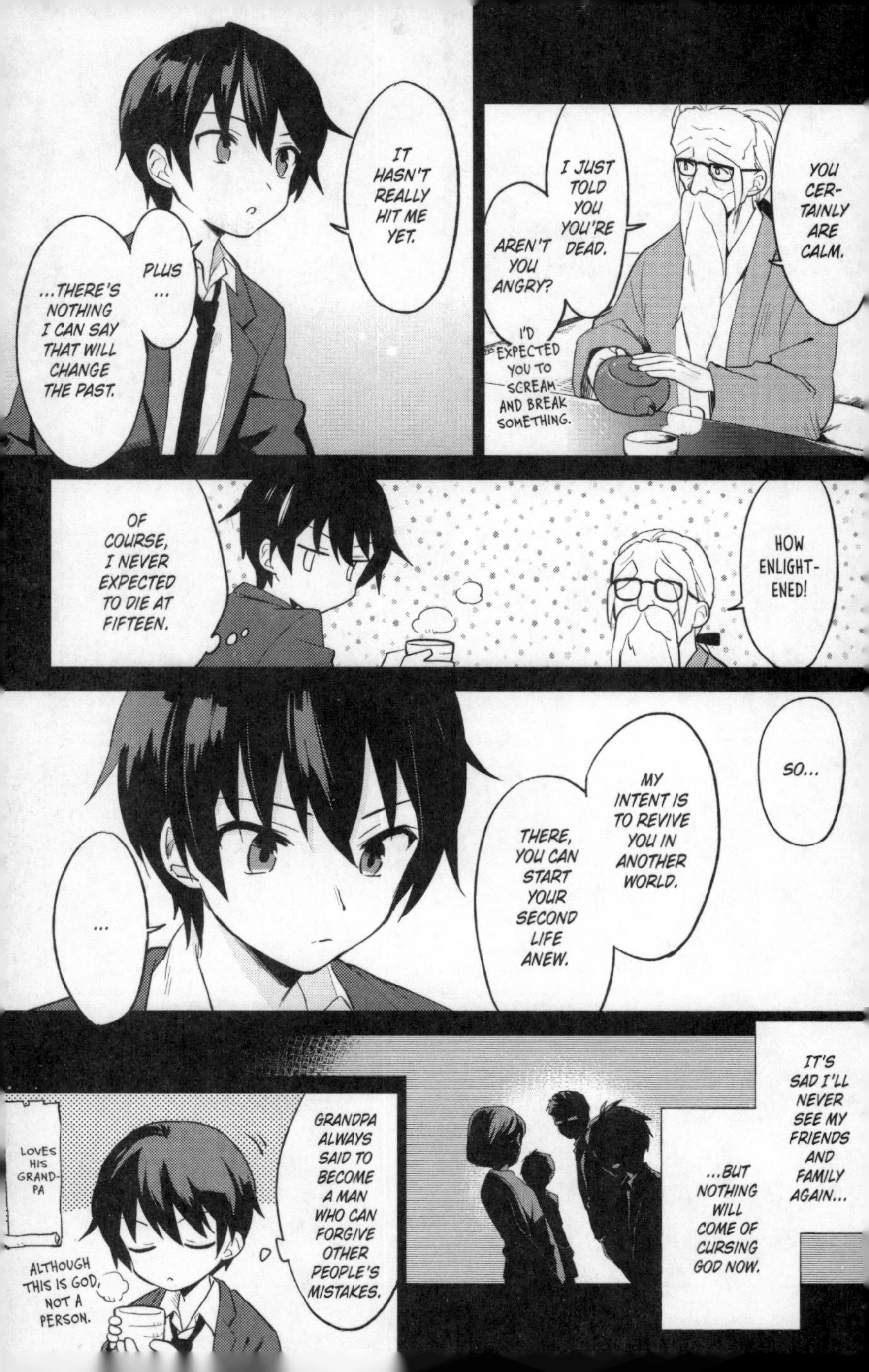
YOU CERTAINLY ARE CALM.
I JUST TOLD YOU YOU'RE DEAD.
AREN'T YOU ANGRY?
I'D EXPECTED YOU TO SCREAM AND BREAK SOMETHING.
IT HASN'T REALLY HIT ME YET.
PLUS...
...THERE'S NOTHING I CAN SAY THAT WILL CHANGE THE PAST.
HOW ENLIGHTENED!
OF COURSE, I NEVER EXPECTED TO DIE AT FIFTEEN.
SO...
MY INTENT IS TO REVIVE YOU IN ANOTHER WORLD.
THERE, YOU CAN START YOUR SECOND LIFE ANEW.
...
IT'S SAD I'LL NEVER SEE MY FRIENDS AND FAMILY AGAIN...
...BUT NOTHING WILL COME OF CURSING GOD NOW.
GRANDPA ALWAYS SAID TO BECOME A MAN WHO CAN FORGIVE OTHER PEOPLE'S MISTAKES.
LOVES HIS GRANDPA
ALTHOUGH THIS IS GOD, NOT A PERSON.

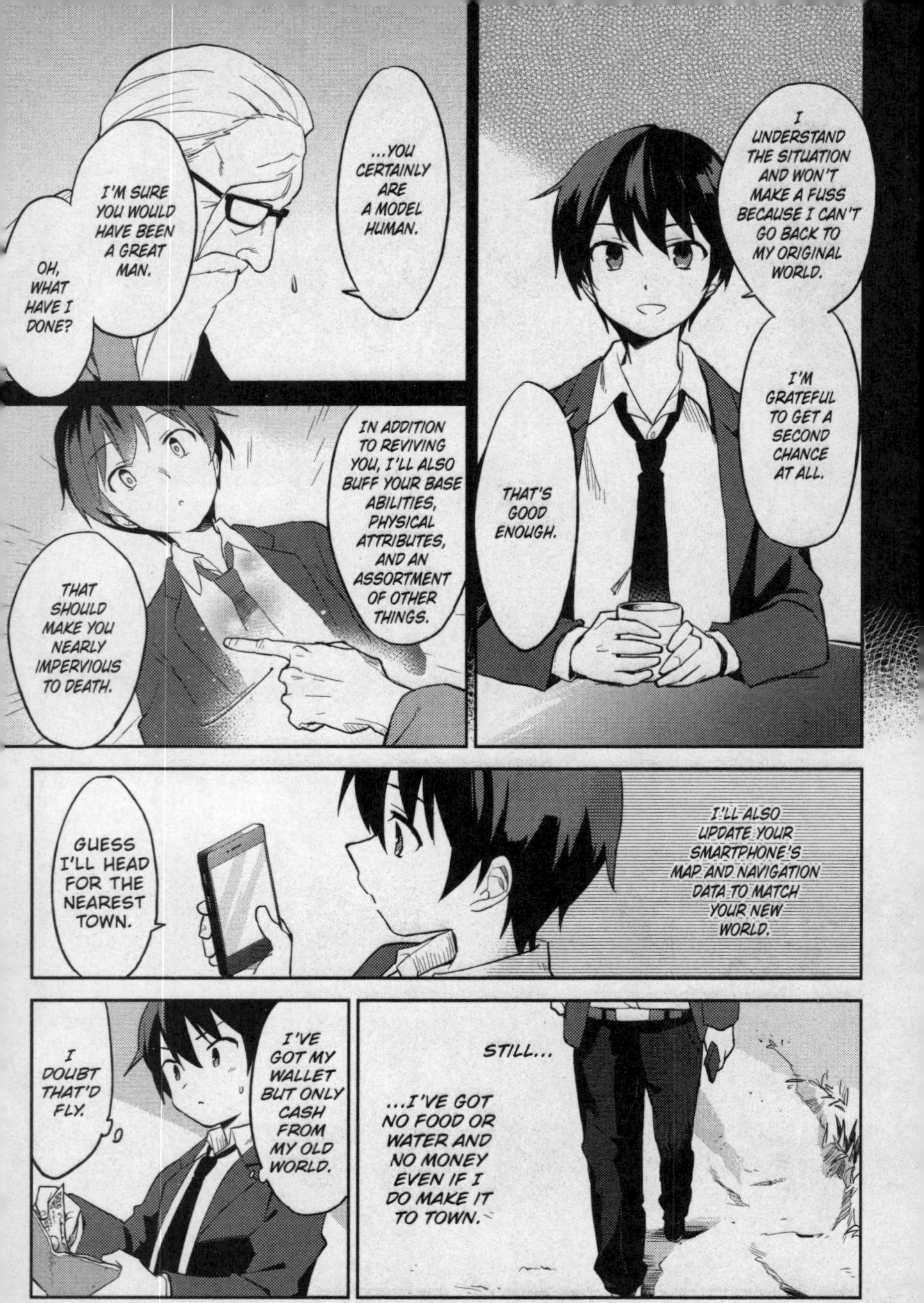
I UNDERSTAND THE SITUATION AND WON'T MAKE A FUSS BECAUSE I CAN'T GO BACK TO MY ORIGINAL WORLD.
I'M GRATEFUL TO GET A SECOND CHANCE AT ALL.
THAT'S GOOD ENOUGH.
...YOU CERTAINLY ARE A MODEL HUMAN.
I'M SURE YOU WOULD HAVE BEEN A GREAT MAN.
OH, WHAT HAVE I DONE?
IN ADDITION TO REVIVING YOU, I'LL ALSO BUFF YOUR BASE ABILITIES, PHYSICAL ATTRIBUTES, AND AN ASSORTMENT OF OTHER THINGS.
THAT SHOULD MAKE YOU NEARLY IMPERVIOUS TO DEATH.
I'LL ALSO UPDATE YOUR SMARTPHONE'S MAP AND NAVIGATION DATA TO MATCH YOUR NEW WORLD.
GUESS I'LL HEAD FOR THE NEAREST TOWN.
STILL...
...I'VE GOT NO FOOD OR WATER AND NO MONEY EVEN IF I DO MAKE IT TO TOWN.
I'VE GOT MY WALLET BUT ONLY CASH FROM MY OLD WORLD.
I DOUBT THAT'D FLY.

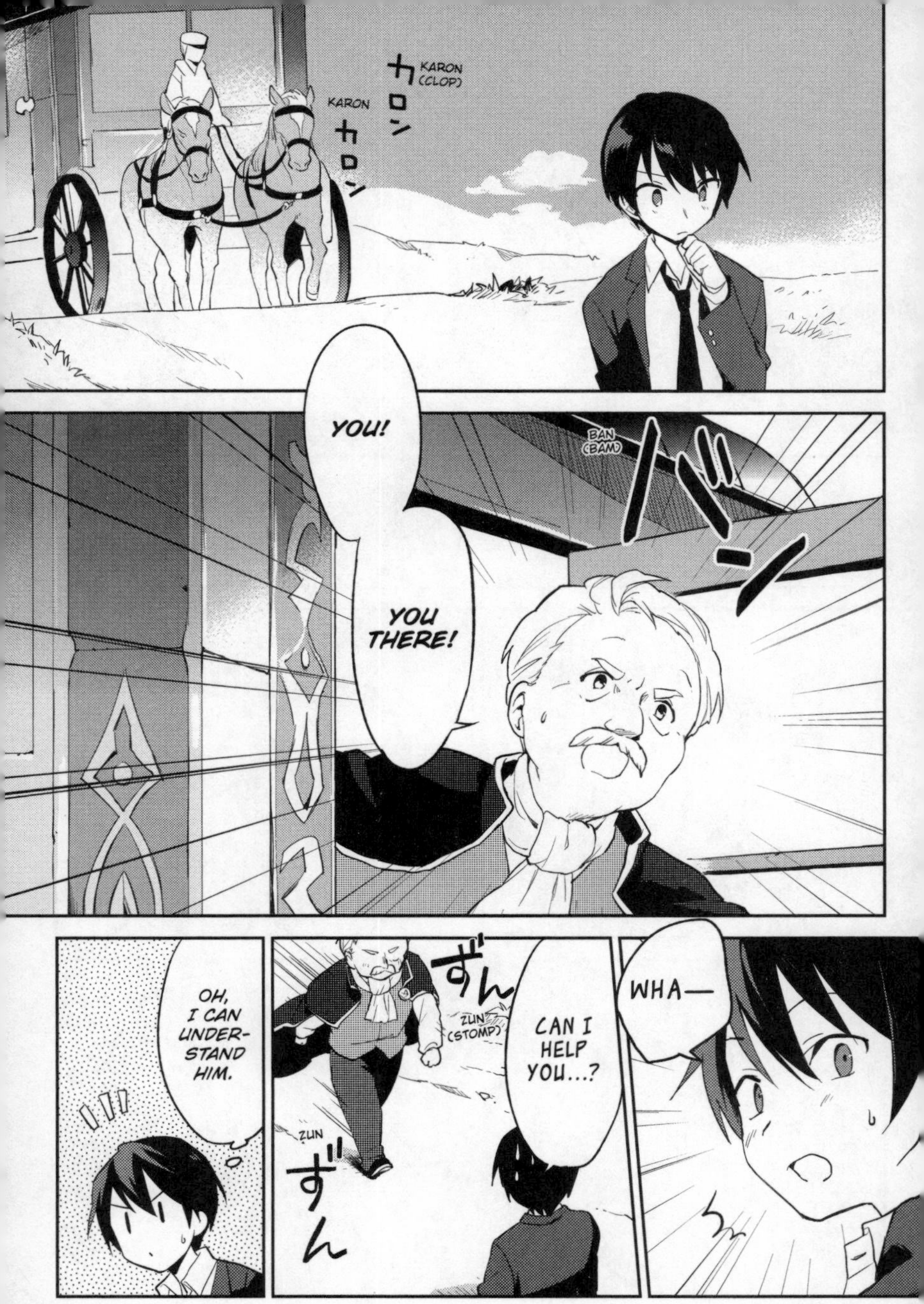
カロン
KARON (CLOP)
カロン
KARON
バン
BAN (BAM)
YOU!
YOU THERE!
WHA—
CAN I HELP YOU...?
ずん
ZUN (STOMP)
ずん
ZUN
OH, I CAN UNDERSTAND HIM.

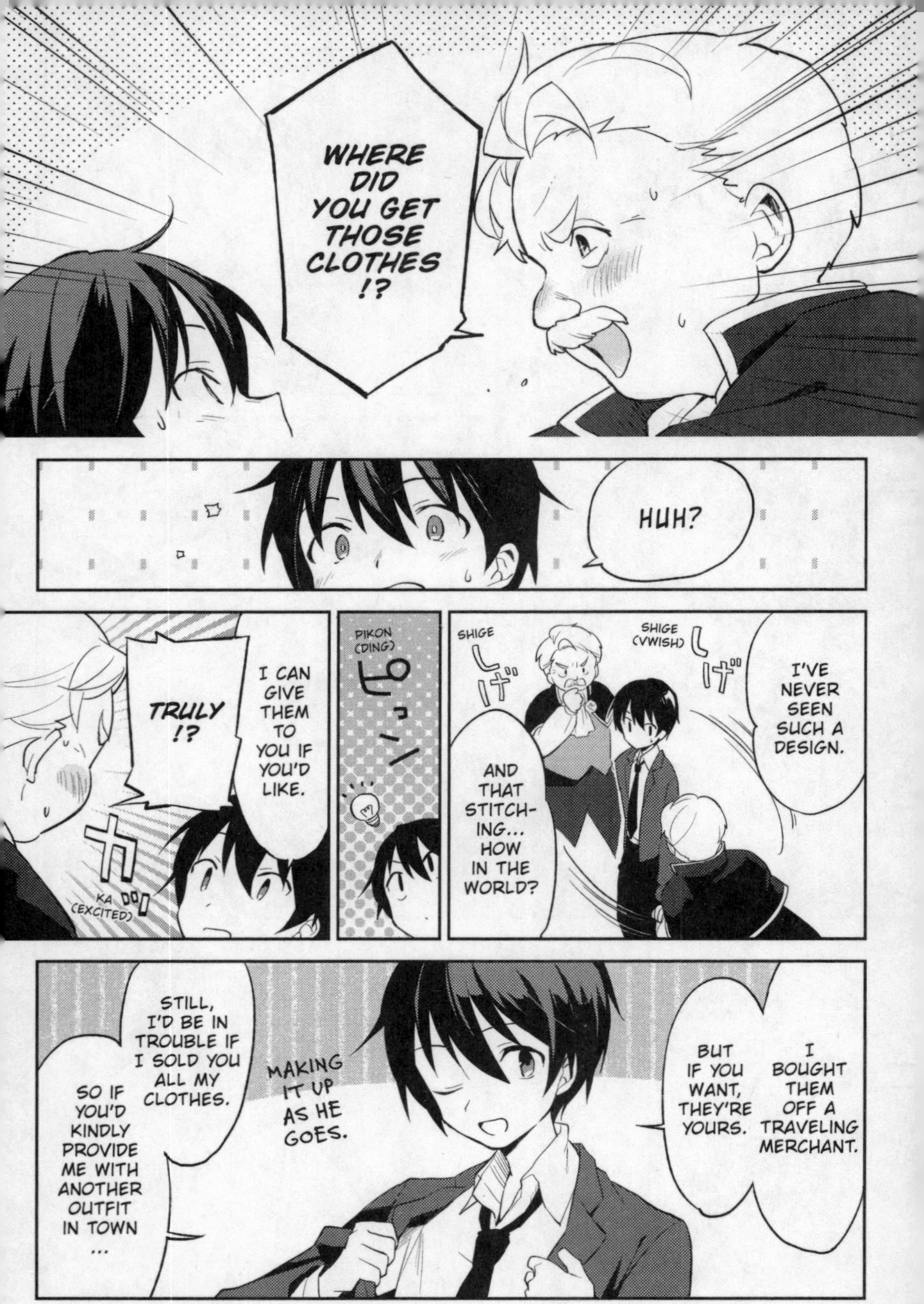
WHERE DID YOU GET THOSE CLOTHES!?
HUH?
SHIGE (VWISH)
SHIGE
I'VE NEVER SEEN SUCH A DESIGN.
AND THAT STITCHING... HOW IN THE WORLD?
PIKON (DING)
I CAN GIVE THEM TO YOU IF YOU'D LIKE.
TRULY!?
KA (EXCITED)
I BOUGHT THEM OFF A TRAVELING MERCHANT.
BUT IF YOU WANT, THEY'RE YOURS.
MAKING IT UP AS HE GOES.
STILL, I'D BE IN TROUBLE IF I SOLD YOU ALL MY CLOTHES.
SO IF YOU'D KINDLY PROVIDE ME WITH ANOTHER OUTFIT IN TOWN...

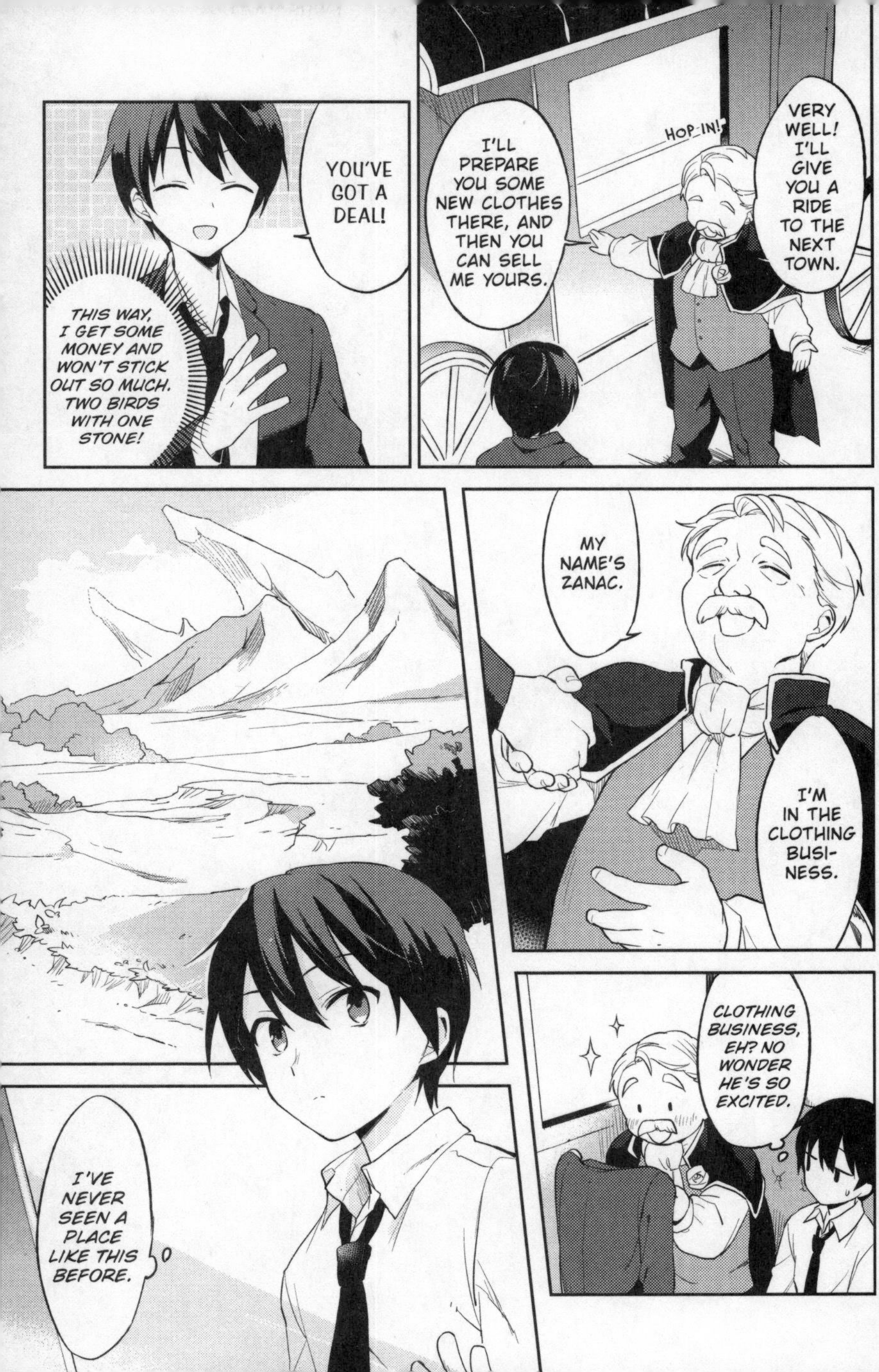
VERY WELL! I'LL GIVE YOU A RIDE TO THE NEXT TOWN.
HOP IN!
I'LL PREPARE YOU SOME NEW CLOTHES THERE, AND THEN YOU CAN SELL ME YOURS.
YOU'VE GOT A DEAL!
THIS WAY, I GET SOME MONEY AND WON'T STICK OUT SO MUCH. TWO BIRDS WITH ONE STONE!
MY NAME'S ZANAC.
I'M IN THE CLOTHING BUSINESS.
CLOTHING BUSINESS, EH? NO WONDER HE'S SO EXCITED.
I'VE NEVER SEEN A PLACE LIKE THIS BEFORE.

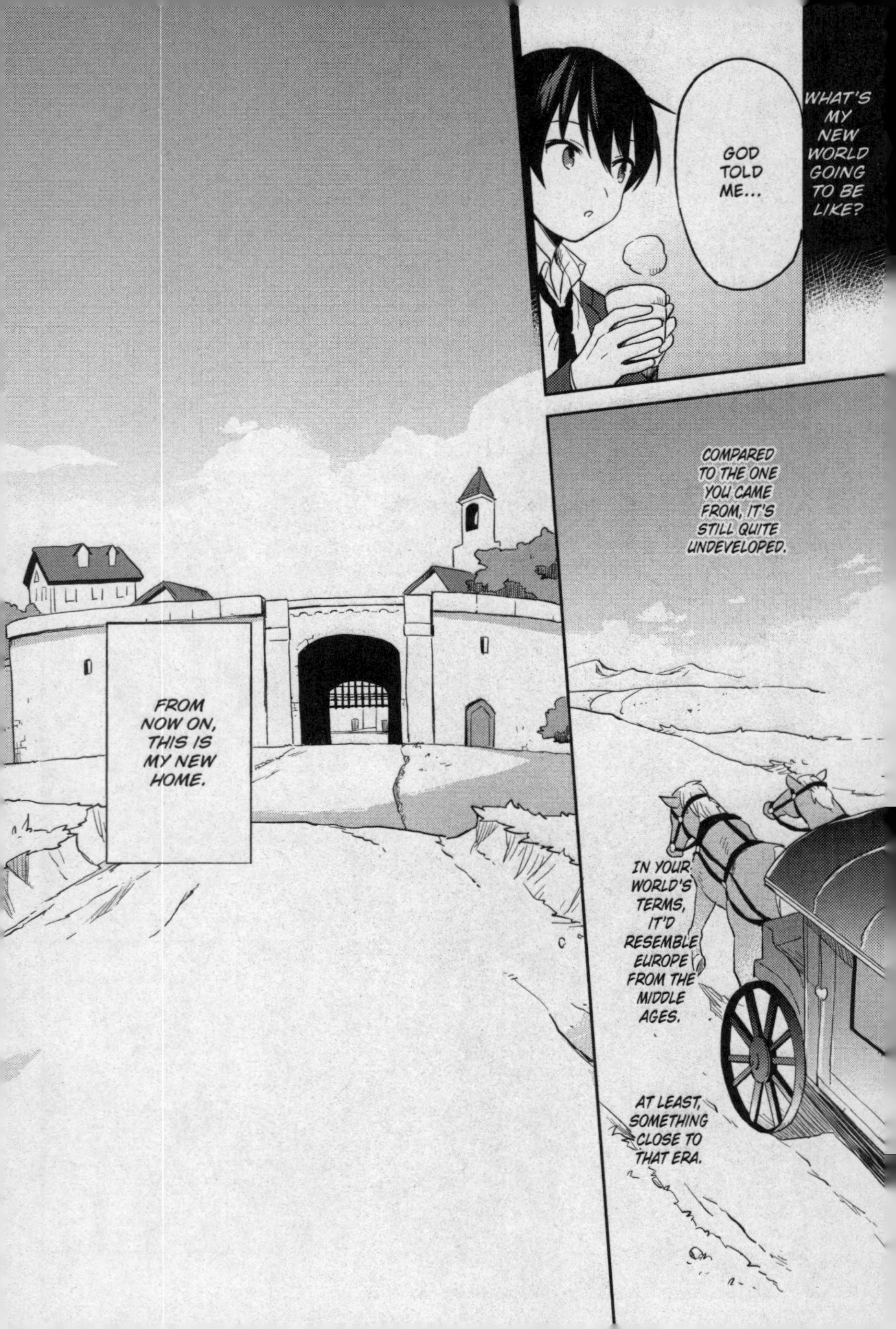
WHAT'S MY NEW WORLD GOING TO BE LIKE?
GOD TOLD ME...
COMPARED TO THE ONE YOU CAME FROM, IT'S STILL QUITE UNDEVELOPED.
IN YOUR WORLD'S TERMS, IT'D RESEMBLE EUROPE FROM THE MIDDLE AGES.
AT LEAST, SOMETHING CLOSE TO THAT ERA.
FROM NOW ON, THIS IS MY NEW HOME.

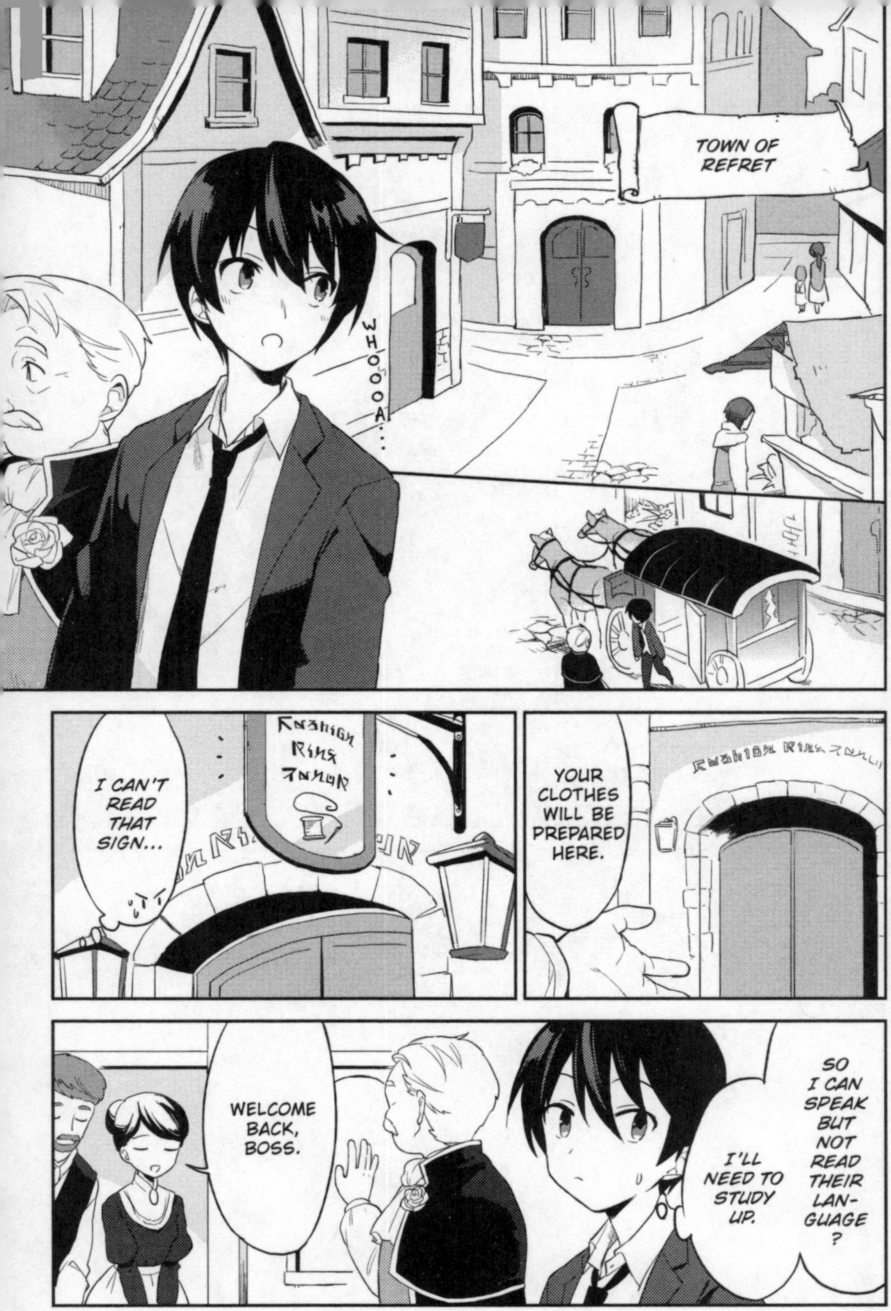
TOWN OF REFRET
WHOOOA...
YOUR CLOTHES WILL BE PREPARED HERE.
...
I CAN'T READ THAT SIGN...
SO I CAN SPEAK BUT NOT READ THEIR LAN-GUAGE?
I'LL NEED TO STUDY UP.
WELCOME BACK, BOSS.

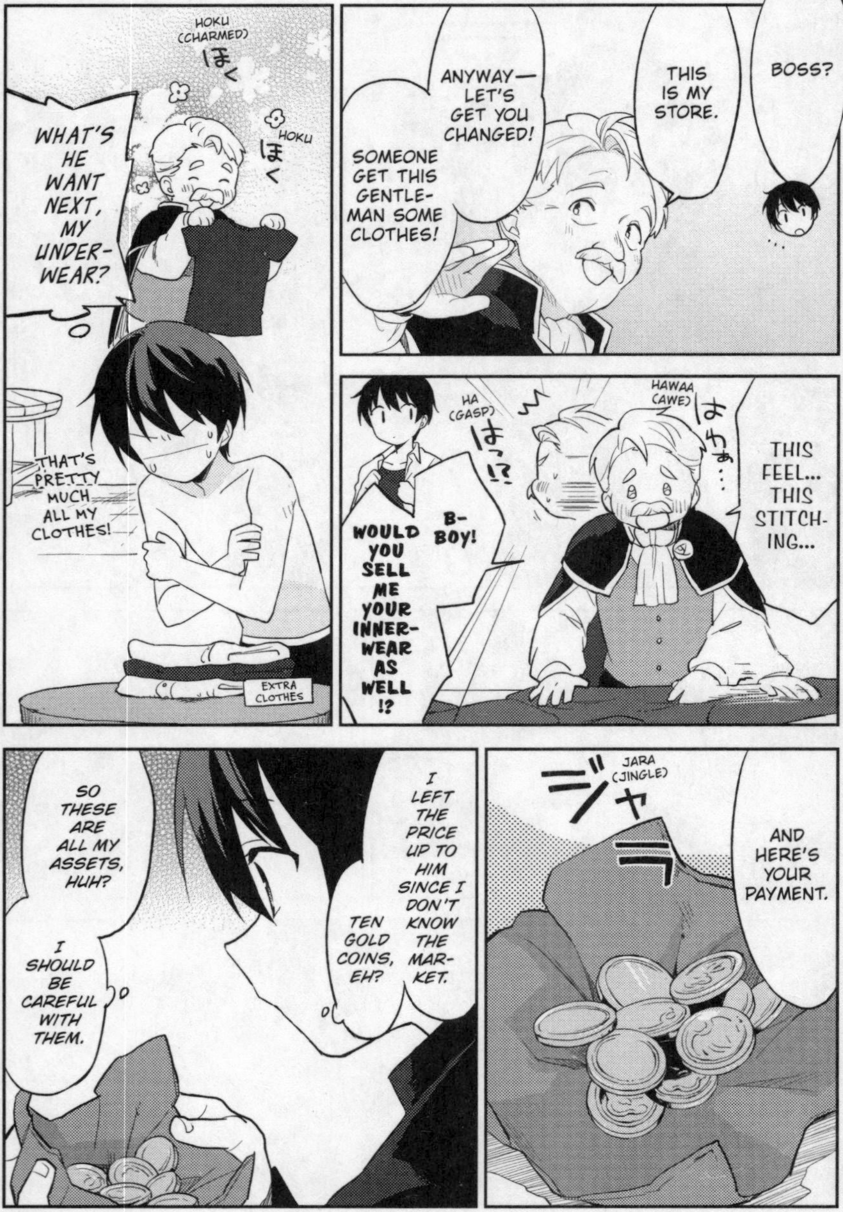
BOSS?
THIS IS MY STORE.
ANYWAY— LET'S GET YOU CHANGED!
SOMEONE GET THIS GENTLE-MAN SOME CLOTHES!
THIS FEEL... THIS STITCH-ING...
HAWAA (AWE)
はわぁ…
HA (GASP)
はっ!?
B-BOY!
WOULD YOU SELL ME YOUR INNER-WEAR AS WELL!?
HOKU (CHARMED)
ほく
HOKU
ほく
WHAT'S HE WANT NEXT, MY UNDER-WEAR?
THAT'S PRETTY MUCH ALL MY CLOTHES!
EXTRA CLOTHES
JARA (JINGLE)
ジャラ
AND HERE'S YOUR PAYMENT.
I LEFT THE PRICE UP TO HIM SINCE I DON'T KNOW THE MAR-KET.
TEN GOLD COINS, EH?
SO THESE ARE ALL MY ASSETS, HUH?
I SHOULD BE CAREFUL WITH THEM.

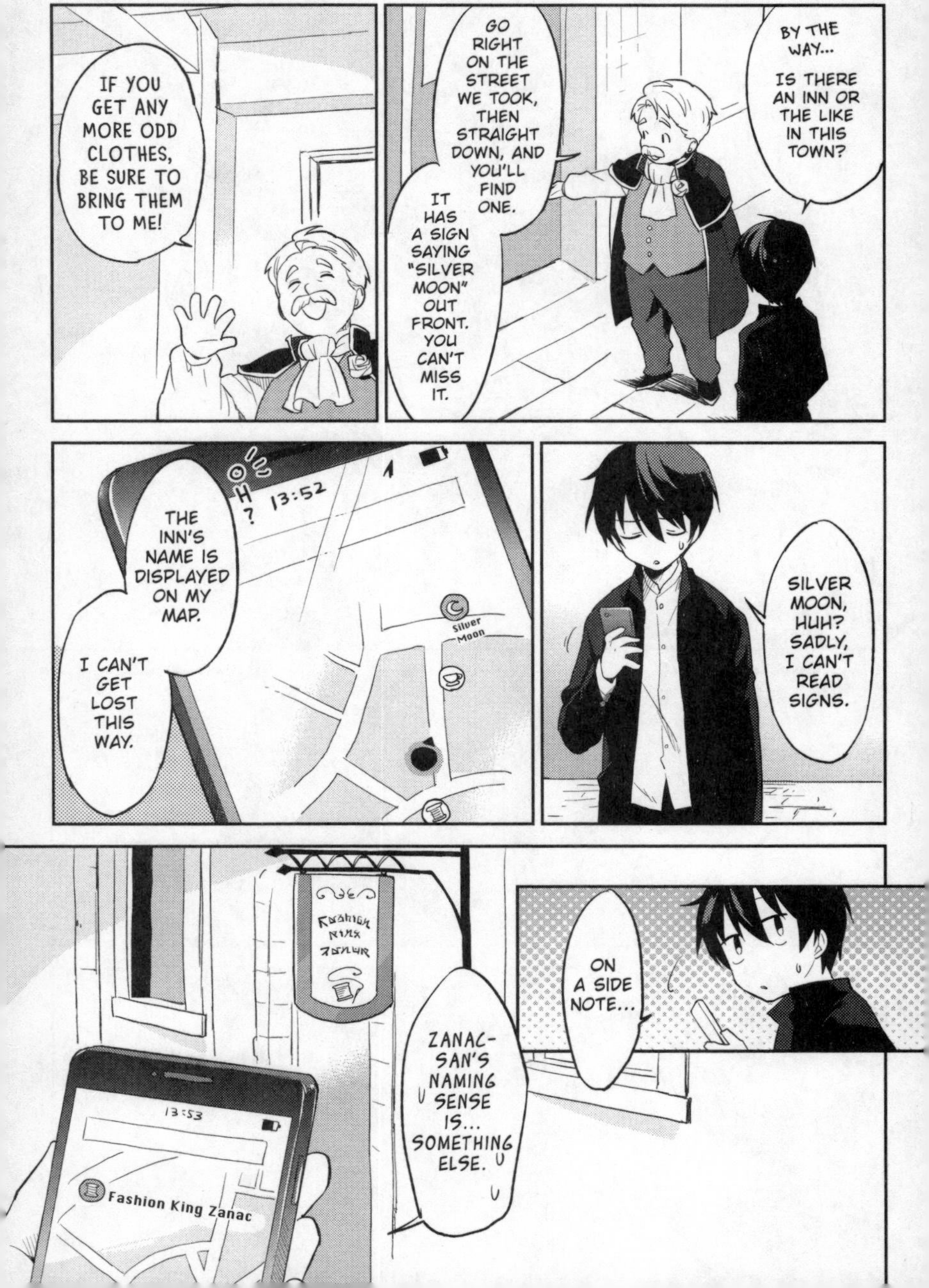
BY THE WAY... IS THERE AN INN OR THE LIKE IN THIS TOWN?
GO RIGHT ON THE STREET WE TOOK, THEN STRAIGHT DOWN, AND YOU'LL FIND ONE.
IT HAS A SIGN SAYING "SILVER MOON" OUT FRONT. YOU CAN'T MISS IT.
IF YOU GET ANY MORE ODD CLOTHES, BE SURE TO BRING THEM TO ME!
SILVER MOON, HUH? SADLY, I CAN'T READ SIGNS.
13:52
Silver Moon
THE INN'S NAME IS DISPLAYED ON MY MAP.
I CAN'T GET LOST THIS WAY.
ON A SIDE NOTE...
ZANAC-SAN'S NAMING SENSE IS... SOMETHING ELSE.
13:53
Fashion King Zanac

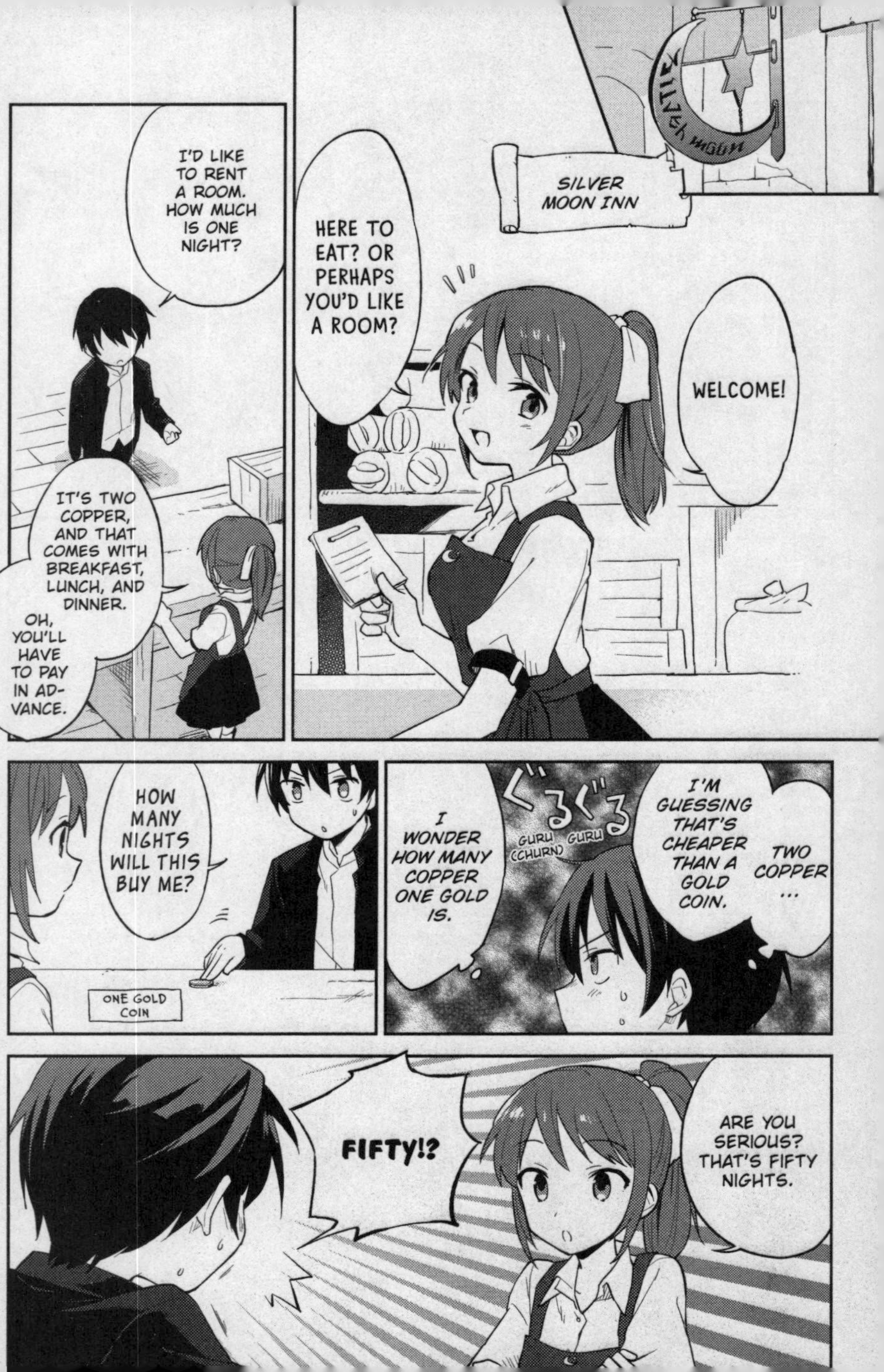
SILVER MOON INN
WELCOME!
HERE TO EAT? OR PERHAPS YOU'D LIKE A ROOM?
I'D LIKE TO RENT A ROOM. HOW MUCH IS ONE NIGHT?
IT'S TWO COPPER, AND THAT COMES WITH BREAKFAST, LUNCH, AND DINNER.
OH, YOU'LL HAVE TO PAY IN ADVANCE.
TWO COPPER ...
I'M GUESSING THAT'S CHEAPER THAN A GOLD COIN.
ぐるぐる
GURU GURU (CHURN)
I WONDER HOW MANY COPPER ONE GOLD IS.
HOW MANY NIGHTS WILL THIS BUY ME?
ONE GOLD COIN
ARE YOU SERIOUS? THAT'S FIFTY NIGHTS.
FIFTY!?

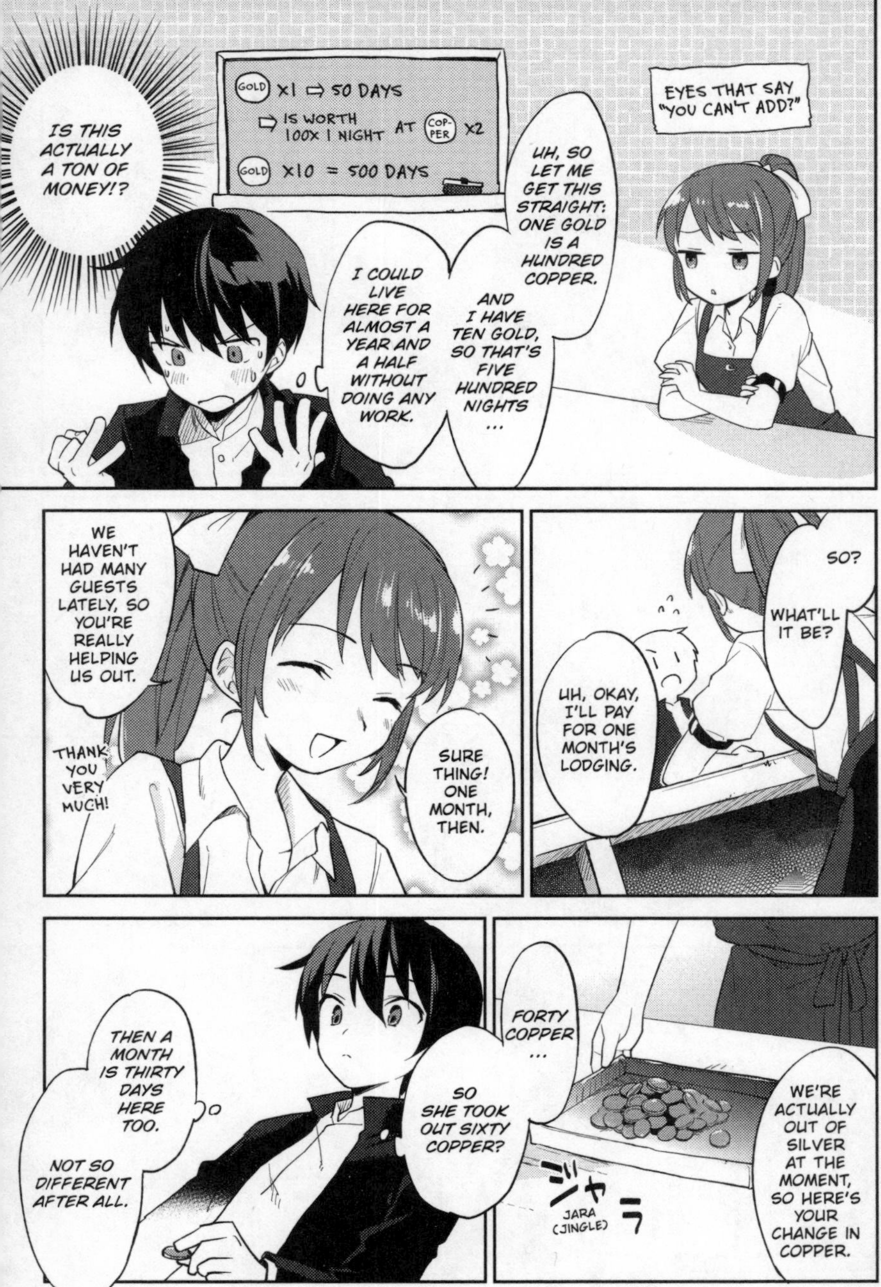
EYES THAT SAY "YOU CAN'T ADD?"
UH, SO LET ME GET THIS STRAIGHT: ONE GOLD IS A HUNDRED COPPER.
AND I HAVE TEN GOLD, SO THAT'S FIVE HUNDRED NIGHTS...
I COULD LIVE HERE FOR ALMOST A YEAR AND A HALF WITHOUT DOING ANY WORK.
GOLD X1 ⇨ 50 DAYS
⇨ IS WORTH 100X 1 NIGHT AT COPPER X2
GOLD X10 = 500 DAYS
IS THIS ACTUALLY A TON OF MONEY!?
SO?
WHAT'LL IT BE?
UH, OKAY, I'LL PAY FOR ONE MONTH'S LODGING.
SURE THING! ONE MONTH, THEN.
WE HAVEN'T HAD MANY GUESTS LATELY, SO YOU'RE REALLY HELPING US OUT.
THANK YOU VERY MUCH!
WE'RE ACTUALLY OUT OF SILVER AT THE MOMENT, SO HERE'S YOUR CHANGE IN COPPER.
ジャラ
JARA (JINGLE)
FORTY COPPER...
SO SHE TOOK OUT SIXTY COPPER?
THEN A MONTH IS THIRTY DAYS HERE TOO.
NOT SO DIFFERENT AFTER ALL.

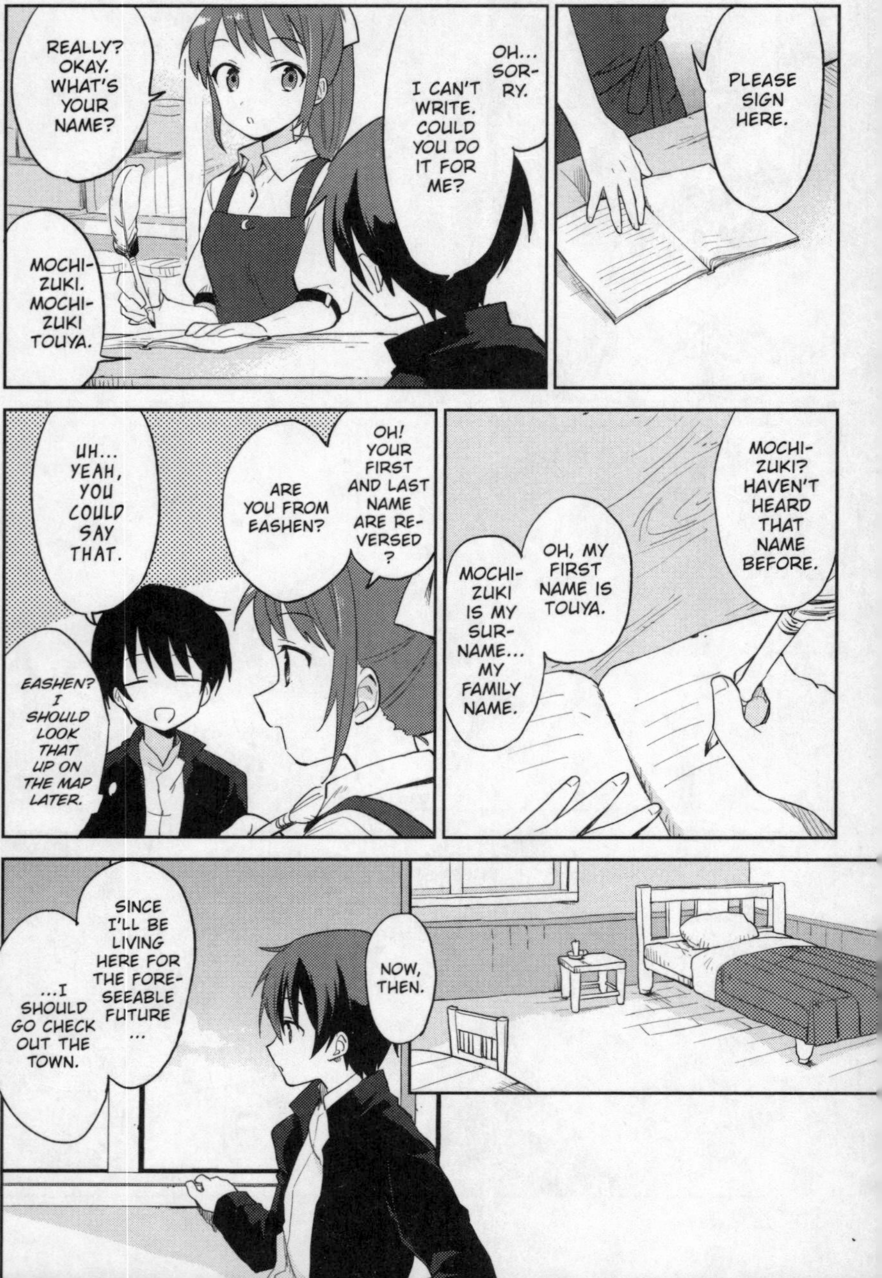
PLEASE SIGN HERE.
OH... SORRY.
I CAN'T WRITE. COULD YOU DO IT FOR ME?
REALLY? OKAY. WHAT'S YOUR NAME?
MOCHIZUKI. MOCHIZUKI TOUYA.
MOCHIZUKI? HAVEN'T HEARD THAT NAME BEFORE.
OH, MY FIRST NAME IS TOUYA.
MOCHIZUKI IS MY SURNAME... MY FAMILY NAME.
OH! YOUR FIRST AND LAST NAME ARE REVERSED?
ARE YOU FROM EASHEN?
UH... YEAH, YOU COULD SAY THAT.
EASHEN? I SHOULD LOOK THAT UP ON THE MAP LATER.
NOW, THEN.
SINCE I'LL BE LIVING HERE FOR THE FORESEEABLE FUTURE...
...I SHOULD GO CHECK OUT THE TOWN.

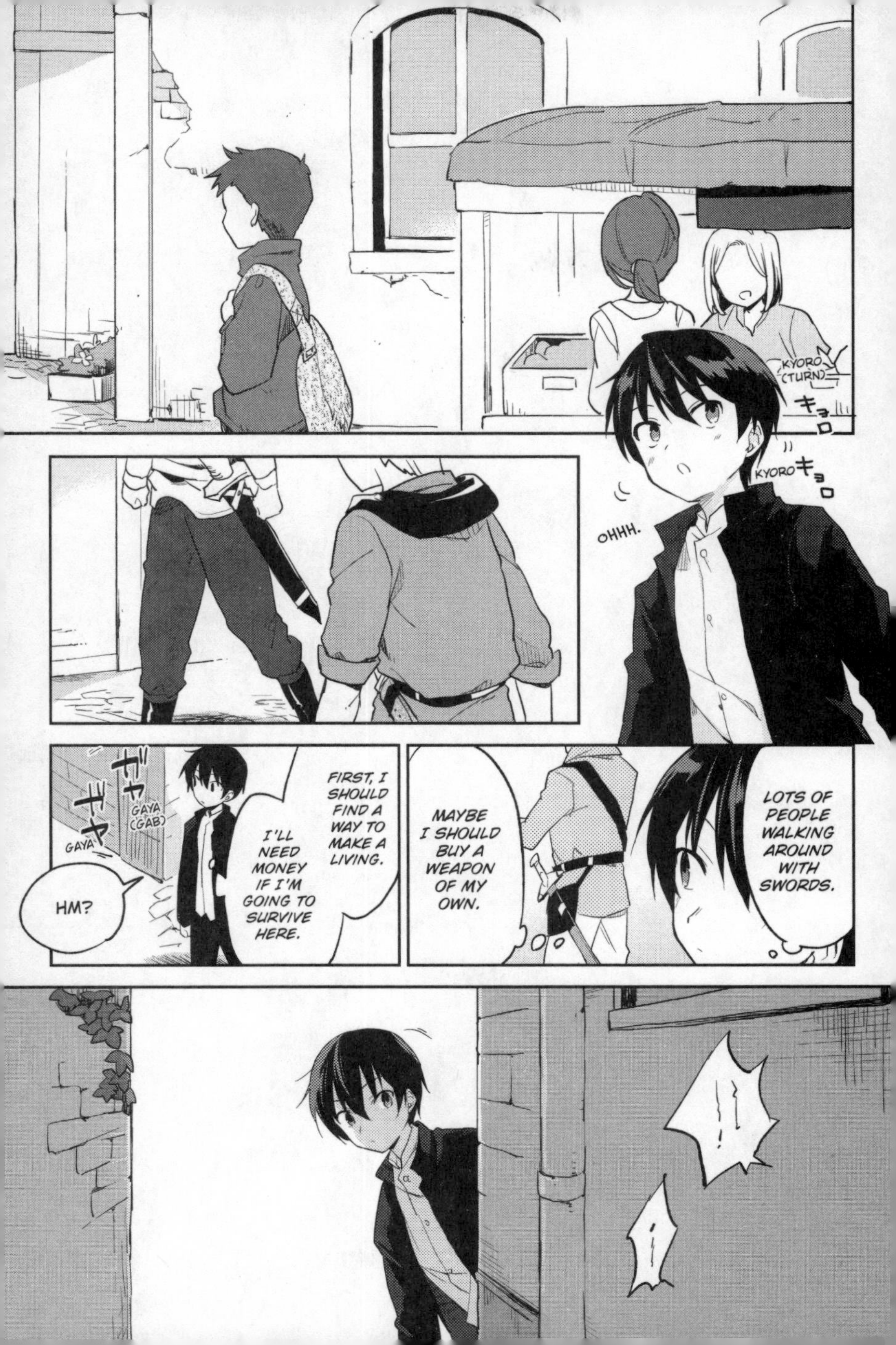
KYORO (TURN)
キョロ
KYORO キョロ
OHHH.
LOTS OF PEOPLE WALKING AROUND WITH SWORDS.
MAYBE I SHOULD BUY A WEAPON OF MY OWN.
FIRST, I SHOULD FIND A WAY TO MAKE A LIVING.
I'LL NEED MONEY IF I'M GOING TO SURVIVE HERE.
ガヤ GAYA (GAB)
ガヤ GAYA
HM?
!
!

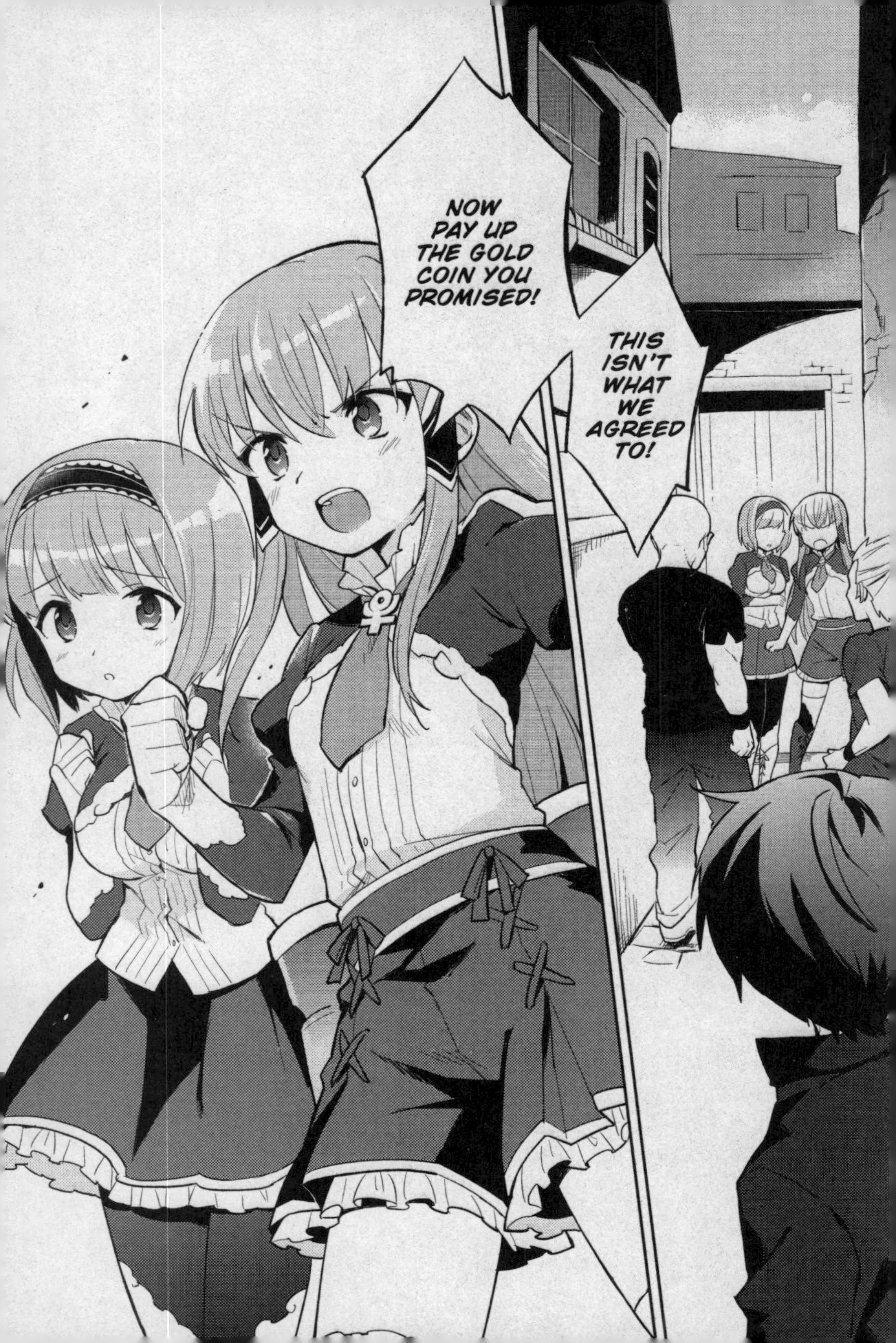
NOW PAY UP THE GOLD COIN YOU PROMISED!
THIS ISN'T WHAT WE AGREED TO!

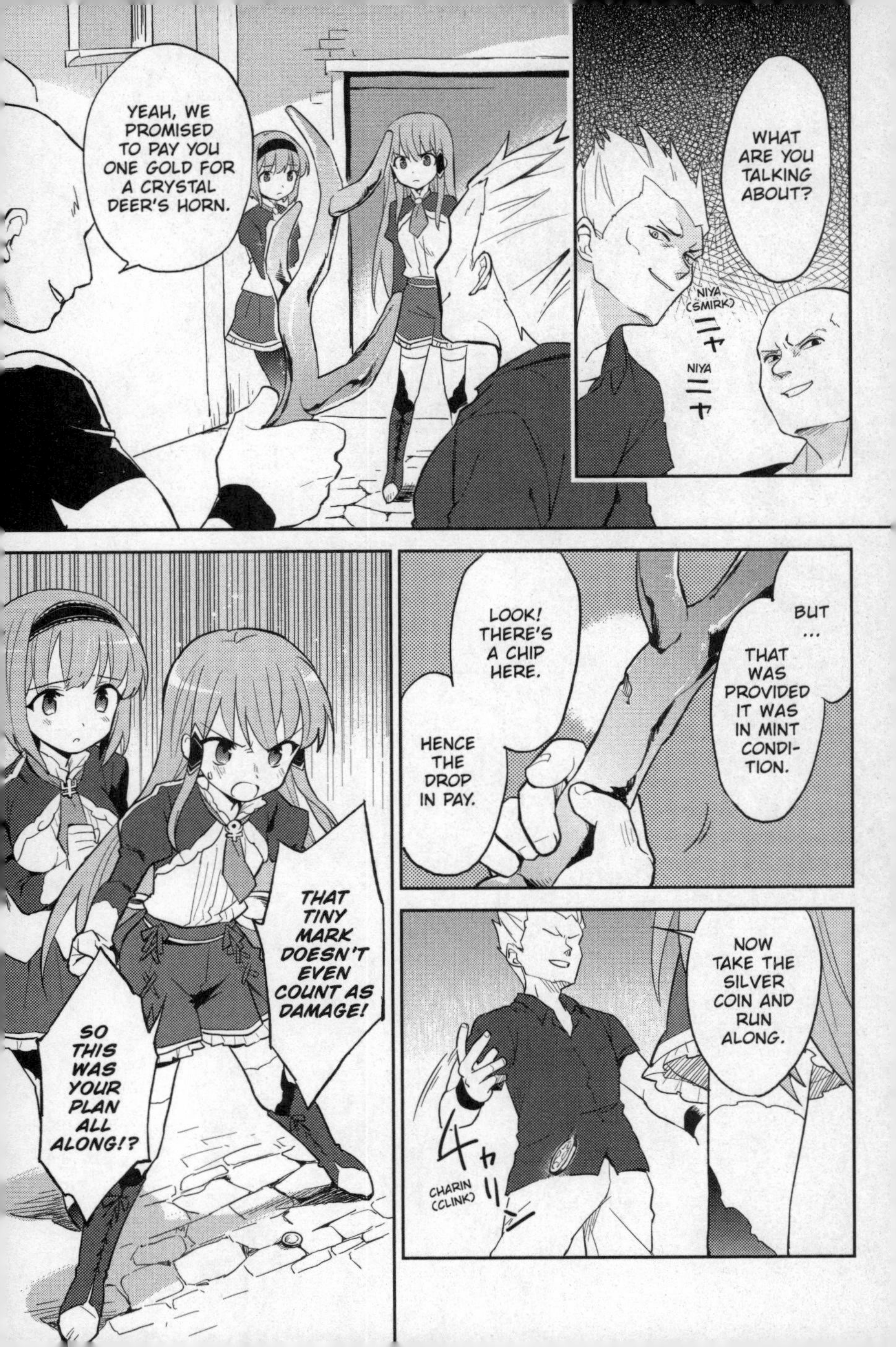

WHAT ARE YOU TALKING ABOUT?
NIYA (SMIRK)
ニヤ
NIYA
ニヤ
YEAH, WE PROMISED TO PAY YOU ONE GOLD FOR A CRYSTAL DEER'S HORN.
BUT ... THAT WAS PROVIDED IT WAS IN MINT CONDITION.
LOOK! THERE'S A CHIP HERE.
HENCE THE DROP IN PAY.
NOW TAKE THE SILVER COIN AND RUN ALONG.
チャリン
CHARIN (CLINK)
THAT TINY MARK DOESN'T EVEN COUNT AS DAMAGE!
SO THIS WAS YOUR PLAN ALL ALONG!?

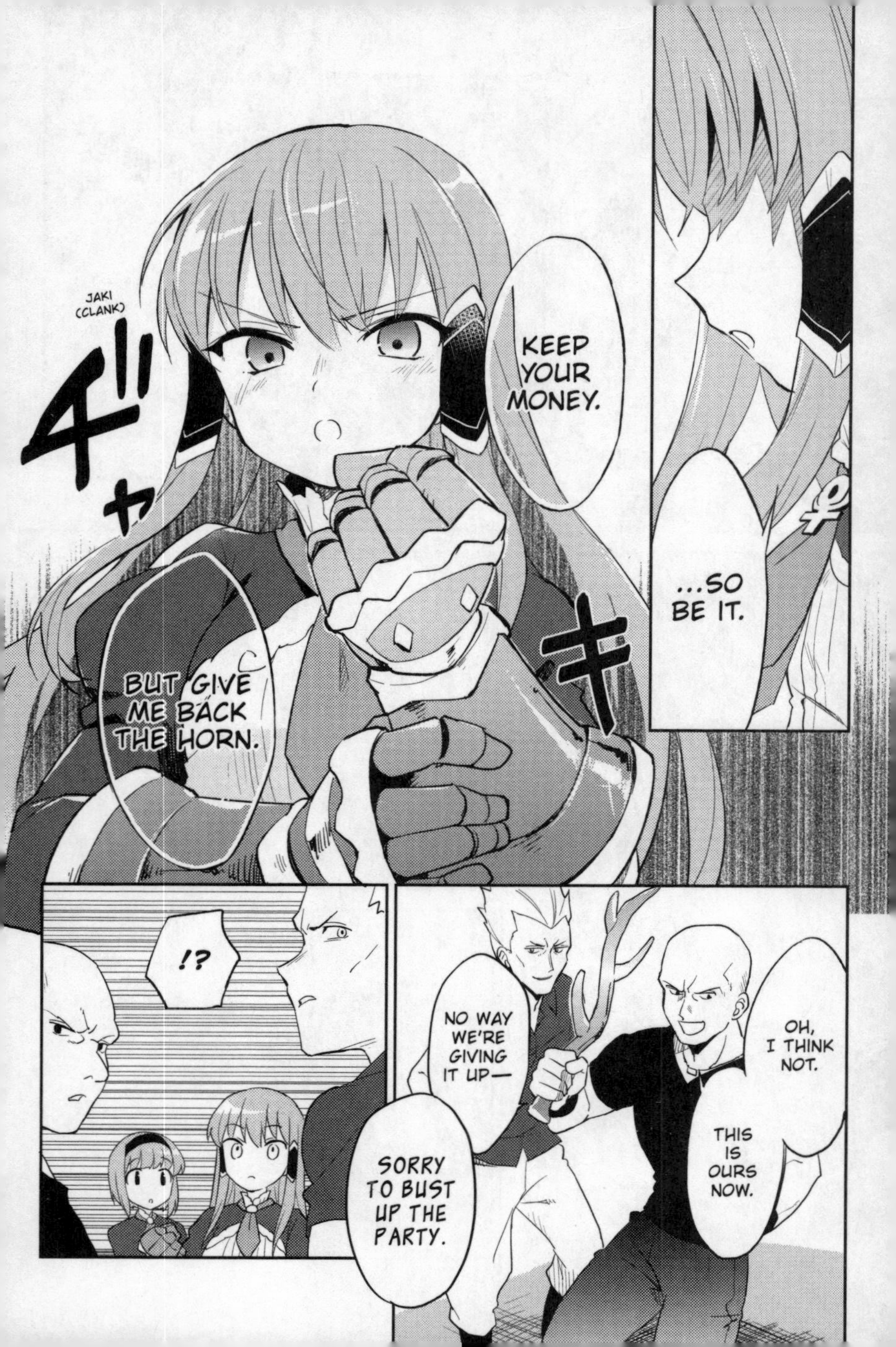
...SO BE IT.
KEEP YOUR MONEY.
JAKI (CLANK)
BUT GIVE ME BACK THE HORN.
OH, I THINK NOT.
THIS IS OURS NOW.
NO WAY WE'RE GIVING IT UP—
SORRY TO BUST UP THE PARTY.
!?

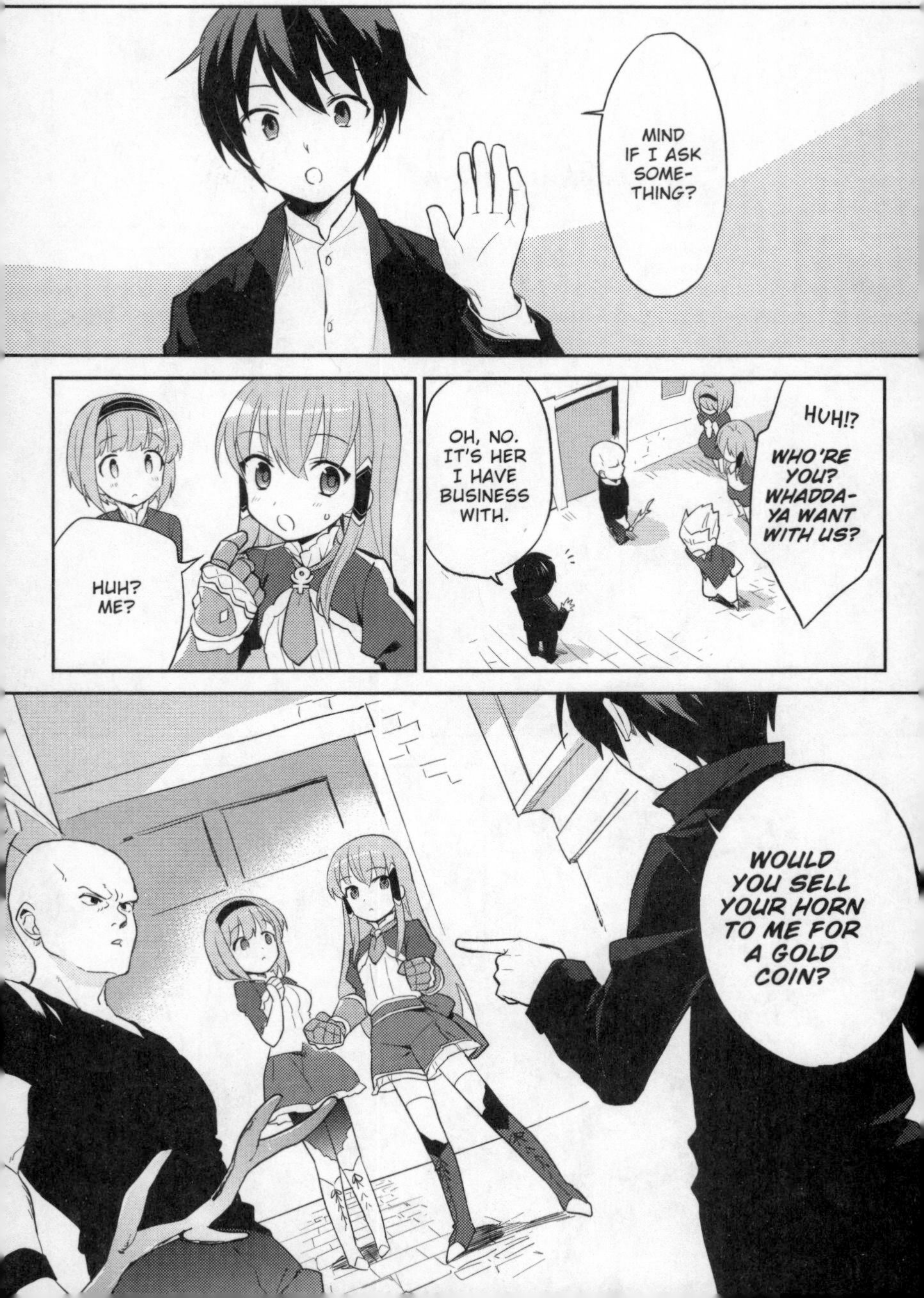
MIND IF I ASK SOME-THING?
HUH!?
WHO'RE YOU? WHADDA-YA WANT WITH US?
OH, NO. IT'S HER I HAVE BUSINESS WITH.
HUH? ME?
WOULD YOU SELL YOUR HORN TO ME FOR A GOLD COIN?

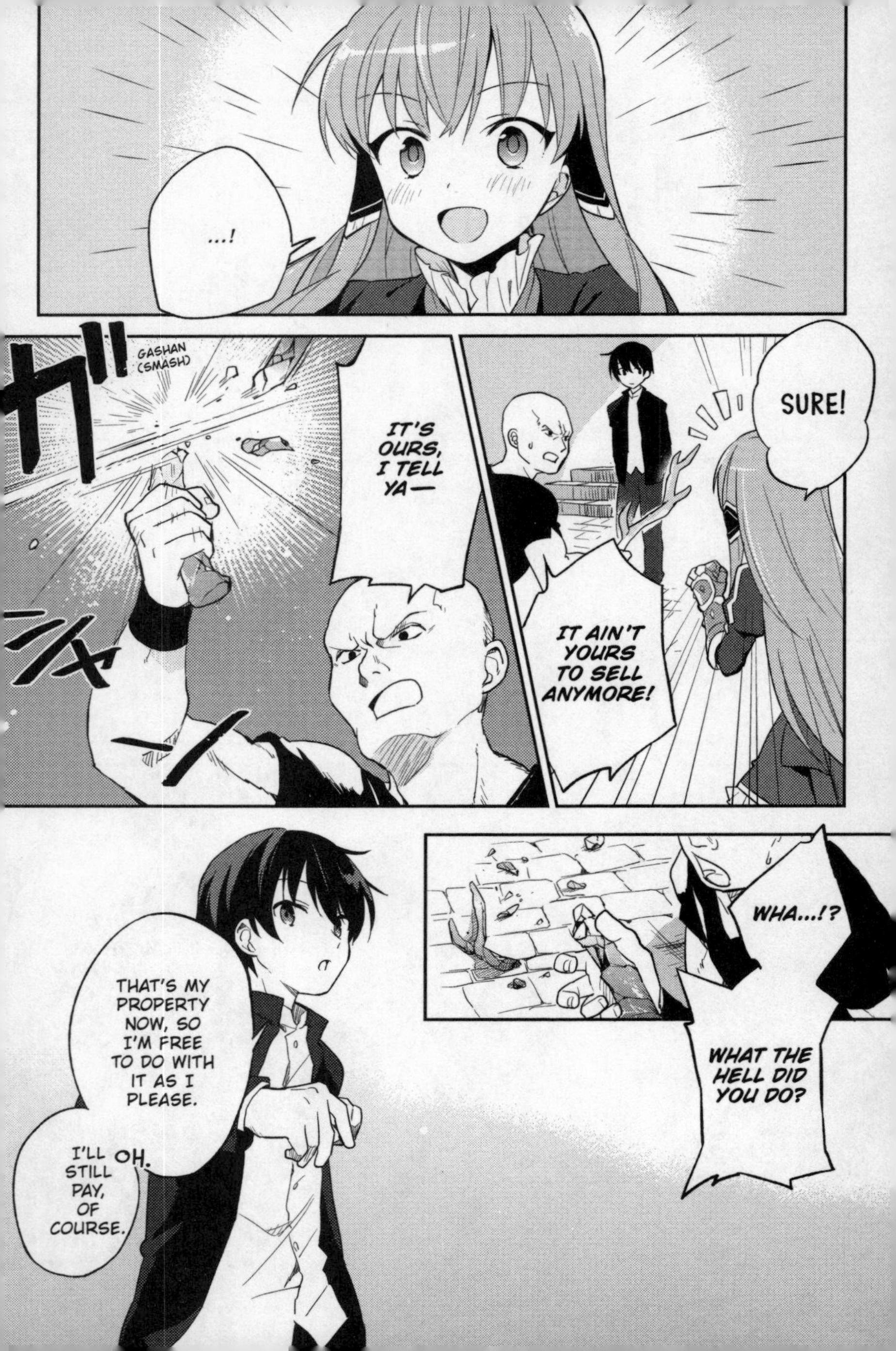
...!
SURE!
IT AIN'T YOURS TO SELL ANYMORE!
IT'S OURS, I TELL YA—
GASHAN (SMASH)
WHA...!?
WHAT THE HELL DID YOU DO?
THAT'S MY PROPERTY NOW, SO I'M FREE TO DO WITH IT AS I PLEASE.
OH.
I'LL STILL PAY, OF COURSE.

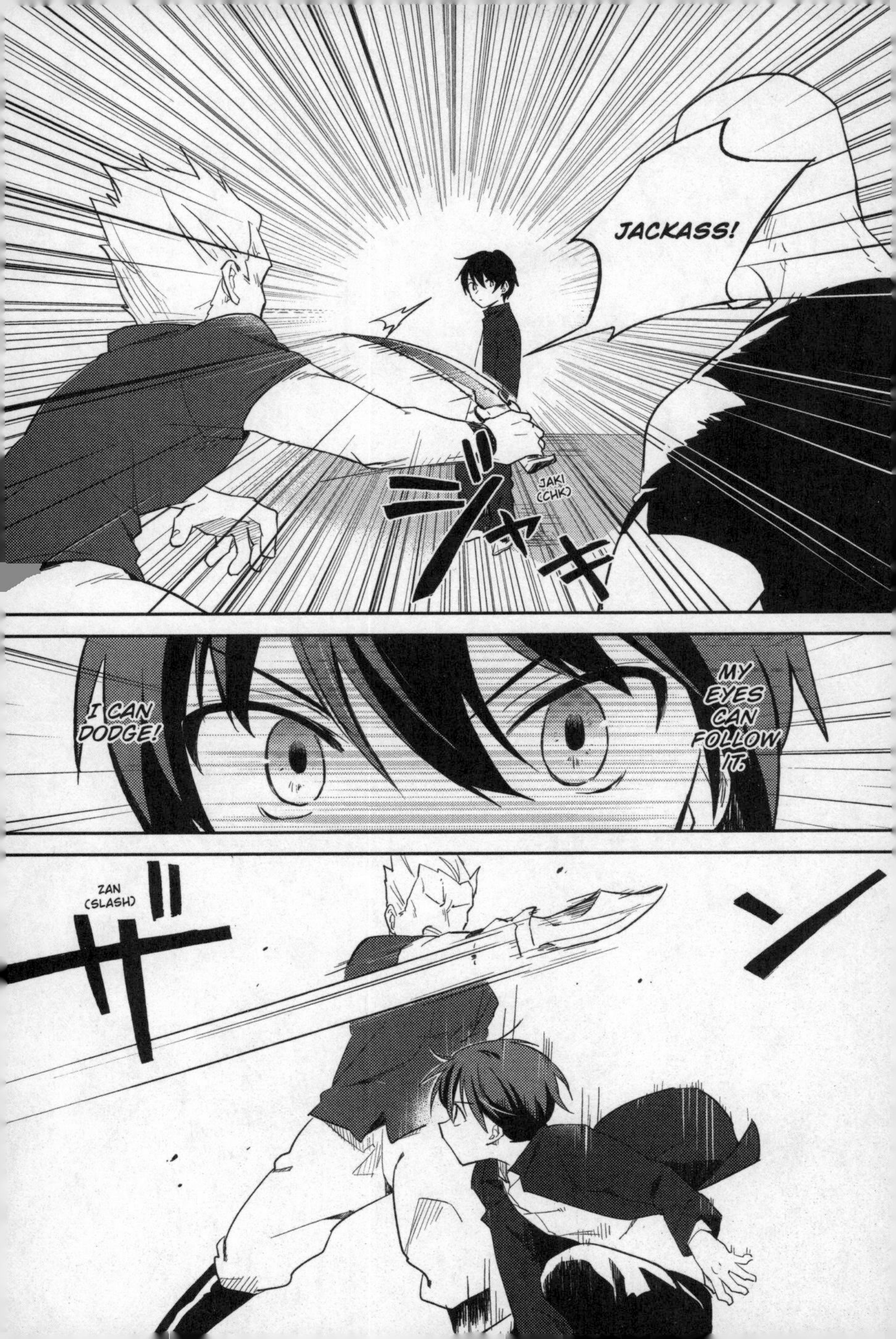
JACKASS!
ジャキ
JAKI (CHK)
MY EYES CAN FOLLOW IT.
I CAN DODGE!
ザン
ZAN (SLASH)

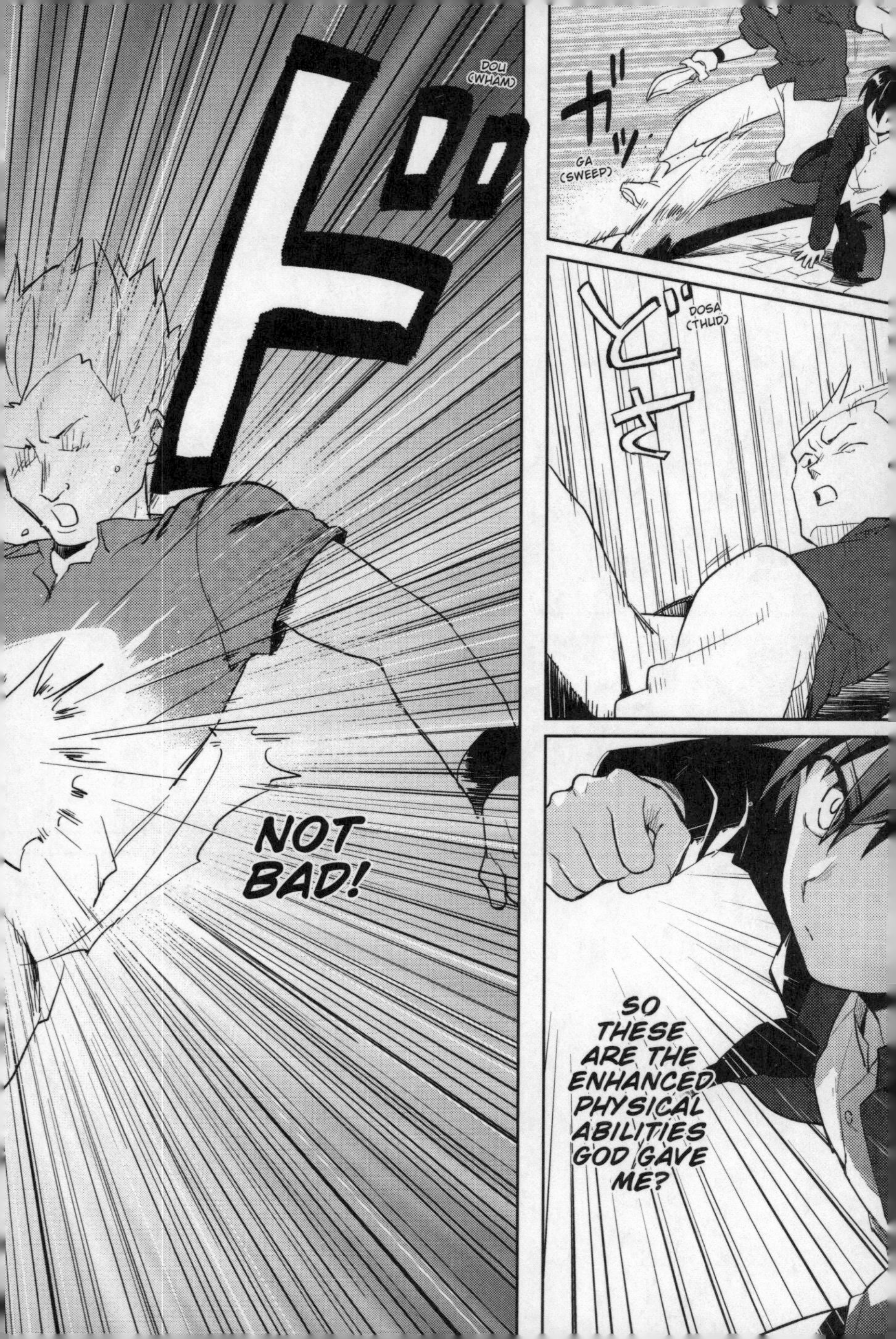
GA (SWEEP)
DOSA (THUD)
SO THESE ARE THE ENHANCED PHYSICAL ABILITIES GOD GAVE ME?
DOU (WHAM)
NOT BAD!

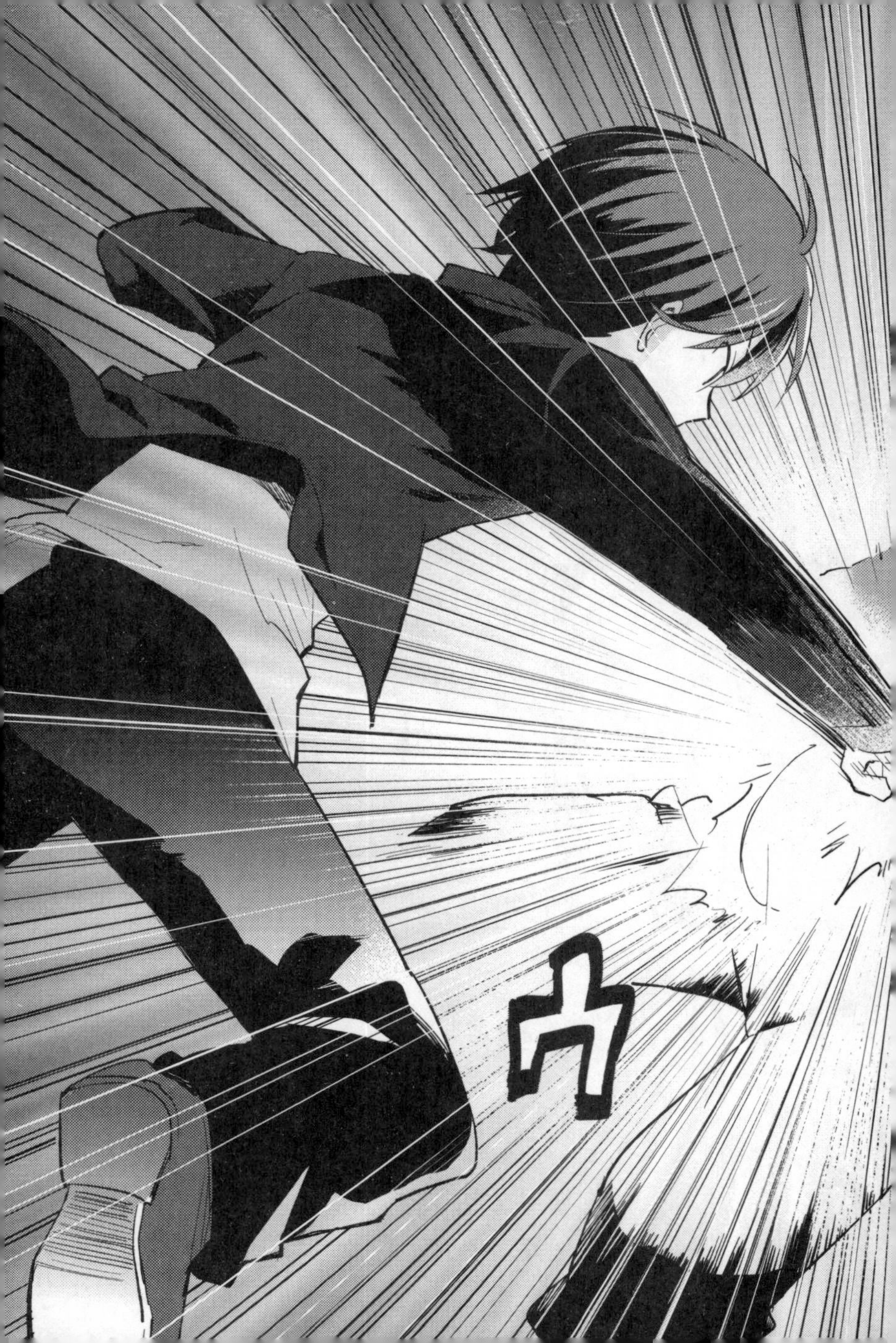
ウ

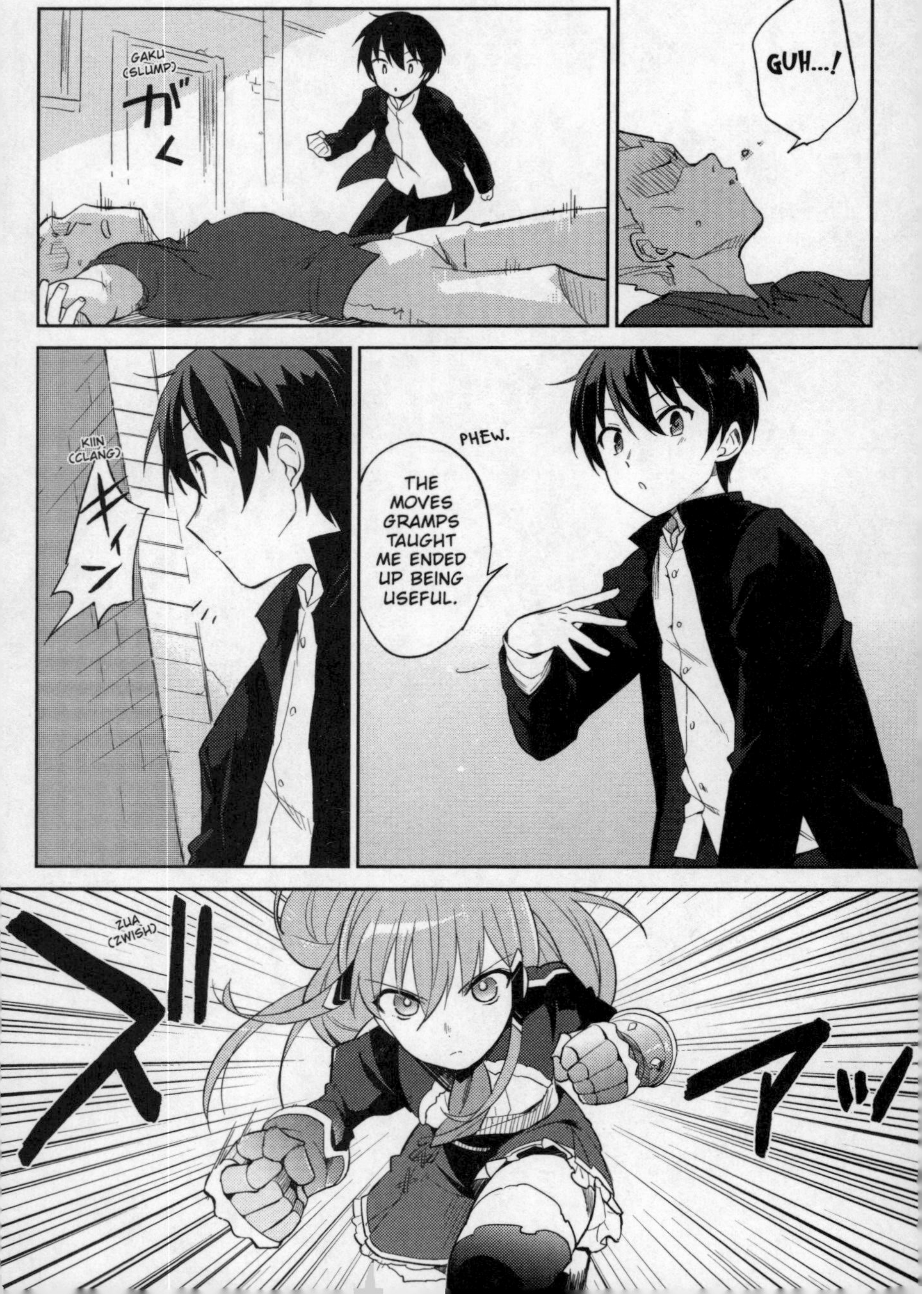
GUH...!
GAKU (SLUMP)
PHEW.
THE MOVES GRAMPS TAUGHT ME ENDED UP BEING USEFUL.
KIIN (CLANG)
ZUA (ZWISH)

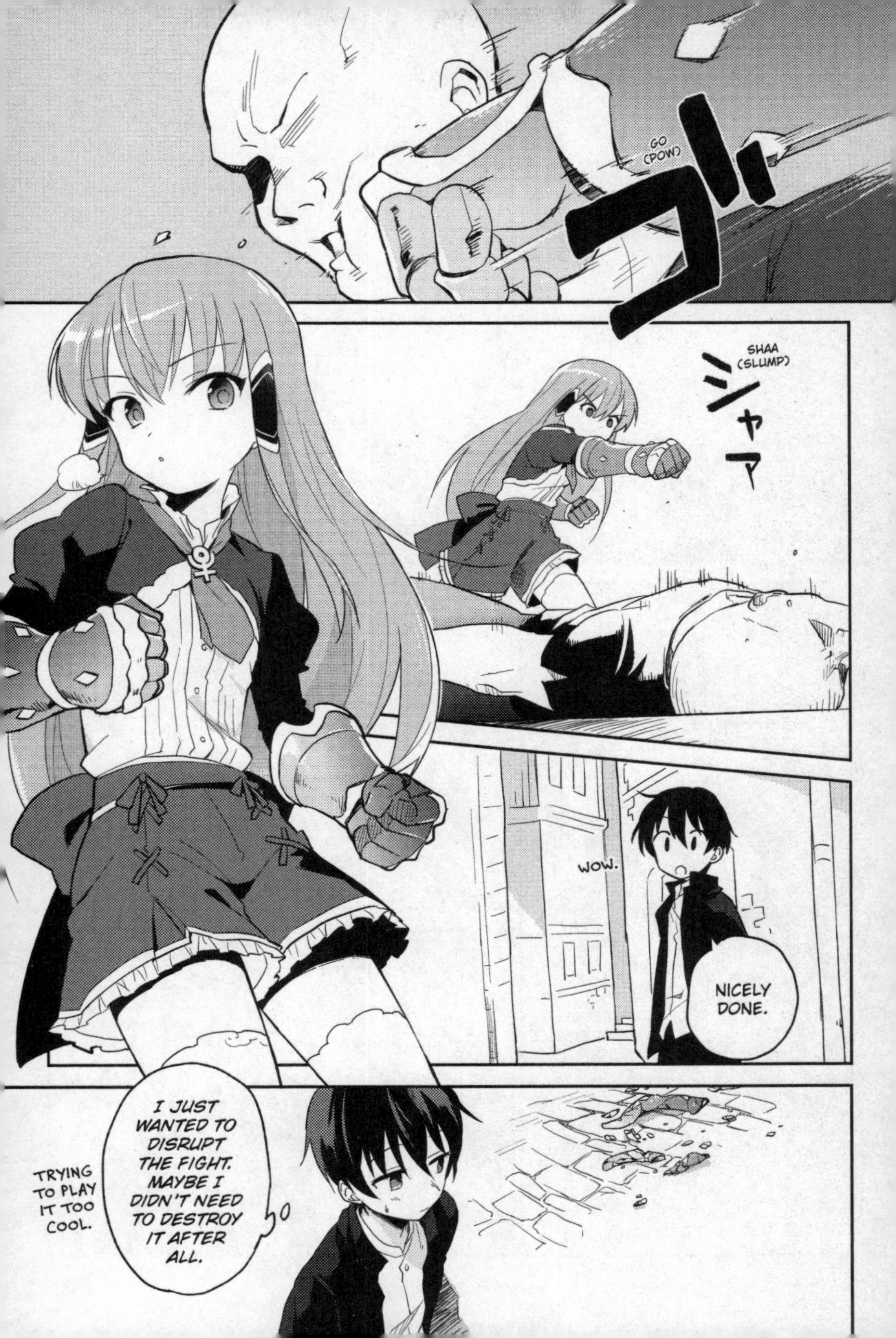
GO
(POW)
ゴッ
SHAA
(SLUMP)
シャア
WOW.
NICELY DONE.
I JUST WANTED TO DISRUPT THE FIGHT. MAYBE I DIDN'T NEED TO DESTROY IT AFTER ALL.
TRYING TO PLAY IT TOO COOL.

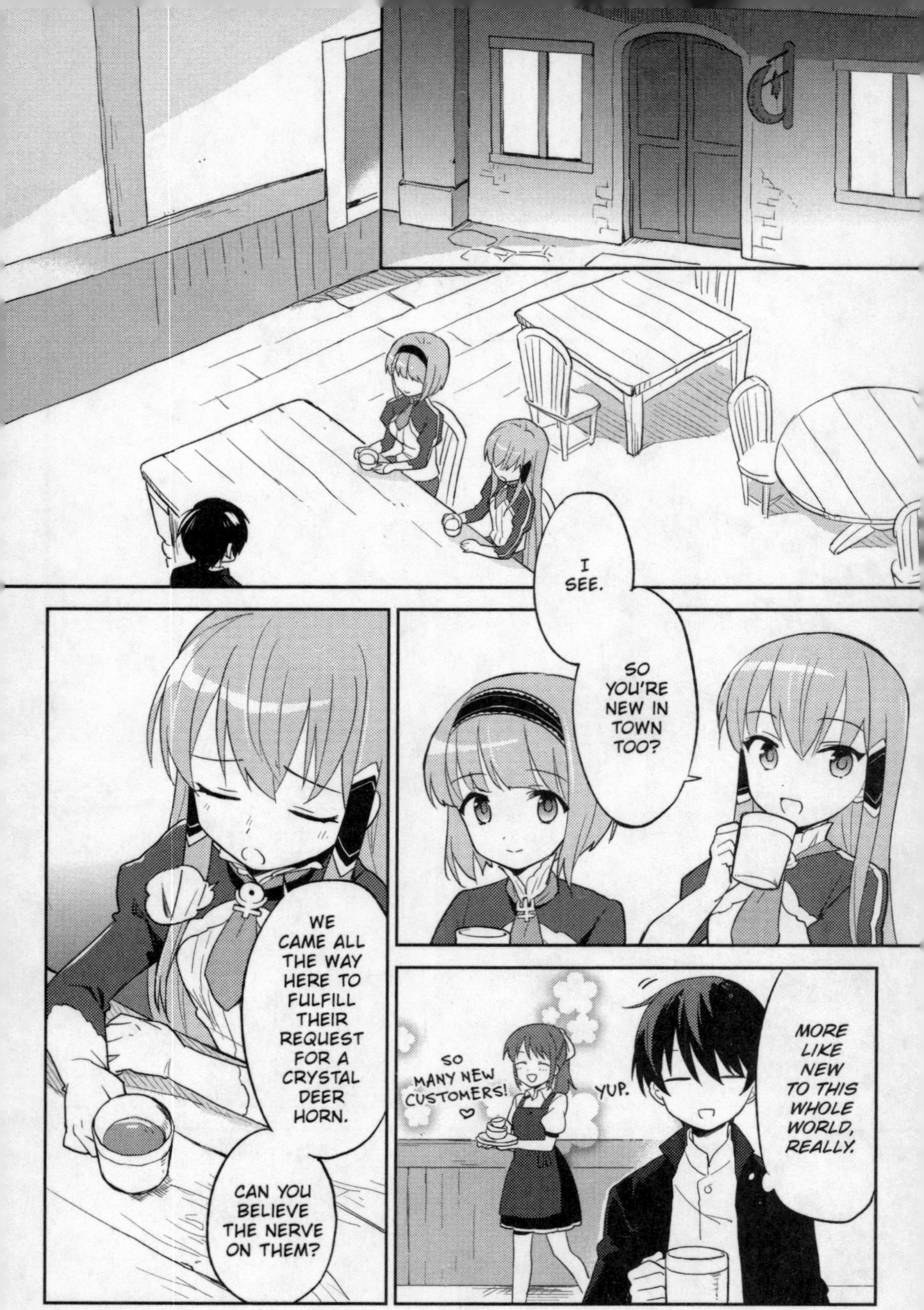
I SEE.
SO YOU'RE NEW IN TOWN TOO?
MORE LIKE NEW TO THIS WHOLE WORLD, REALLY.
YUP.
SO MANY NEW CUSTOMERS! ♥
WE CAME ALL THE WAY HERE TO FULFILL THEIR REQUEST FOR A CRYSTAL DEER HORN.
CAN YOU BELIEVE THE NERVE ON THEM?

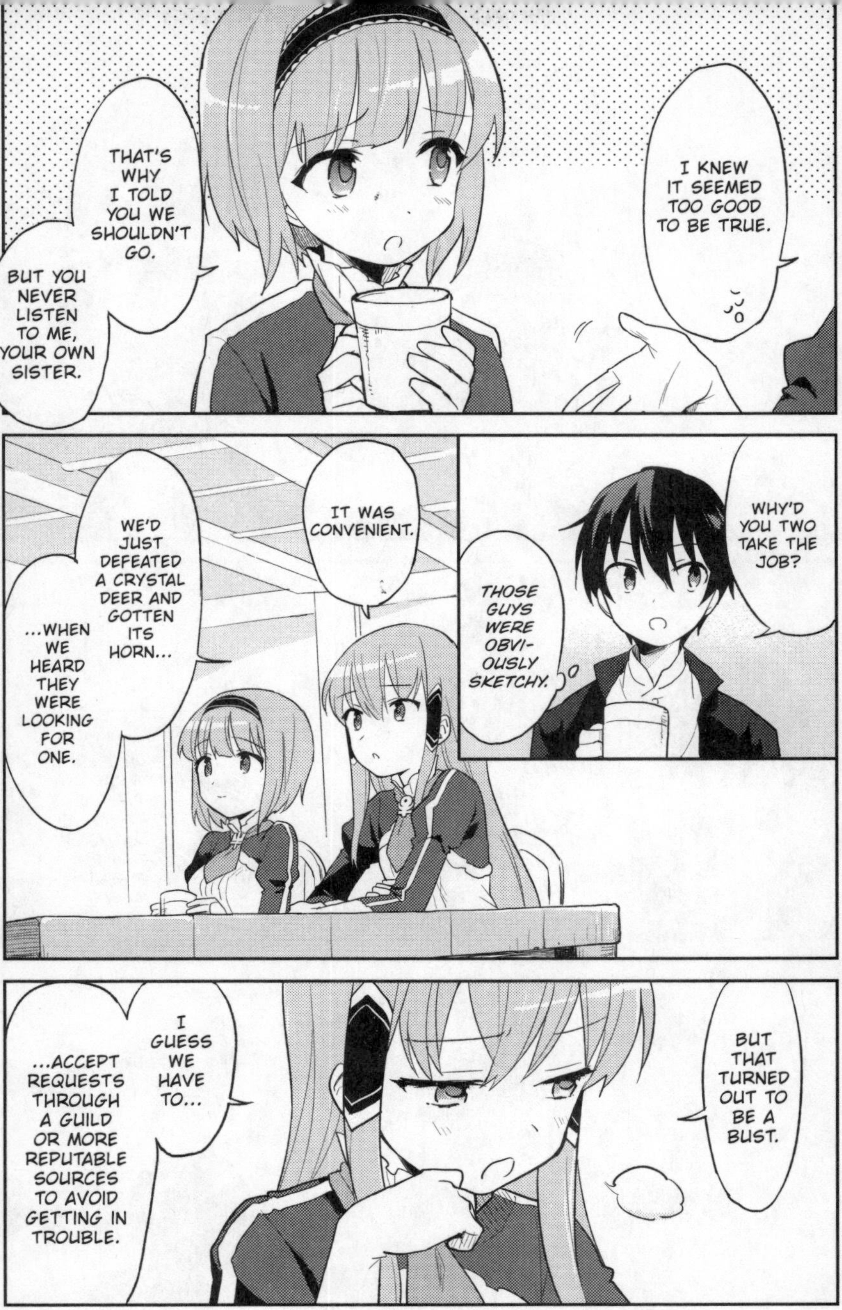
I KNEW IT SEEMED TOO GOOD TO BE TRUE.
THAT'S WHY I TOLD YOU WE SHOULDN'T GO.
BUT YOU NEVER LISTEN TO ME, YOUR OWN SISTER.
WHY'D YOU TWO TAKE THE JOB?
THOSE GUYS WERE OBVI-OUSLY SKETCHY.
IT WAS CONVENIENT.
WE'D JUST DEFEATED A CRYSTAL DEER AND GOTTEN ITS HORN...
...WHEN WE HEARD THEY WERE LOOKING FOR ONE.
BUT THAT TURNED OUT TO BE A BUST.
I GUESS WE HAVE TO...
...ACCEPT REQUESTS THROUGH A GUILD OR MORE REPUTABLE SOURCES TO AVOID GETTING IN TROUBLE.

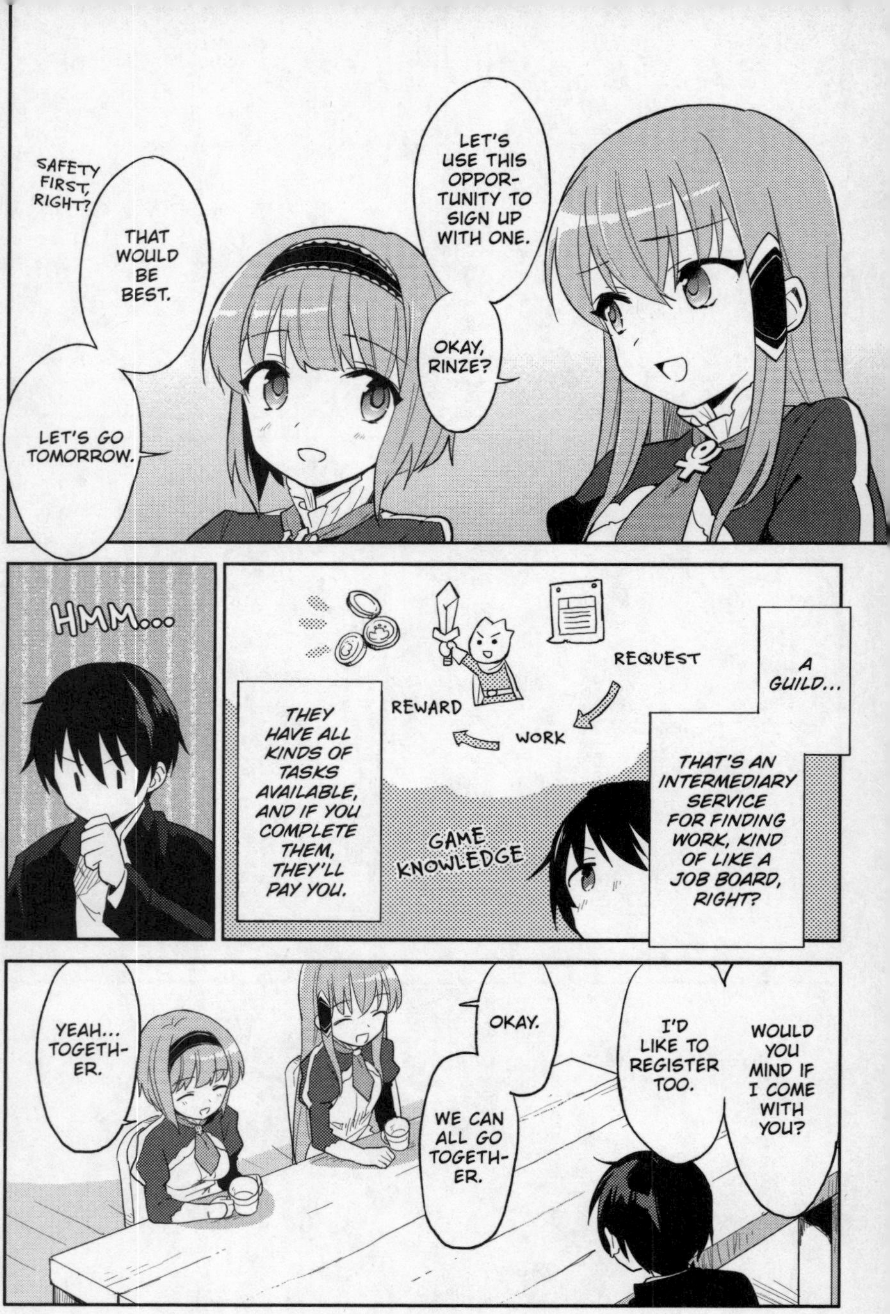
LET'S USE THIS OPPORTUNITY TO SIGN UP WITH ONE.
OKAY, RINZE?
SAFETY FIRST, RIGHT?
THAT WOULD BE BEST.
LET'S GO TOMORROW.
A GUILD...
THAT'S AN INTERMEDIARY SERVICE FOR FINDING WORK, KIND OF LIKE A JOB BOARD, RIGHT?
REQUEST
WORK
REWARD
GAME KNOWLEDGE
THEY HAVE ALL KINDS OF TASKS AVAILABLE, AND IF YOU COMPLETE THEM, THEY'LL PAY YOU.
HMM...
WOULD YOU MIND IF I COME WITH YOU?
I'D LIKE TO REGISTER TOO.
OKAY.
WE CAN ALL GO TOGETHER.
YEAH... TOGETHER.

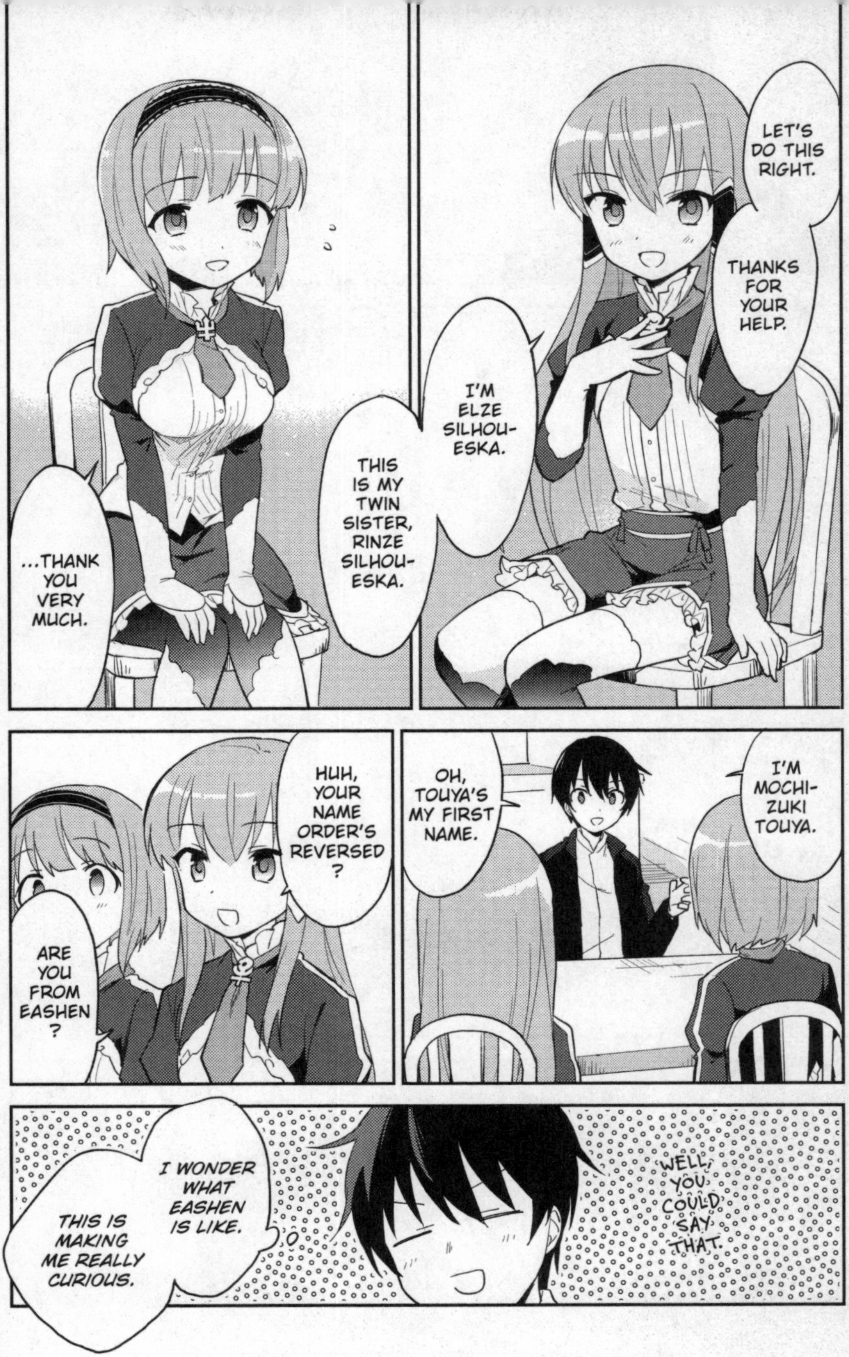
LET'S DO THIS RIGHT.
THANKS FOR YOUR HELP.
I'M ELZE SILHOUESKA.
THIS IS MY TWIN SISTER, RINZE SILHOUESKA.
...THANK YOU VERY MUCH.
I'M MOCHIZUKI TOUYA.
OH, TOUYA'S MY FIRST NAME.
HUH, YOUR NAME ORDER'S REVERSED?
ARE YOU FROM EASHEN?
WELL, YOU COULD SAY THAT.
I WONDER WHAT EASHEN IS LIKE.
THIS IS MAKING ME REALLY CURIOUS.

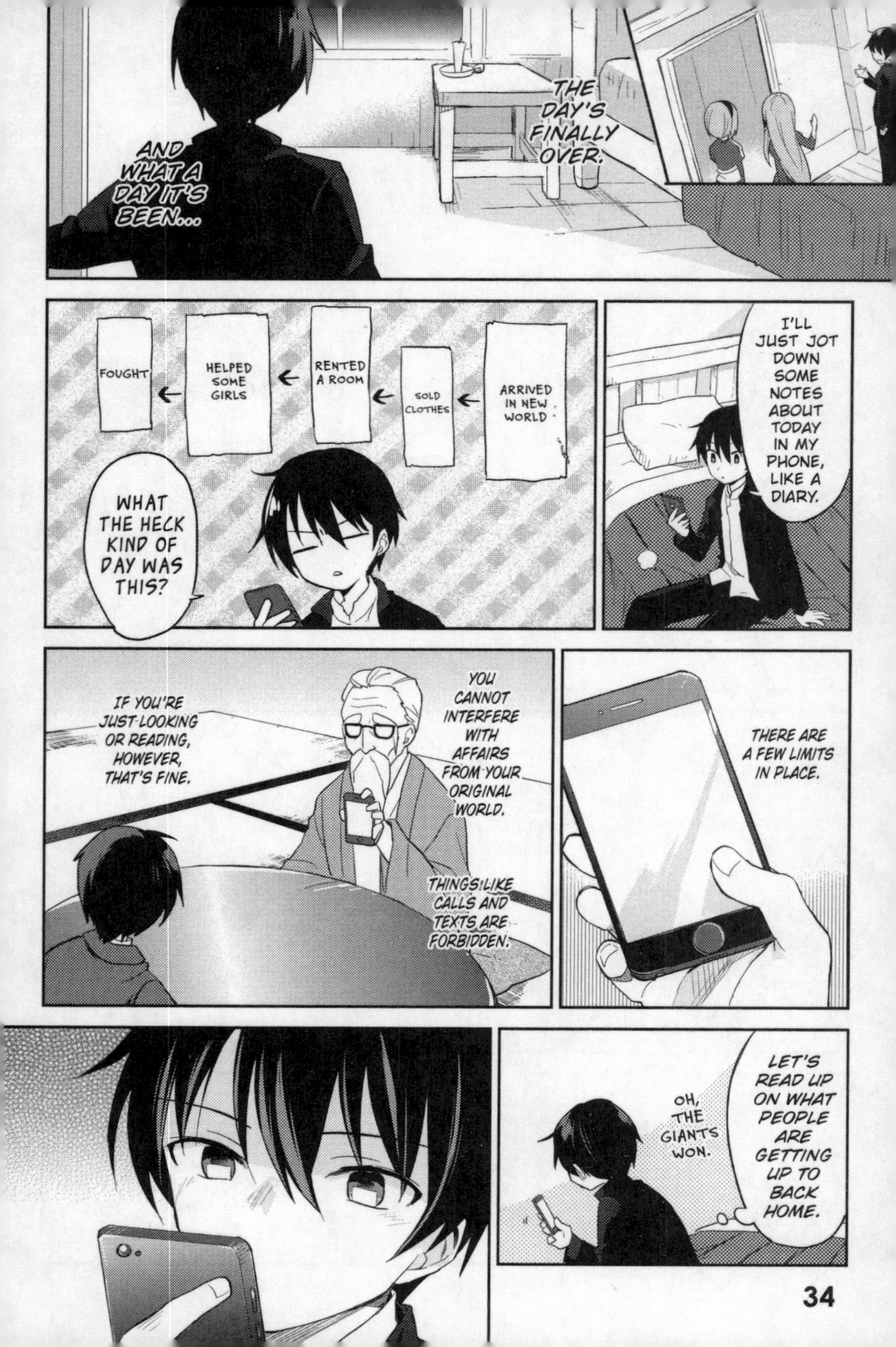

THE DAY'S FINALLY OVER.
AND WHAT A DAY IT'S BEEN...
I'LL JUST JOT DOWN SOME NOTES ABOUT TODAY IN MY PHONE, LIKE A DIARY.
ARRIVED IN NEW WORLD
SOLD CLOTHES
RENTED A ROOM
HELPED SOME GIRLS
FOUGHT
WHAT THE HECK KIND OF DAY WAS THIS?
THERE ARE A FEW LIMITS IN PLACE.
YOU CANNOT INTERFERE WITH AFFAIRS FROM YOUR ORIGINAL WORLD.
IF YOU'RE JUST LOOKING OR READING, HOWEVER, THAT'S FINE.
THINGS LIKE CALLS AND TEXTS ARE FORBIDDEN.
LET'S READ UP ON WHAT PEOPLE ARE GETTING UP TO BACK HOME.
OH, THE GIANTS WON.

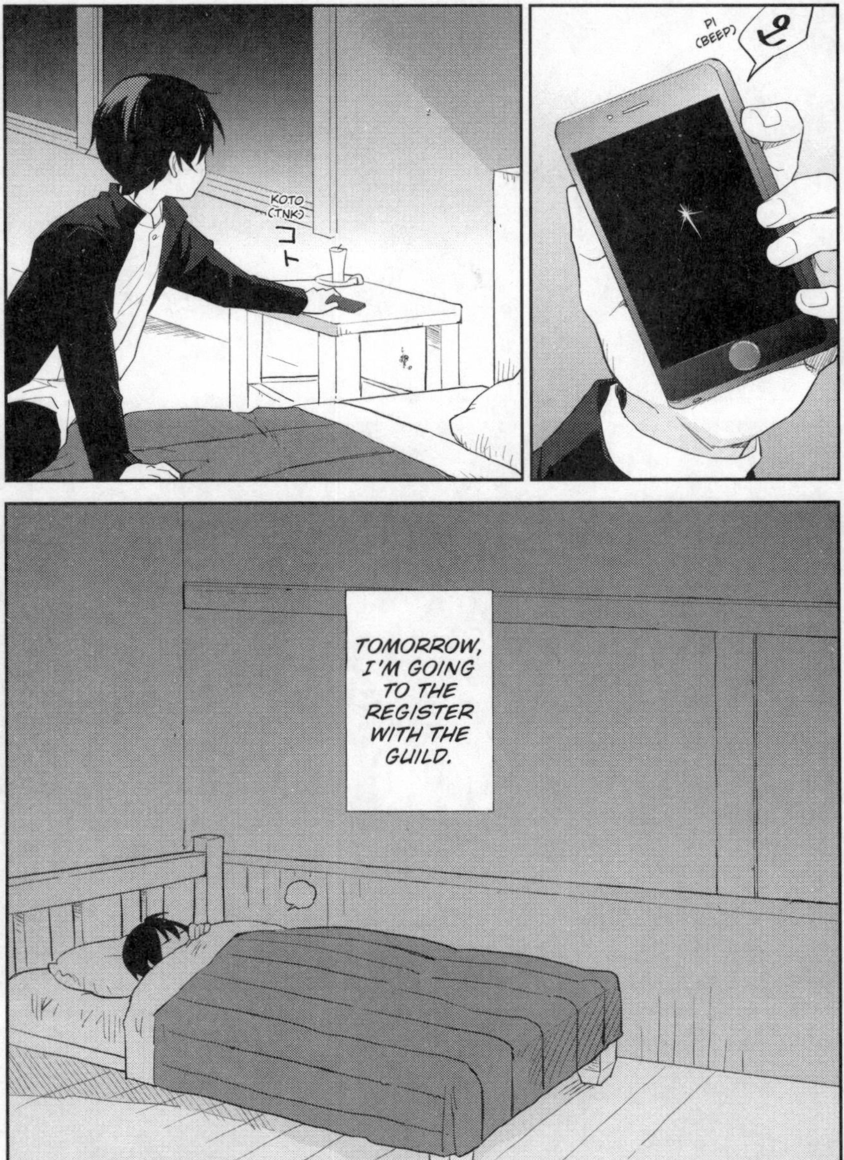
PI (BEEP)
KOTO (TNK)
TOMORROW, I'M GOING TO THE REGISTER WITH THE GUILD.

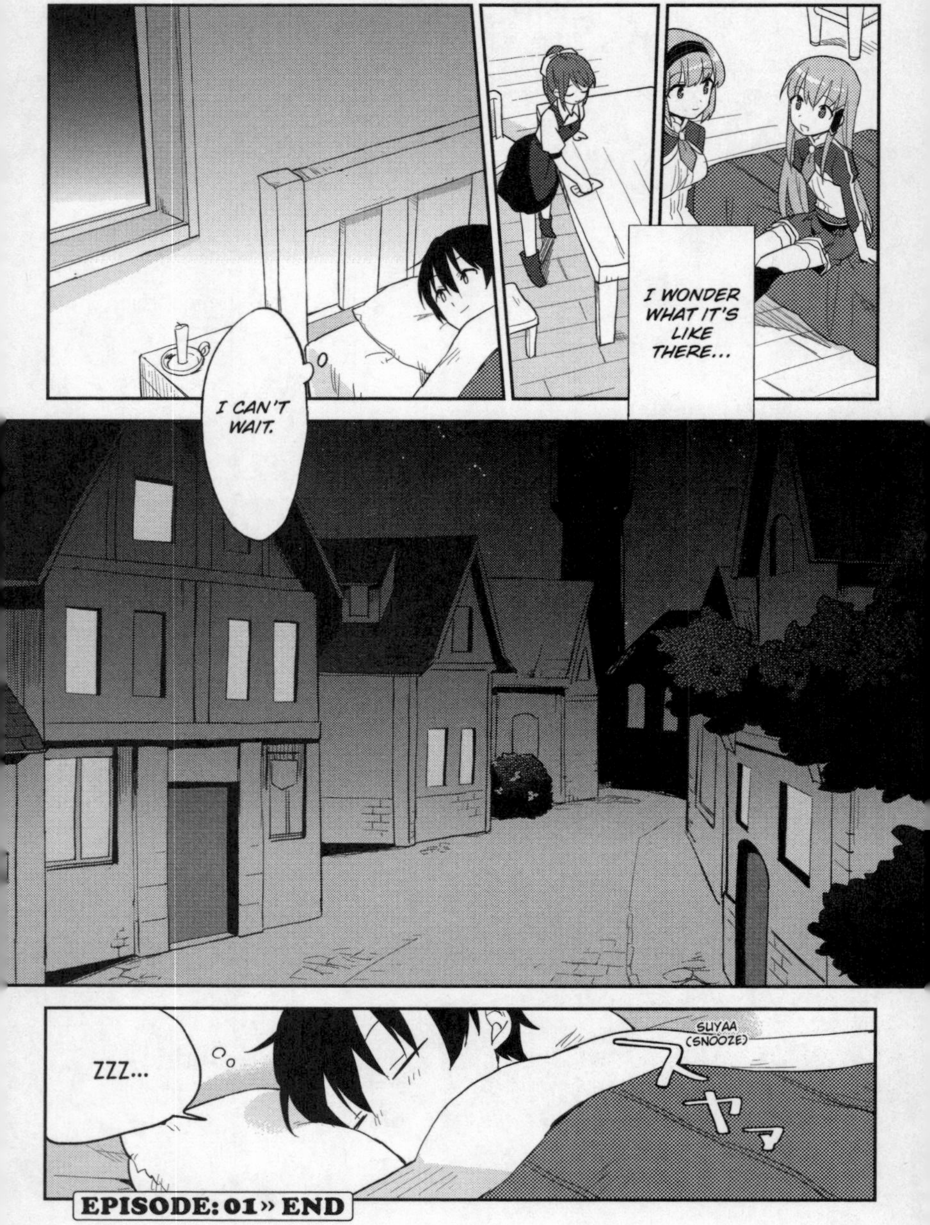
I WONDER WHAT IT'S LIKE THERE...
I CAN'T WAIT.
SUYAA (SNOOZE)
スヤァ
ZZZ...

EPISODE: 01 » END

In Another World with
My Smartphone

In Another World with My Smartphone

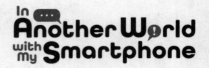

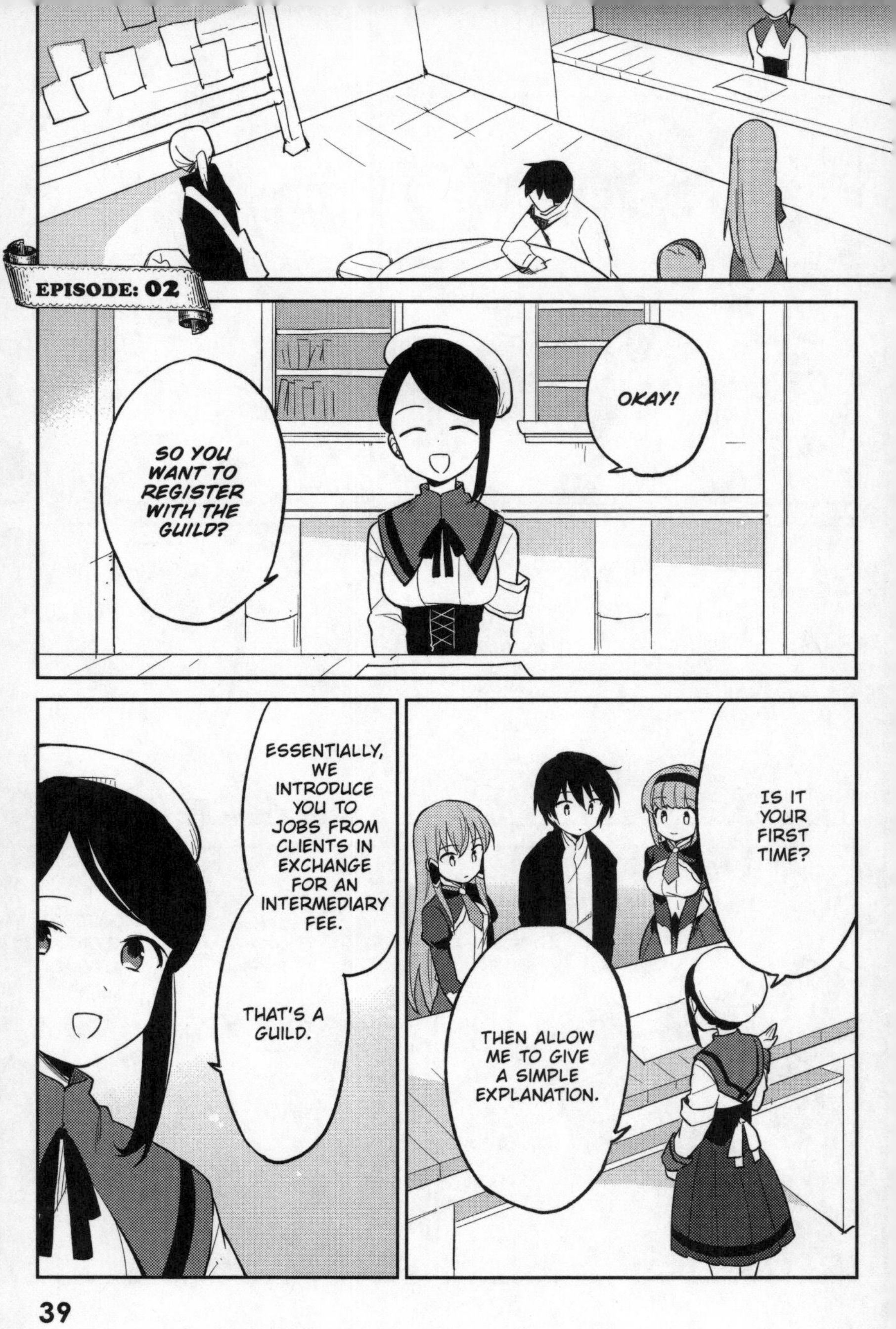
EPISODE: 02
OKAY!
SO YOU WANT TO REGISTER WITH THE GUILD?
IS IT YOUR FIRST TIME?
THEN ALLOW ME TO GIVE A SIMPLE EXPLANATION.
ESSENTIALLY, WE INTRODUCE YOU TO JOBS FROM CLIENTS IN EXCHANGE FOR AN INTERMEDIARY FEE.
THAT'S A GUILD.

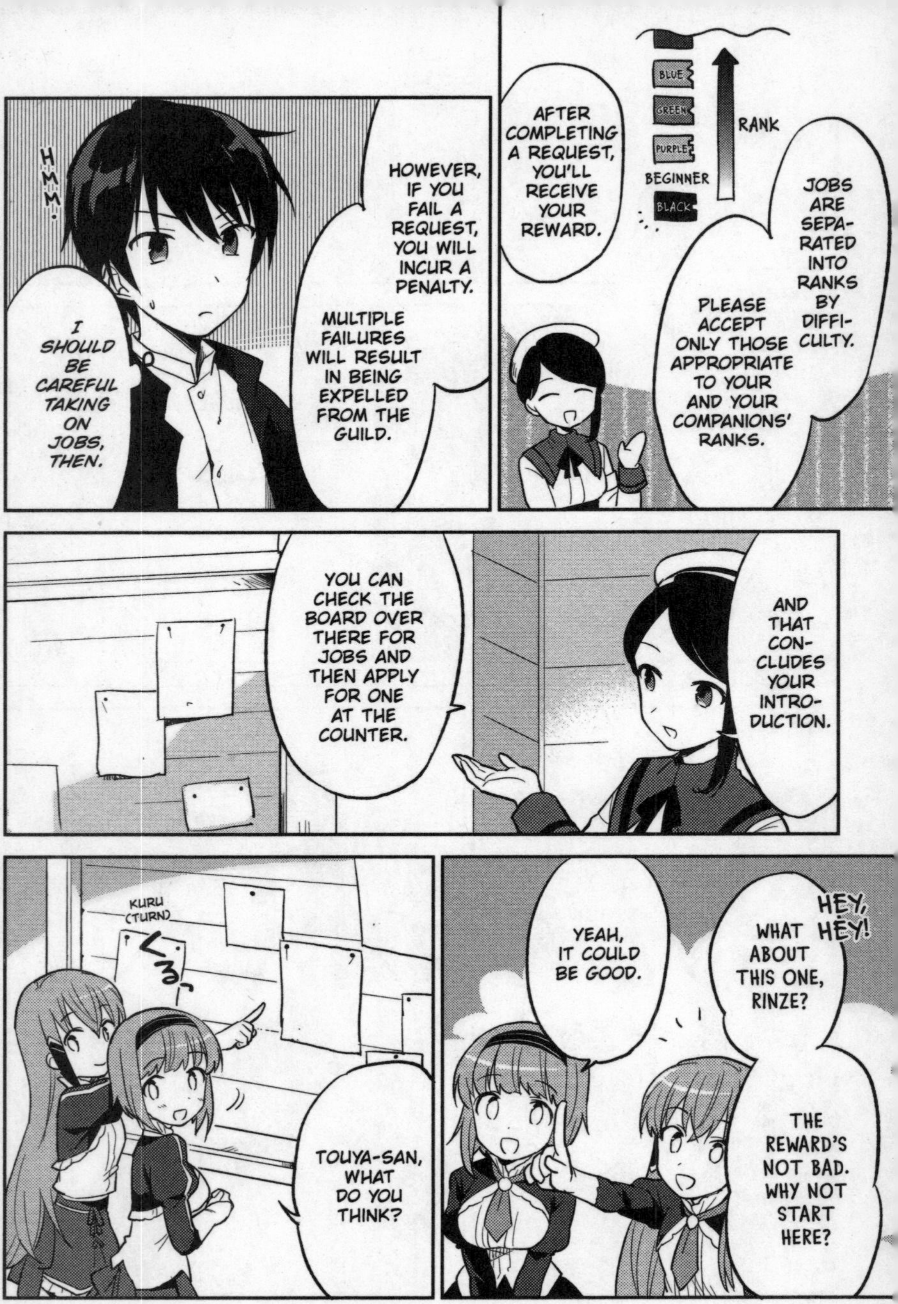
BLUE
GREEN
PURPLE
BEGINNER
BLACK
RANK
JOBS ARE SEPARATED INTO RANKS BY DIFFICULTY.
PLEASE ACCEPT ONLY THOSE APPROPRIATE TO YOUR AND YOUR COMPANIONS' RANKS.
AFTER COMPLETING A REQUEST, YOU'LL RECEIVE YOUR REWARD.
HOWEVER, IF YOU FAIL A REQUEST, YOU WILL INCUR A PENALTY.
MULTIPLE FAILURES WILL RESULT IN BEING EXPELLED FROM THE GUILD.
HMM!
I SHOULD BE CAREFUL TAKING ON JOBS, THEN.
AND THAT CONCLUDES YOUR INTRODUCTION.
YOU CAN CHECK THE BOARD OVER THERE FOR JOBS AND THEN APPLY FOR ONE AT THE COUNTER.
HEY, HEY!
WHAT ABOUT THIS ONE, RINZE?
YEAH, IT COULD BE GOOD.
THE REWARD'S NOT BAD. WHY NOT START HERE?
KURU (TURN)
くる
TOUYA-SAN, WHAT DO YOU THINK?

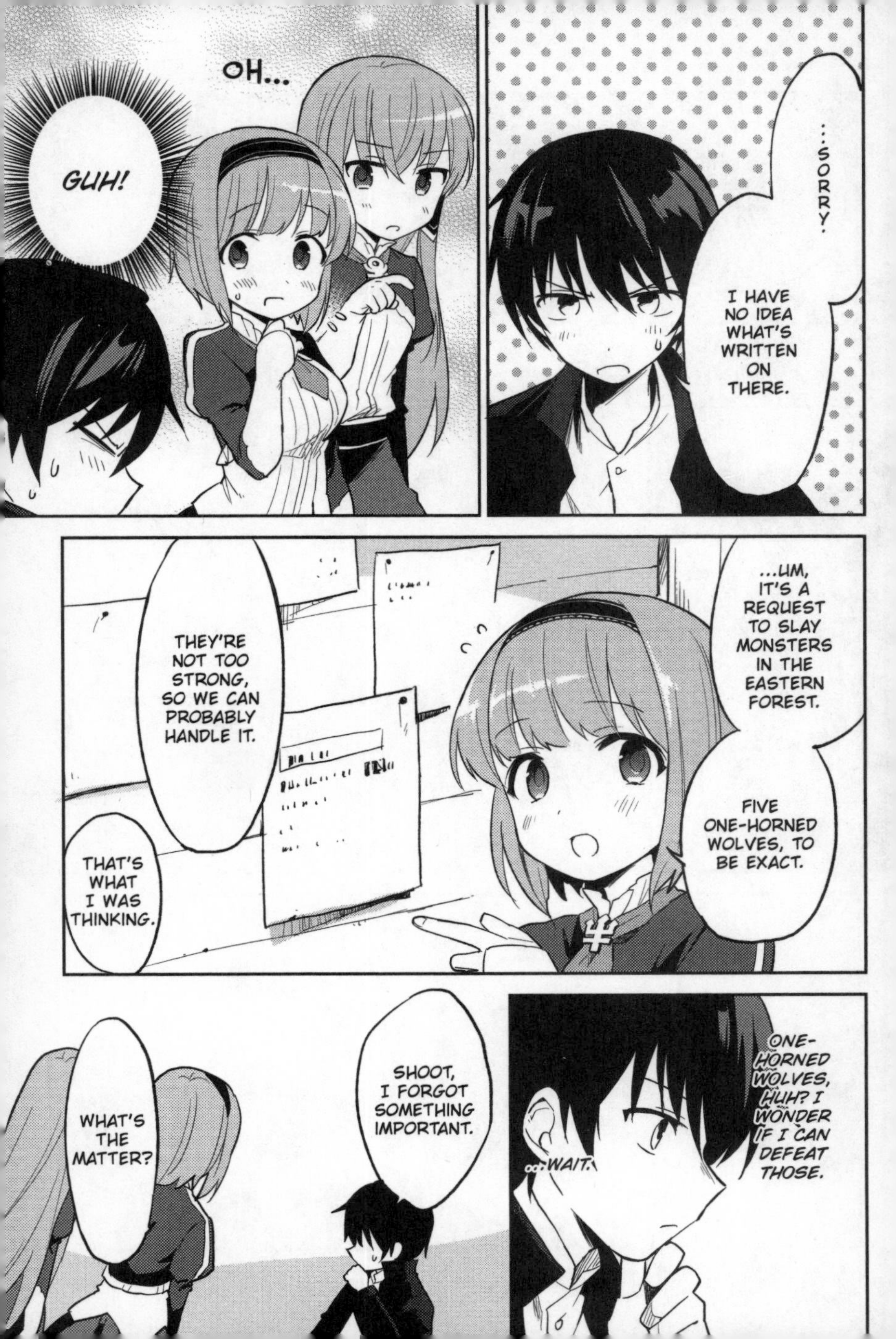
...SORRY.
I HAVE NO IDEA WHAT'S WRITTEN ON THERE.
OH...
GUH!
...UM, IT'S A REQUEST TO SLAY MONSTERS IN THE EASTERN FOREST.
FIVE ONE-HORNED WOLVES, TO BE EXACT.
THEY'RE NOT TOO STRONG, SO WE CAN PROBABLY HANDLE IT.
THAT'S WHAT I WAS THINKING.
ONE-HORNED WOLVES, HUH? I WONDER IF I CAN DEFEAT THOSE.
...WAIT.
SHOOT, I FORGOT SOMETHING IMPORTANT.
WHAT'S THE MATTER?

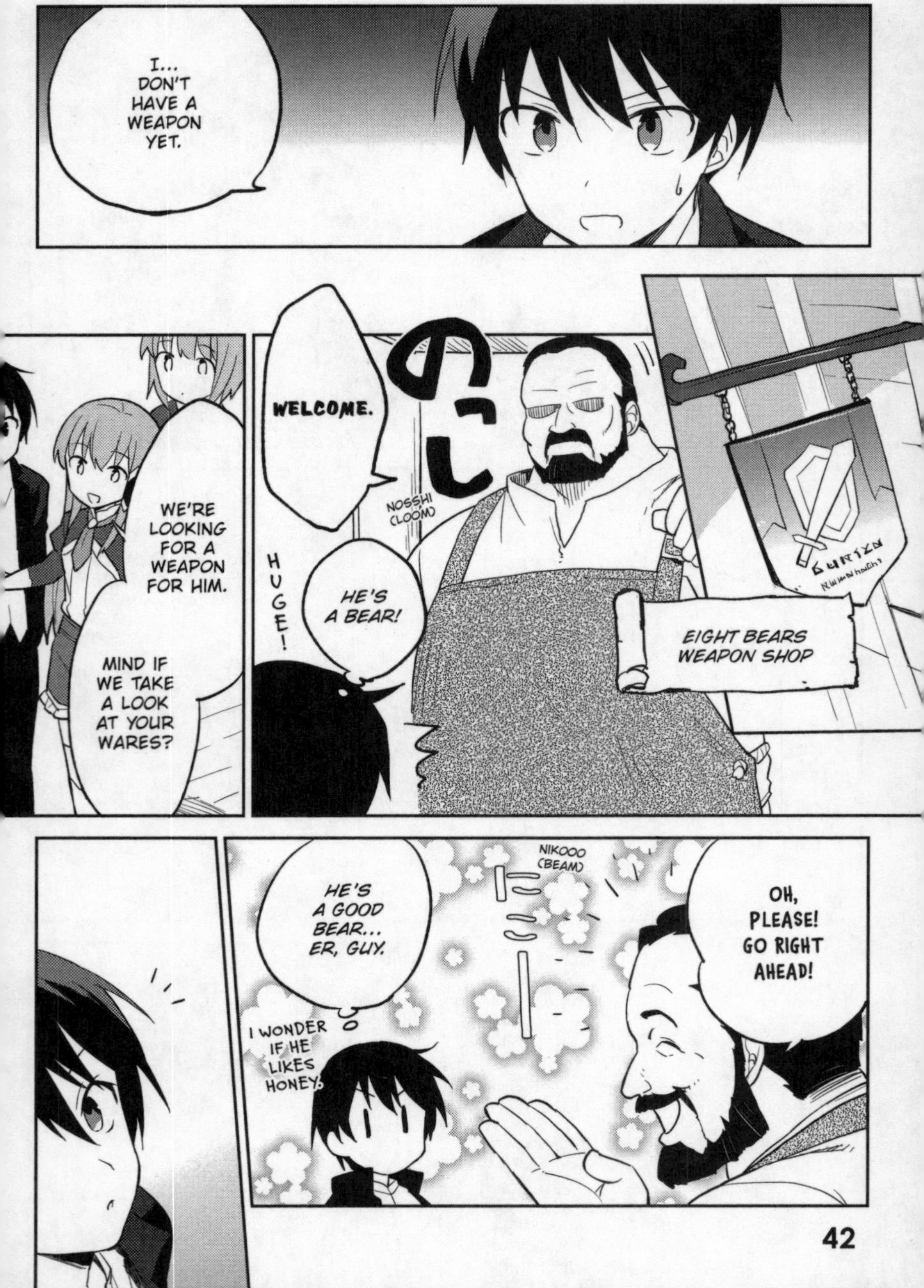

I... DON'T HAVE A WEAPON YET.
EIGHT BEARS WEAPON SHOP
WELCOME.
NOSSHI (LOOM)
HUGE!
HE'S A BEAR!
WE'RE LOOKING FOR A WEAPON FOR HIM.
MIND IF WE TAKE A LOOK AT YOUR WARES?
OH, PLEASE! GO RIGHT AHEAD!
NIKOOO (BEAM)
HE'S A GOOD BEAR... ER, GUY.
I WONDER IF HE LIKES HONEY.

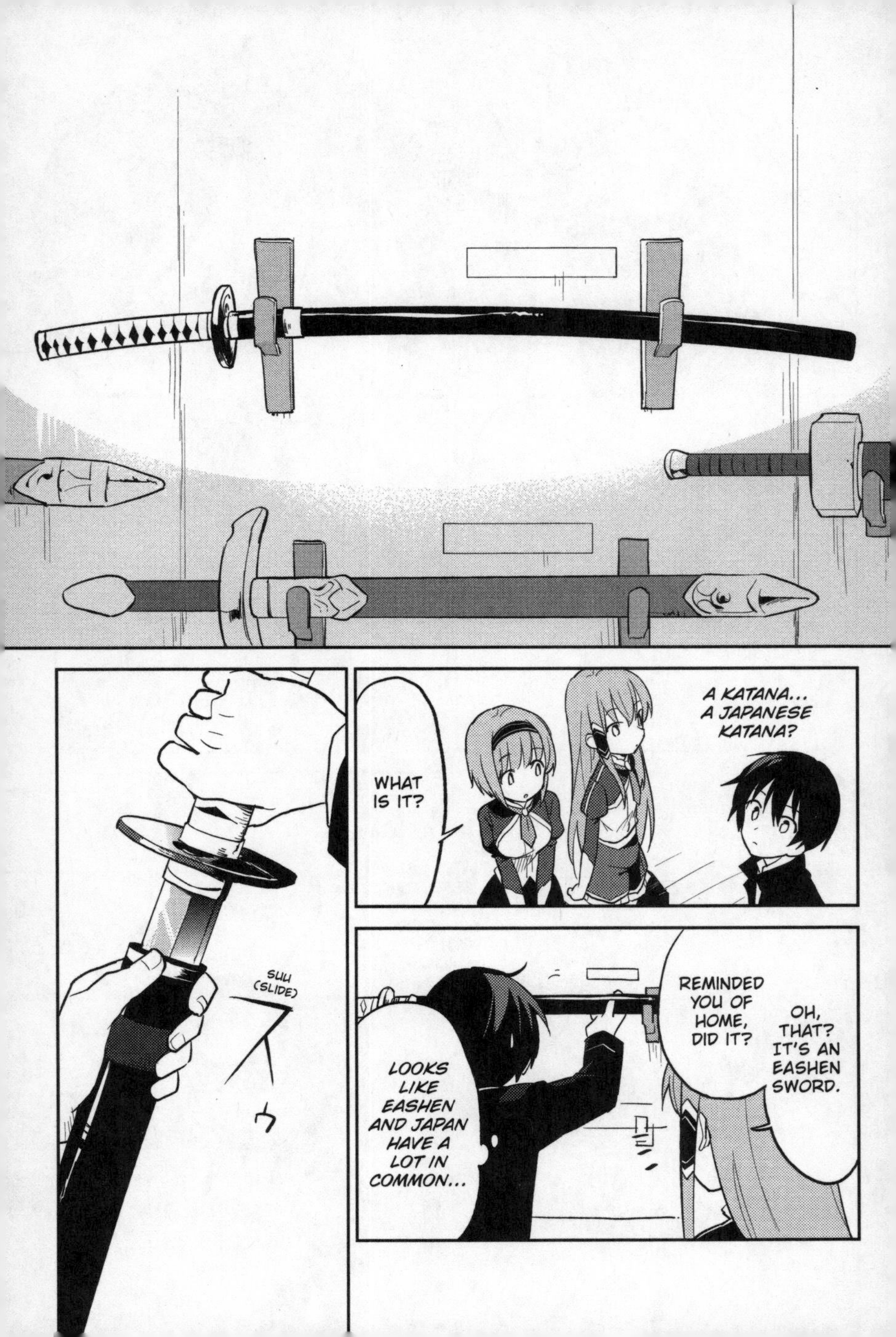
A KATANA... A JAPANESE KATANA?
WHAT IS IT?
OH, THAT? IT'S AN EASHEN SWORD.
REMINDED YOU OF HOME, DID IT?
LOOKS LIKE EASHEN AND JAPAN HAVE A LOT IN COMMON...
SUU (SLIDE)

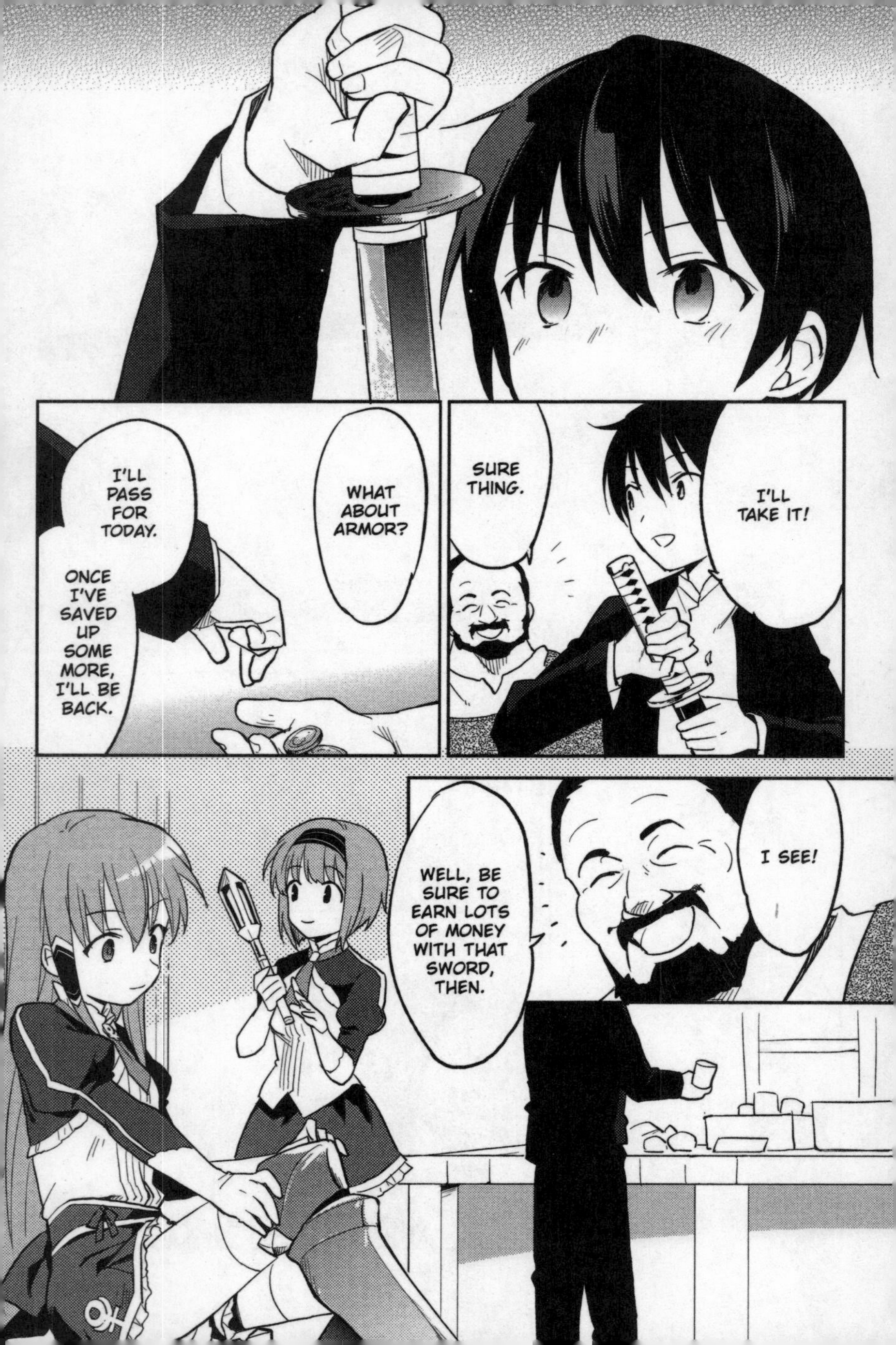
I'LL TAKE IT!
SURE THING.
WHAT ABOUT ARMOR?
I'LL PASS FOR TODAY.
ONCE I'VE SAVED UP SOME MORE, I'LL BE BACK.
I SEE!
WELL, BE SURE TO EARN LOTS OF MONEY WITH THAT SWORD, THEN.

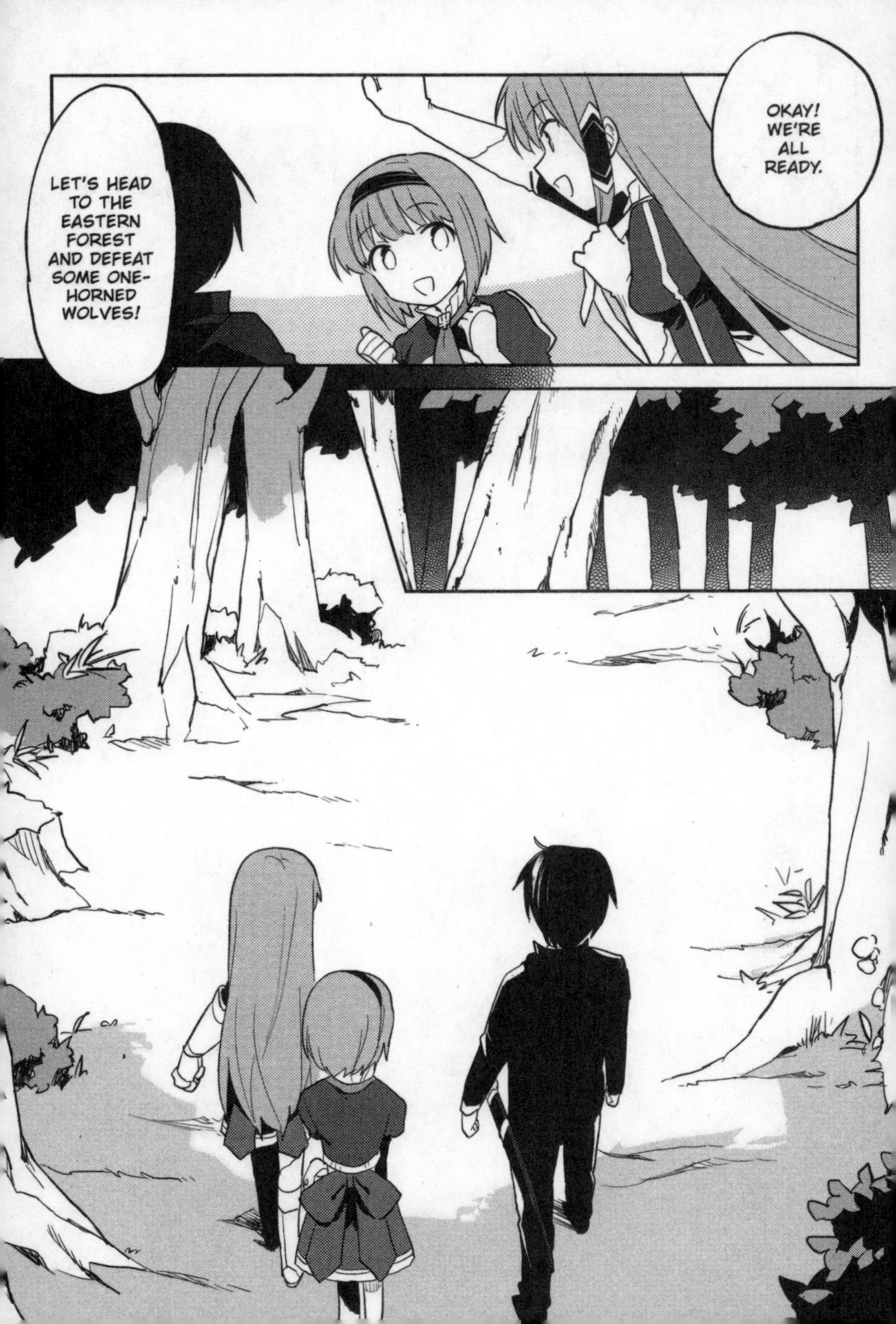
OKAY! WE'RE ALL READY.
LET'S HEAD TO THE EASTERN FOREST AND DEFEAT SOME ONE-HORNED WOLVES!

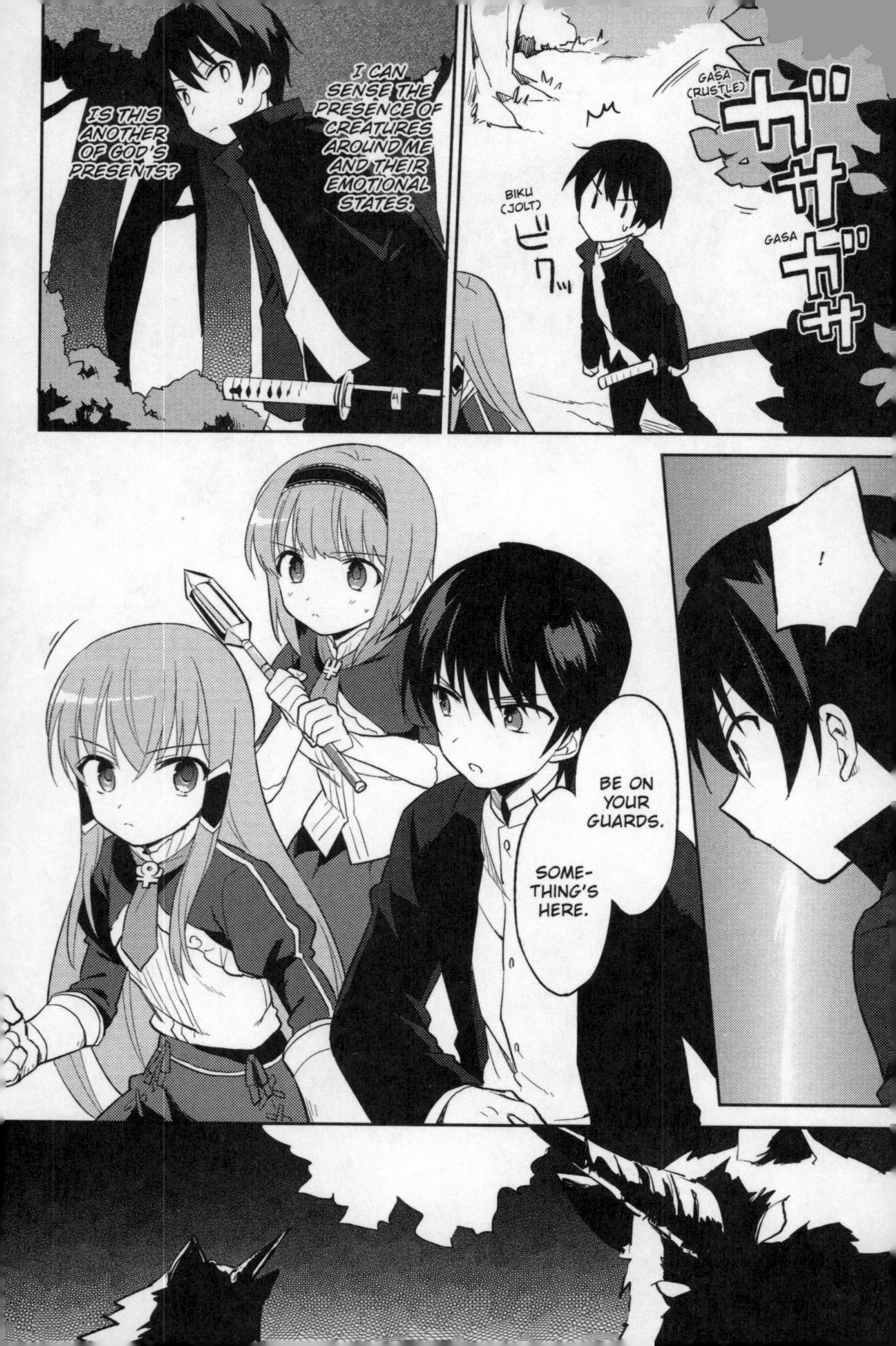
GASA (RUSTLE)
ガサ
GASA
ガサ
BIKU (JOLT)
ビクッ
I CAN SENSE THE PRESENCE OF CREATURES AROUND ME AND THEIR EMOTIONAL STATES.
IS THIS ANOTHER OF GOD'S PRESENTS?
!
BE ON YOUR GUARDS.
SOME-THING'S HERE.

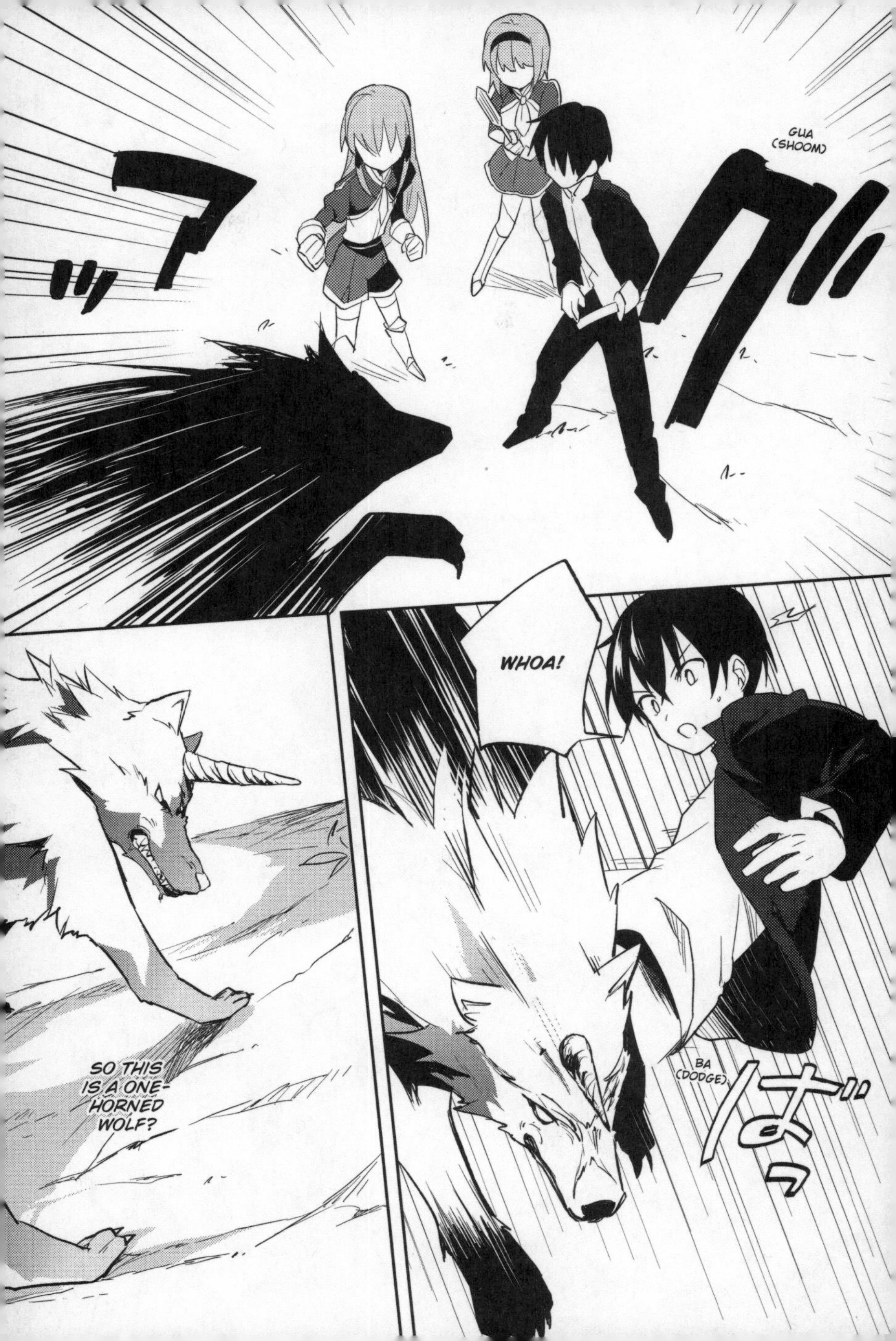
GUA
(SHOOM)
WHOA!
BA
(DODGE)
SO THIS IS A ONE-HORNED WOLF?

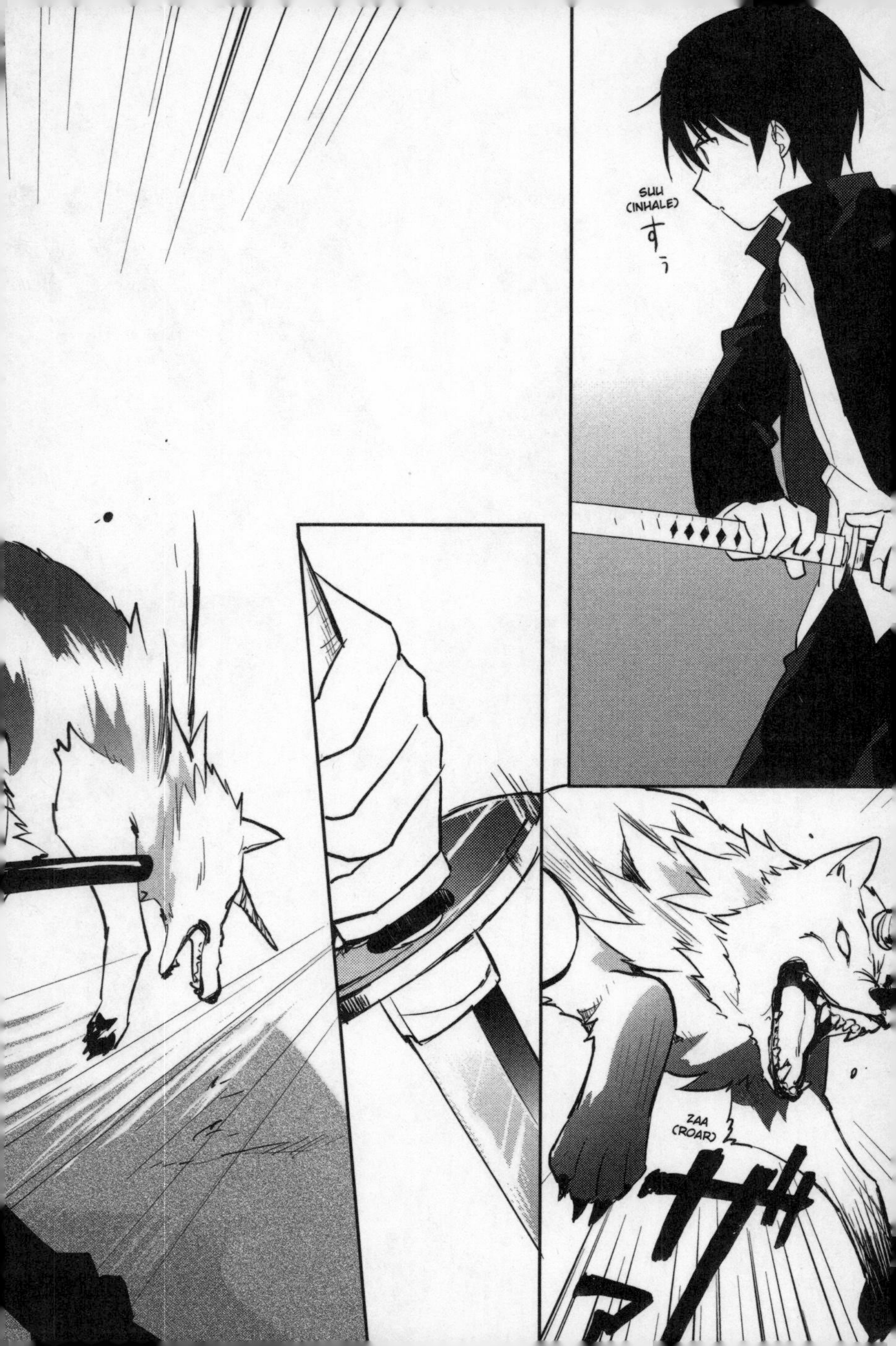
SUU
(INHALE)
すぅ
ZAA
(ROAR)

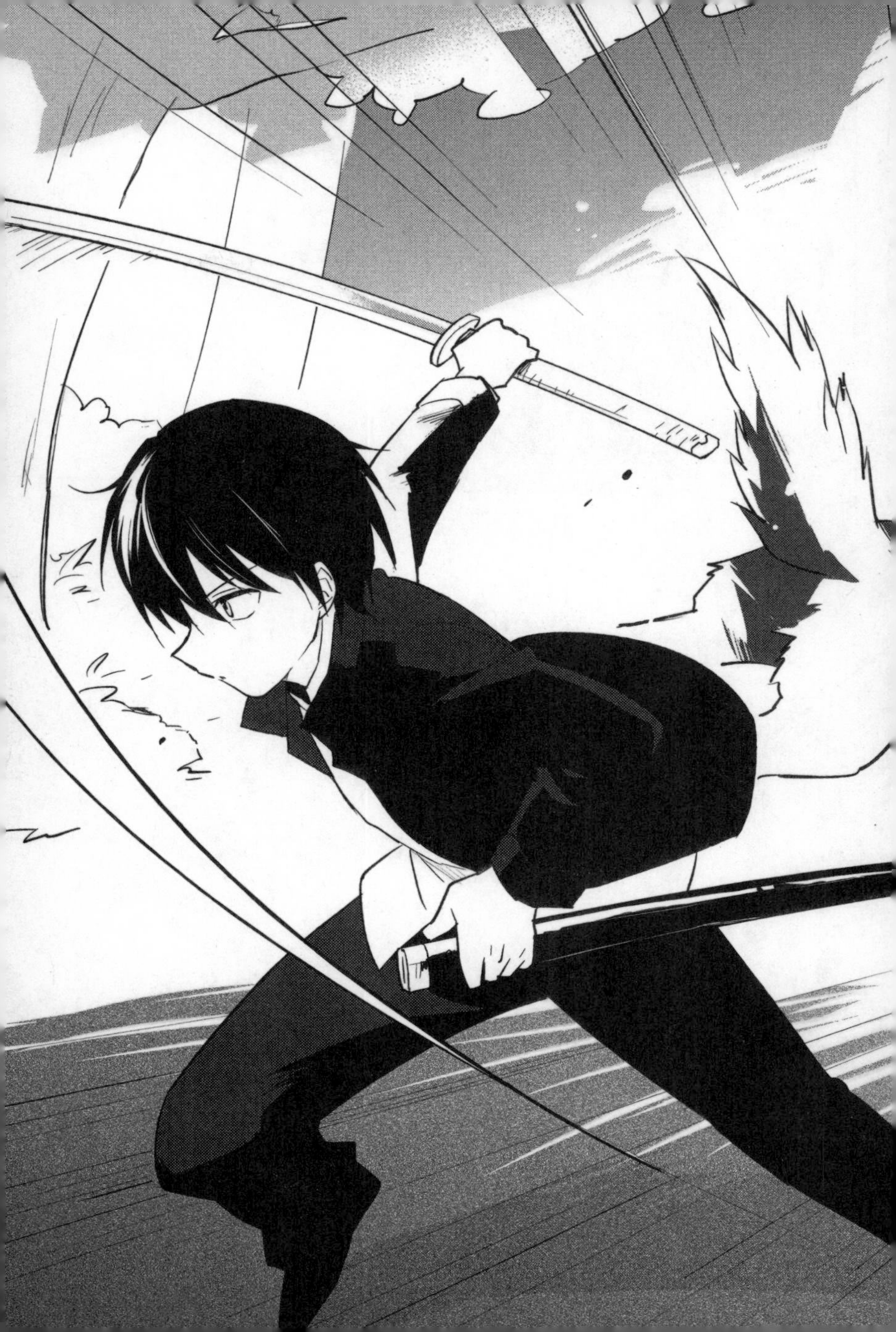

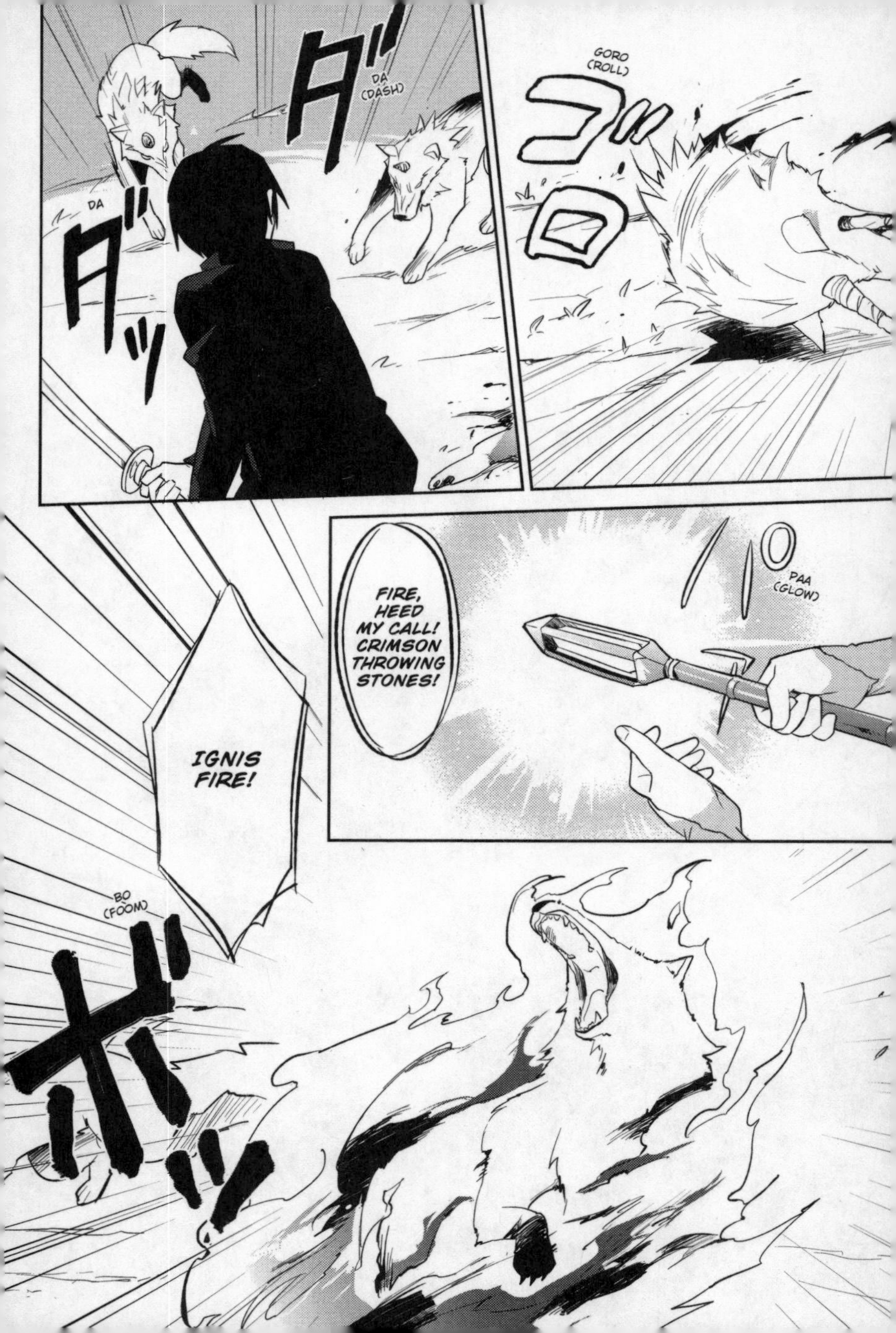

GORO (ROLL)
ゴロ
DA (DASH)
ダ
DA
ダッ
FIRE, HEED MY CALL! CRIMSON THROWING STONES!
PAA (GLOW)
パァ
IGNIS FIRE!
BO (FOOM)
ボッ

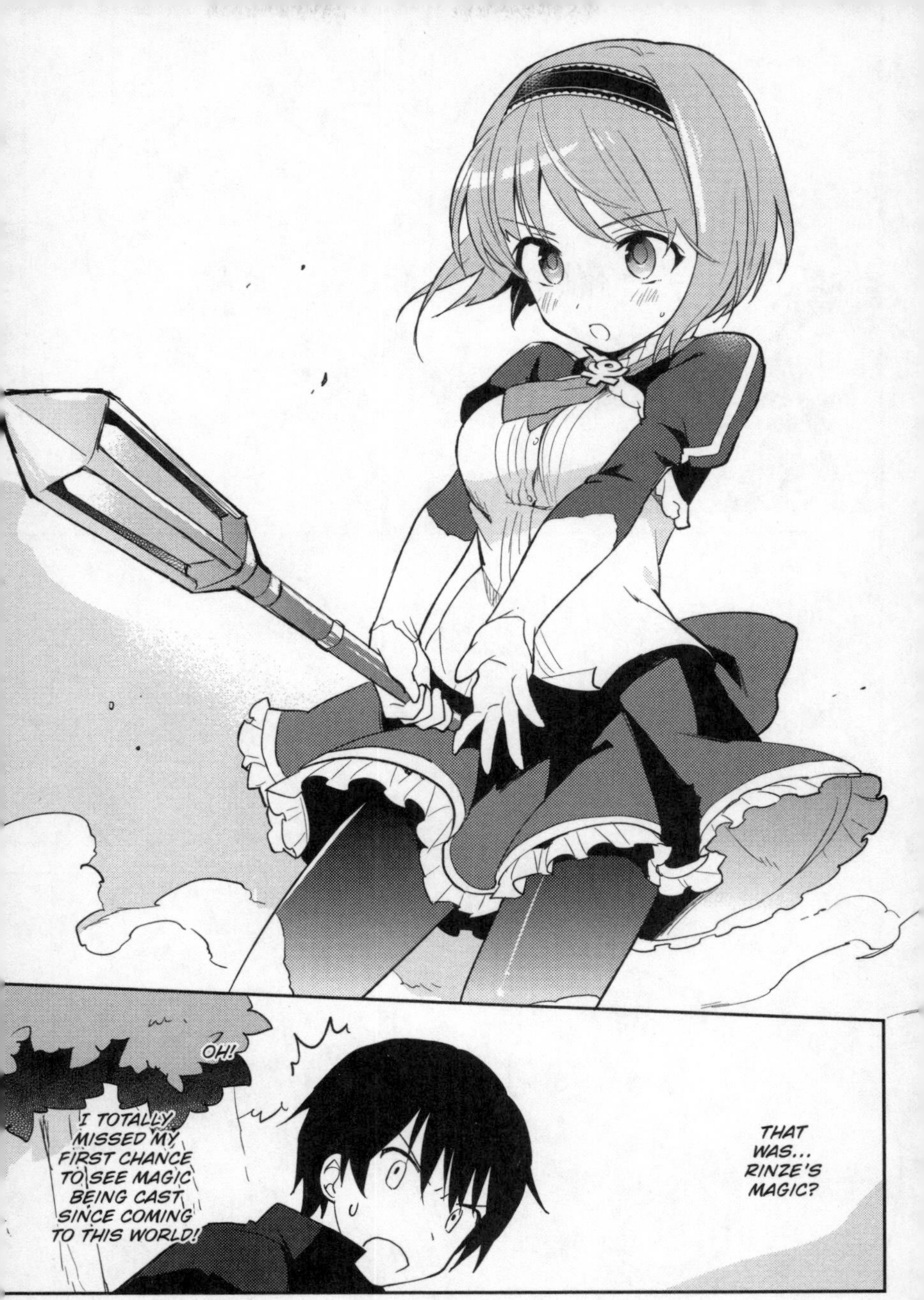
THAT WAS... RINZE'S MAGIC?
OH!
I TOTALLY MISSED MY FIRST CHANCE TO SEE MAGIC BEING CAST SINCE COMING TO THIS WORLD!

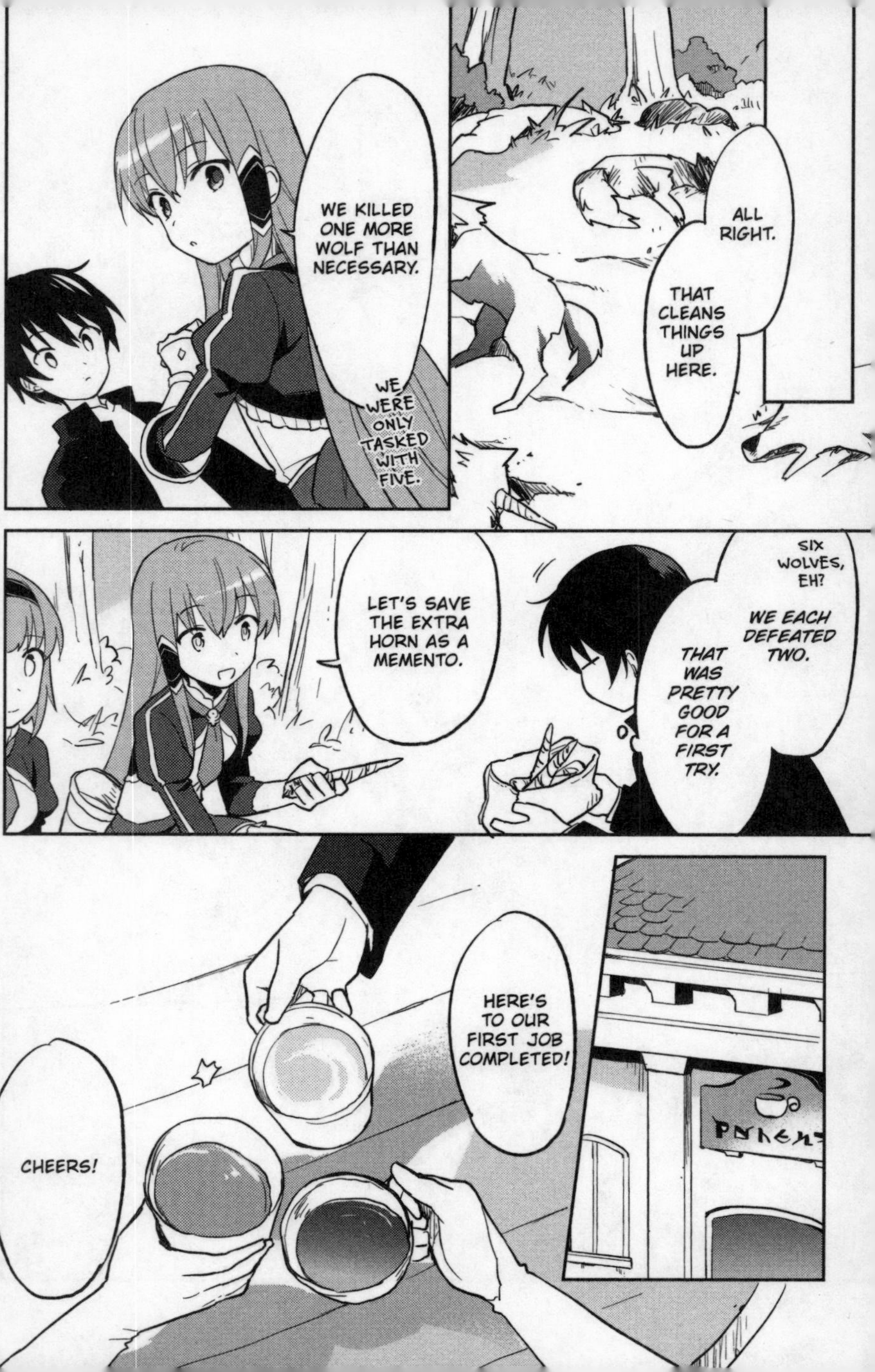
ALL RIGHT.
THAT CLEANS THINGS UP HERE.
WE KILLED ONE MORE WOLF THAN NECESSARY.
WE WERE ONLY TASKED WITH FIVE.
SIX WOLVES, EH?
WE EACH DEFEATED TWO.
THAT WAS PRETTY GOOD FOR A FIRST TRY.
LET'S SAVE THE EXTRA HORN AS A MEMENTO.
HERE'S TO OUR FIRST JOB COMPLETED!
CHEERS!

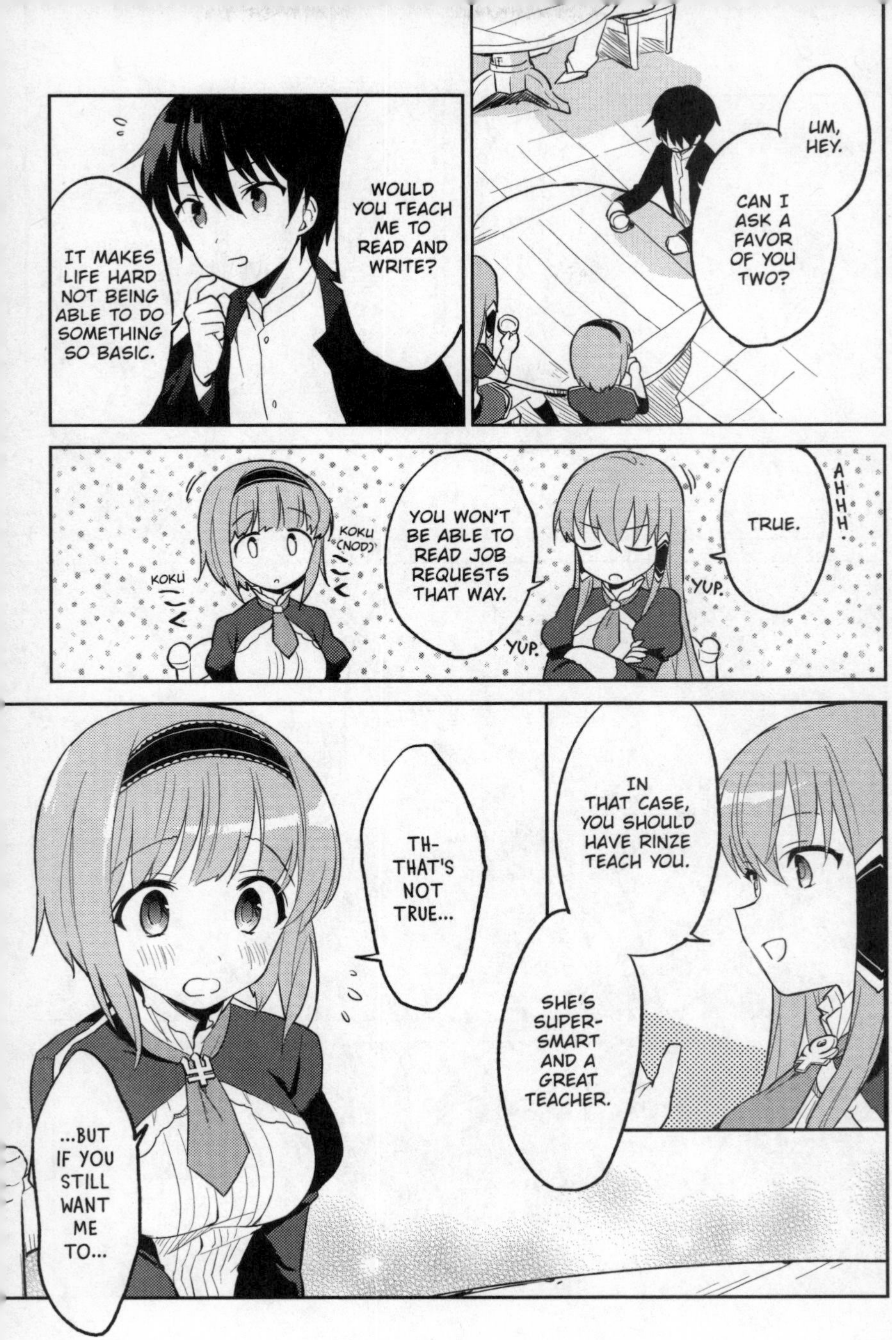
UM, HEY.
CAN I ASK A FAVOR OF YOU TWO?
WOULD YOU TEACH ME TO READ AND WRITE?
IT MAKES LIFE HARD NOT BEING ABLE TO DO SOMETHING SO BASIC.
AHHH.
TRUE.
YUP.
YOU WON'T BE ABLE TO READ JOB REQUESTS THAT WAY.
YUP.
KOKU (NOD)
KOKU
IN THAT CASE, YOU SHOULD HAVE RINZE TEACH YOU.
SHE'S SUPER-SMART AND A GREAT TEACHER.
TH-THAT'S NOT TRUE...
...BUT IF YOU STILL WANT ME TO...

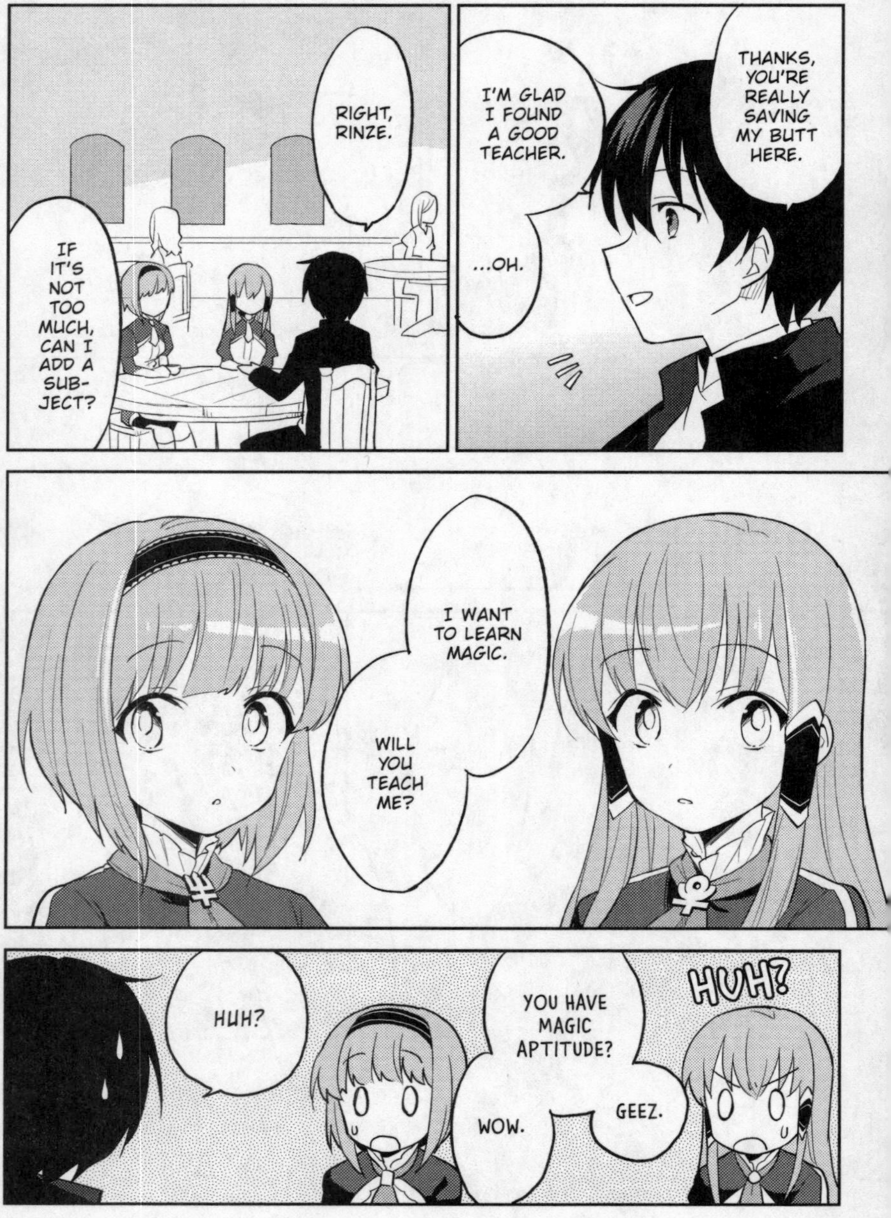
THANKS, YOU'RE REALLY SAVING MY BUTT HERE.
I'M GLAD I FOUND A GOOD TEACHER.
...OH.
RIGHT, RINZE.
IF IT'S NOT TOO MUCH, CAN I ADD A SUB-JECT?
I WANT TO LEARN MAGIC.
WILL YOU TEACH ME?
HUH?
YOU HAVE MAGIC APTITUDE?
GEEZ.
WOW.
HUH?

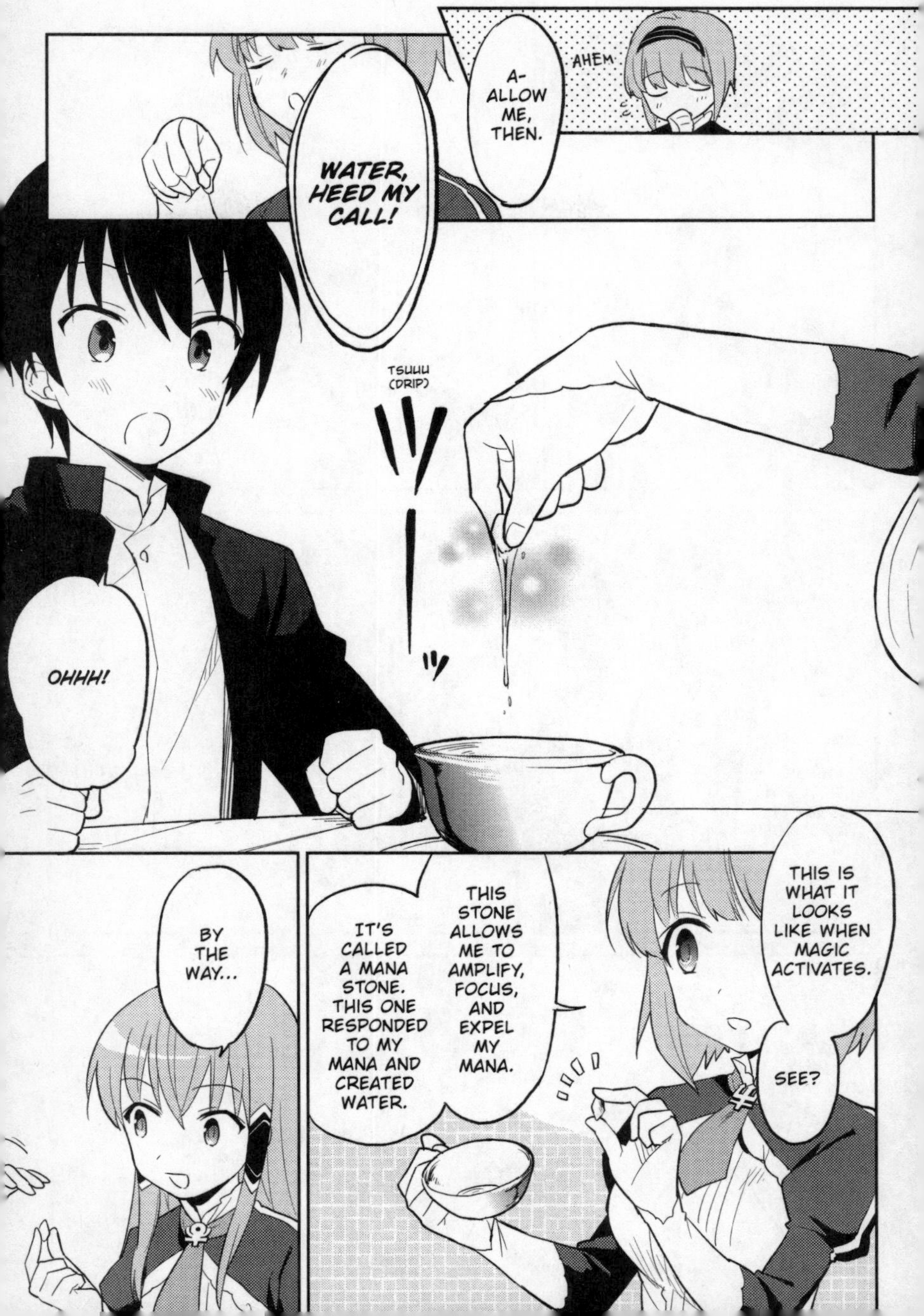
AHEM
A-ALLOW ME, THEN.
WATER, HEED MY CALL!
TSUUU (DRIP)
OHHH!
THIS IS WHAT IT LOOKS LIKE WHEN MAGIC ACTIVATES.
SEE?
THIS STONE ALLOWS ME TO AMPLIFY, FOCUS, AND EXPEL MY MANA.
IT'S CALLED A MANA STONE. THIS ONE RESPONDED TO MY MANA AND CREATED WATER.
BY THE WAY...

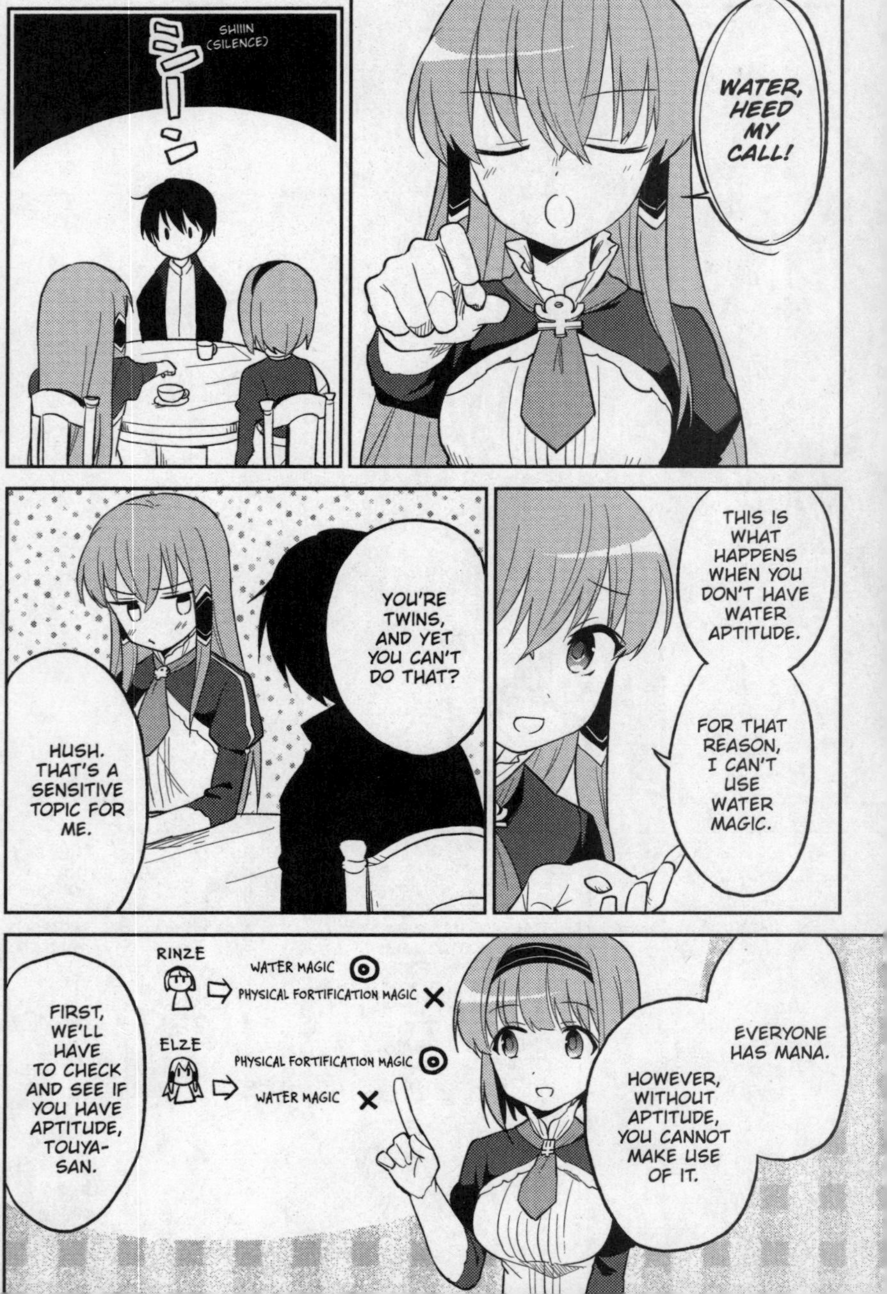
WATER, HEED MY CALL!
SHIIIN (SILENCE)
THIS IS WHAT HAPPENS WHEN YOU DON'T HAVE WATER APTITUDE.
FOR THAT REASON, I CAN'T USE WATER MAGIC.
YOU'RE TWINS, AND YET YOU CAN'T DO THAT?
HUSH. THAT'S A SENSITIVE TOPIC FOR ME.
EVERYONE HAS MANA.
HOWEVER, WITHOUT APTITUDE, YOU CANNOT MAKE USE OF IT.
RINZE
WATER MAGIC ◎
PHYSICAL FORTIFICATION MAGIC ✕
ELZE
PHYSICAL FORTIFICATION MAGIC ◎
WATER MAGIC ✕
FIRST, WE'LL HAVE TO CHECK AND SEE IF YOU HAVE APTITUDE, TOUYA-SAN.

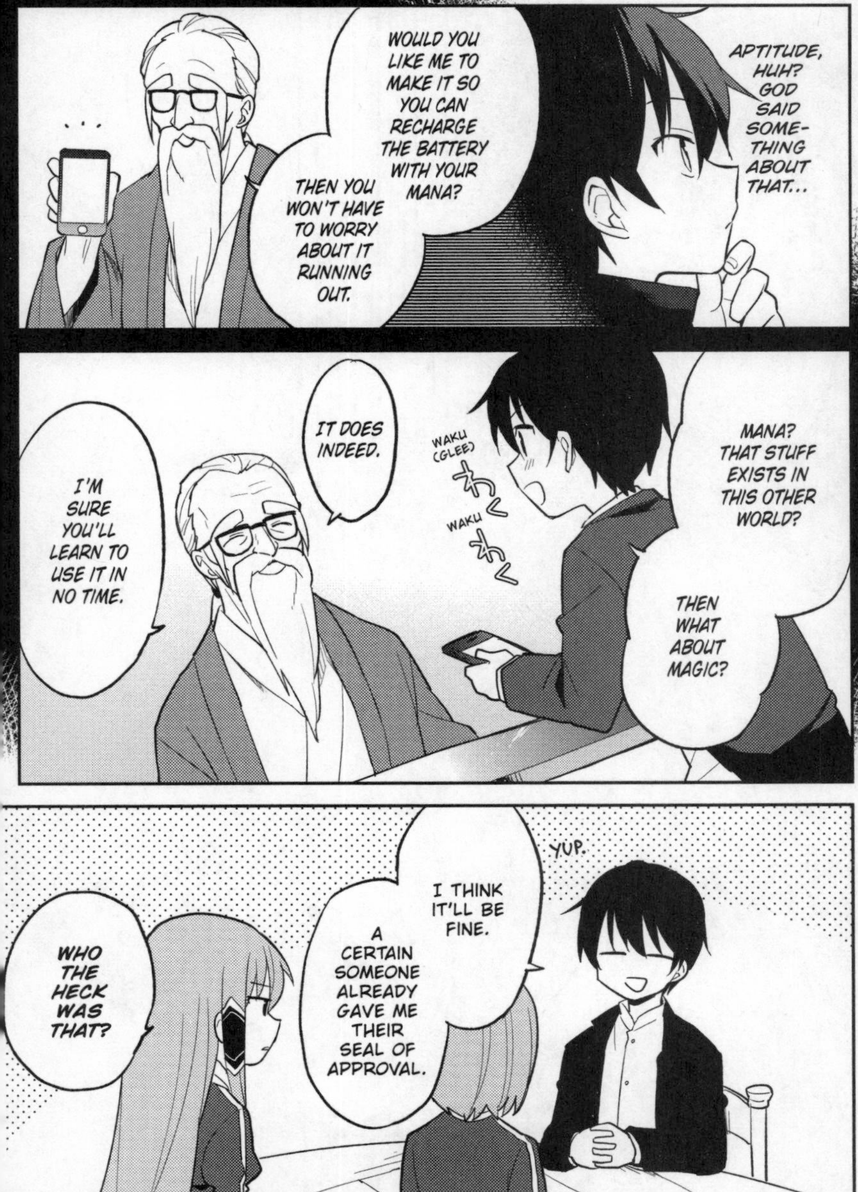
APTITUDE, HUH? GOD SAID SOME-THING ABOUT THAT...
WOULD YOU LIKE ME TO MAKE IT SO YOU CAN RECHARGE THE BATTERY WITH YOUR MANA?
THEN YOU WON'T HAVE TO WORRY ABOUT IT RUNNING OUT.
...
MANA? THAT STUFF EXISTS IN THIS OTHER WORLD?
THEN WHAT ABOUT MAGIC?
WAKU (GLEE)
WAKU
IT DOES INDEED.
I'M SURE YOU'LL LEARN TO USE IT IN NO TIME.
YUP.
I THINK IT'LL BE FINE.
A CERTAIN SOMEONE ALREADY GAVE ME THEIR SEAL OF APPROVAL.
WHO THE HECK WAS THAT?

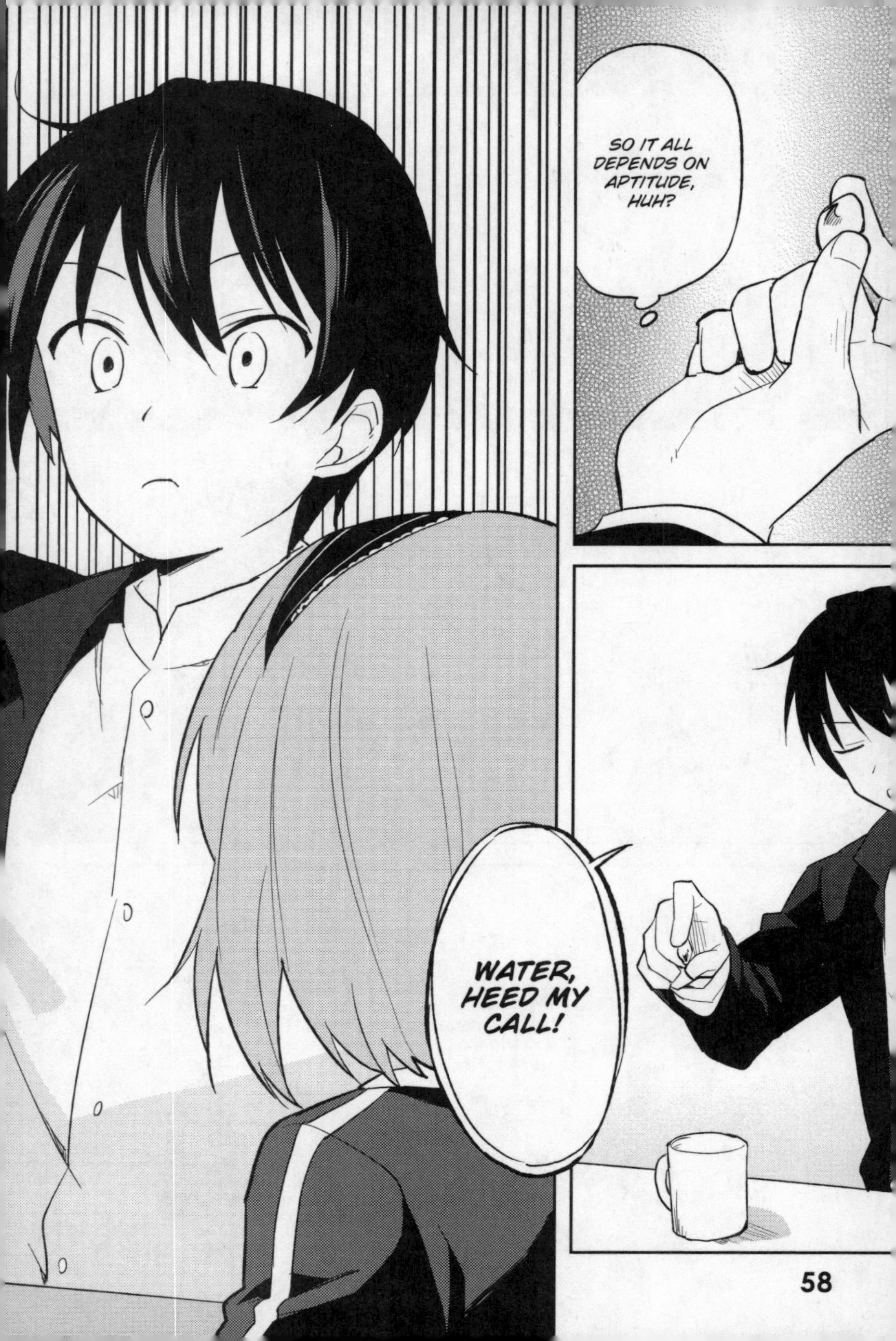
SO IT ALL DEPENDS ON APTITUDE, HUH?
WATER, HEED MY CALL!

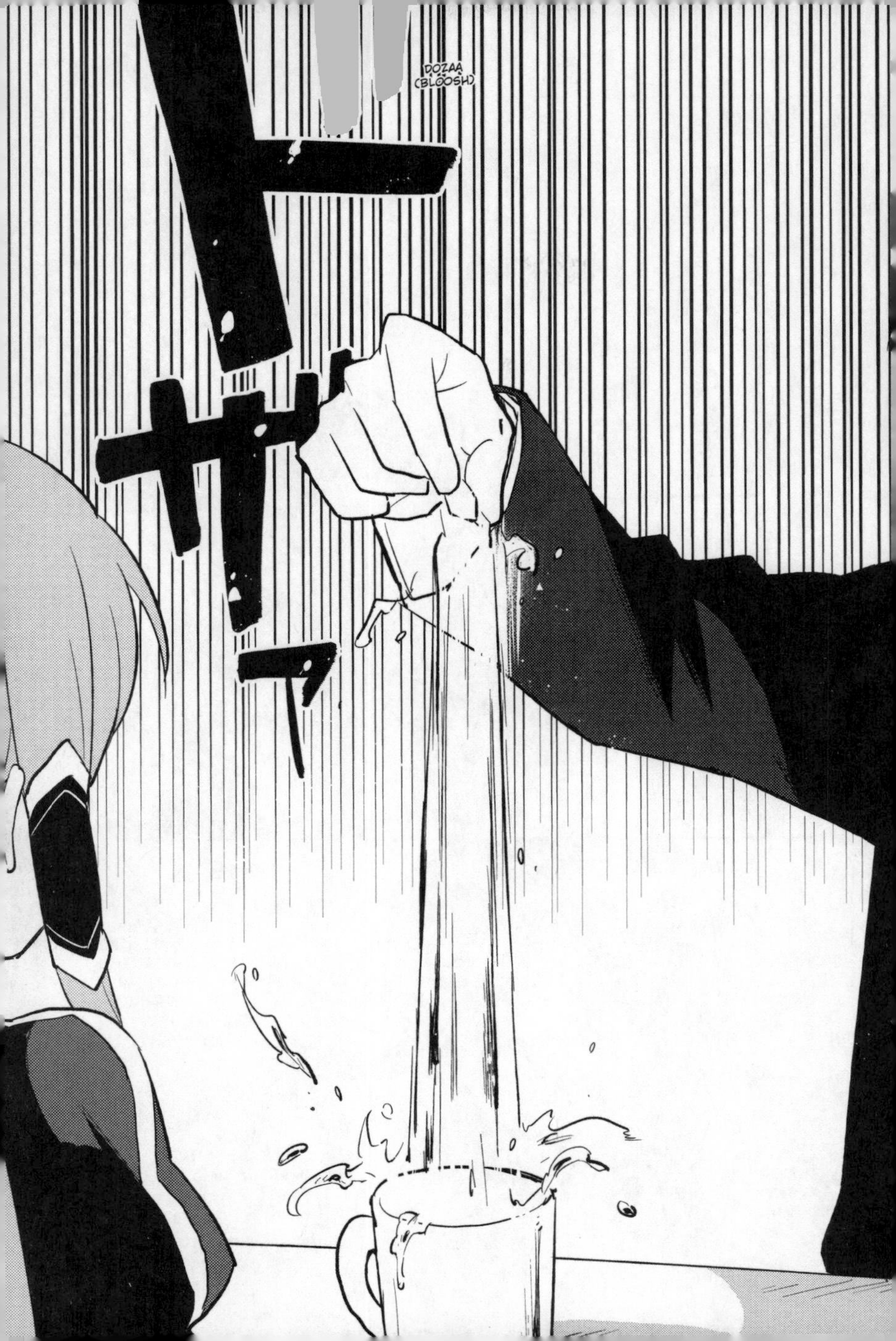
DOZAA
(BLOOSH)

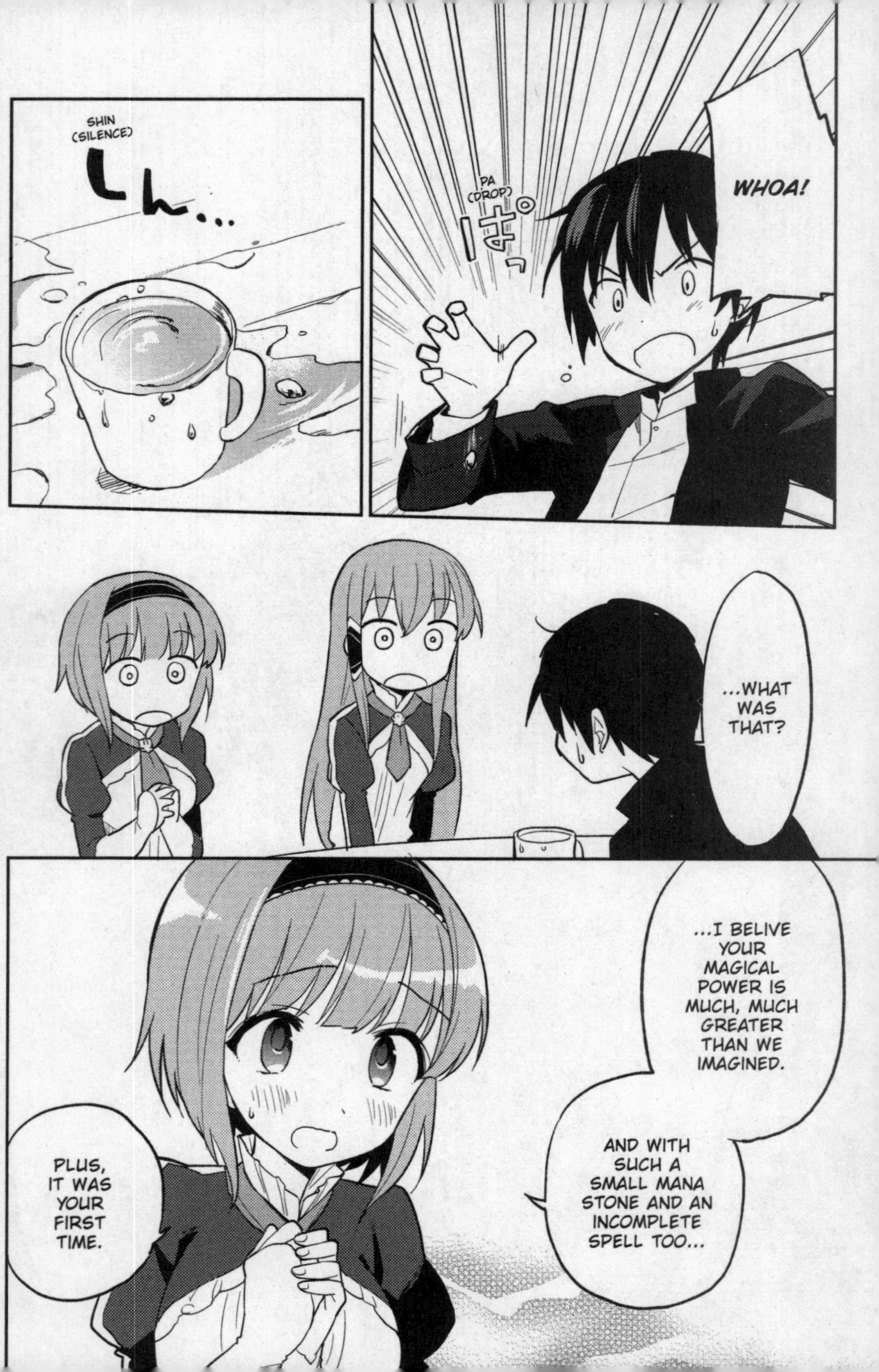
WHOA!
PA (DROP)
ぱっ
SHIN (SILENCE)
しん…
...WHAT WAS THAT?
...I BELIVE YOUR MAGICAL POWER IS MUCH, MUCH GREATER THAN WE IMAGINED.
AND WITH SUCH A SMALL MANA STONE AND AN INCOMPLETE SPELL TOO...
PLUS, IT WAS YOUR FIRST TIME.

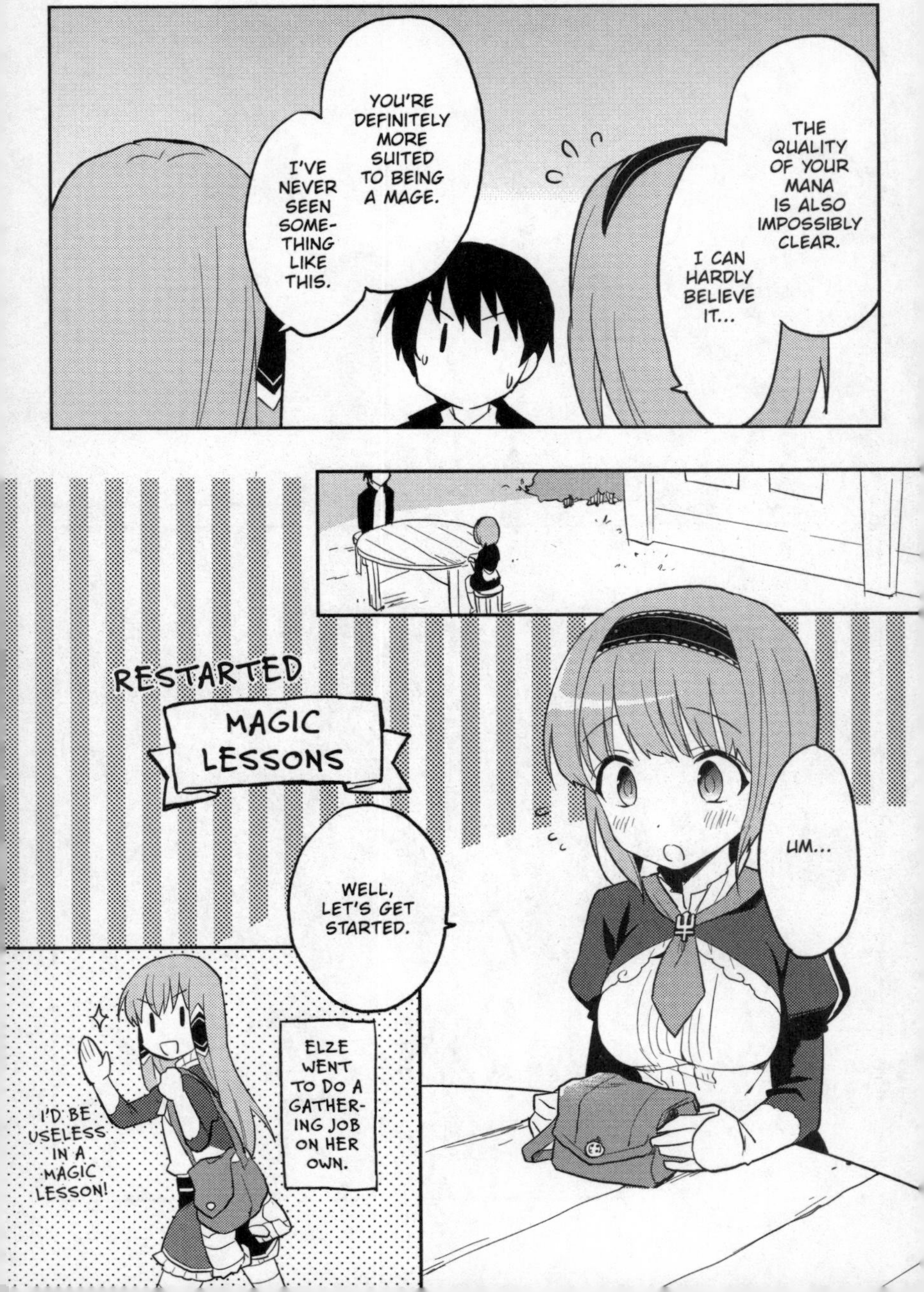
THE QUALITY OF YOUR MANA IS ALSO IMPOSSIBLY CLEAR.
I CAN HARDLY BELIEVE IT...
YOU'RE DEFINITELY MORE SUITED TO BEING A MAGE.
I'VE NEVER SEEN SOME-THING LIKE THIS.
UM...
RESTARTED
MAGIC LESSONS
WELL, LET'S GET STARTED.
ELZE WENT TO DO A GATHER-ING JOB ON HER OWN.
I'D BE USELESS IN A MAGIC LESSON!

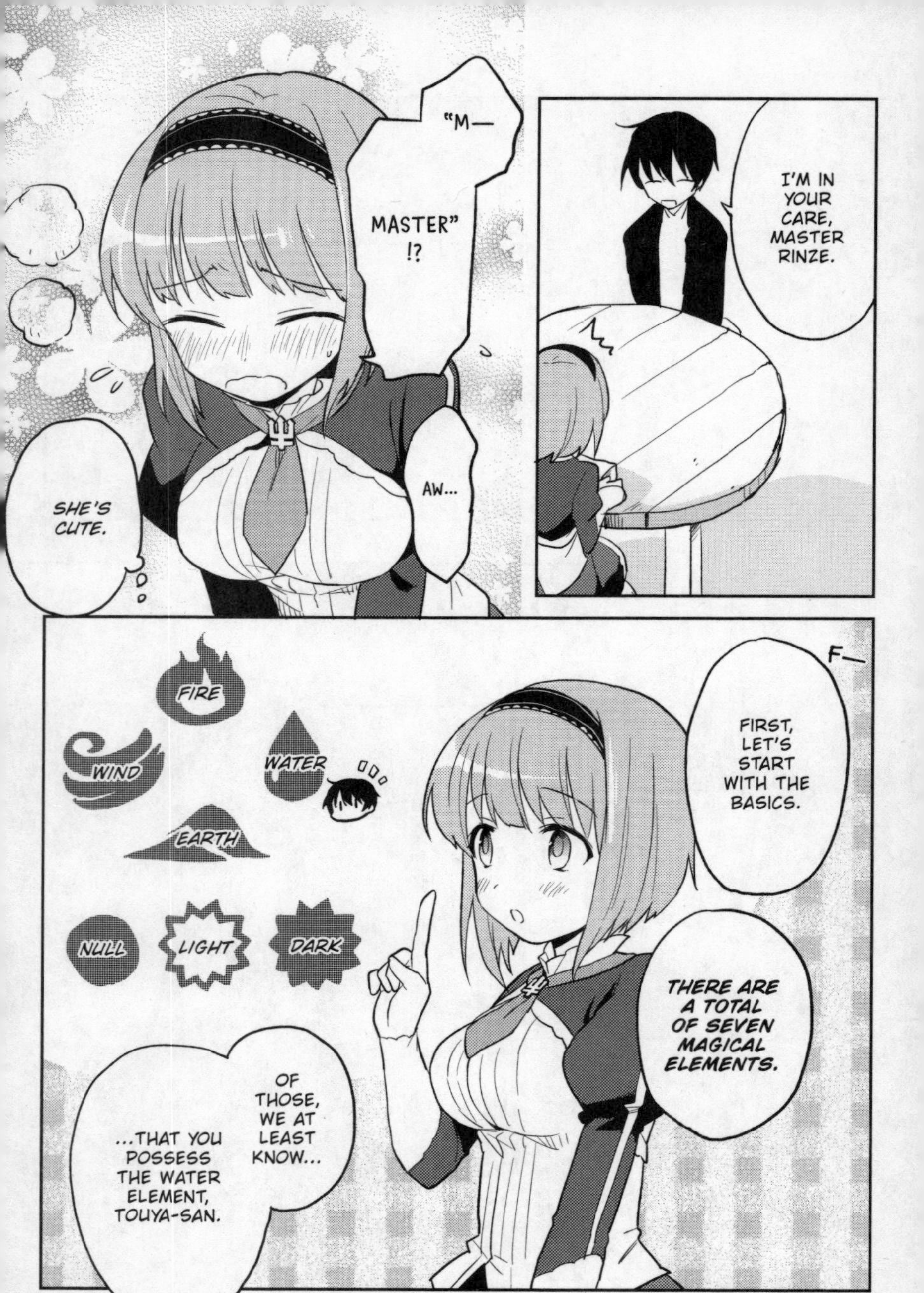
I'M IN YOUR CARE, MASTER RINZE.
"M—
MASTER" !?
AW...
SHE'S CUTE.
F—
FIRST, LET'S START WITH THE BASICS.
FIRE
WIND
WATER
EARTH
NULL
LIGHT
DARK
THERE ARE A TOTAL OF SEVEN MAGICAL ELEMENTS.
OF THOSE, WE AT LEAST KNOW...
...THAT YOU POSSESS THE WATER ELEMENT, TOUYA-SAN.

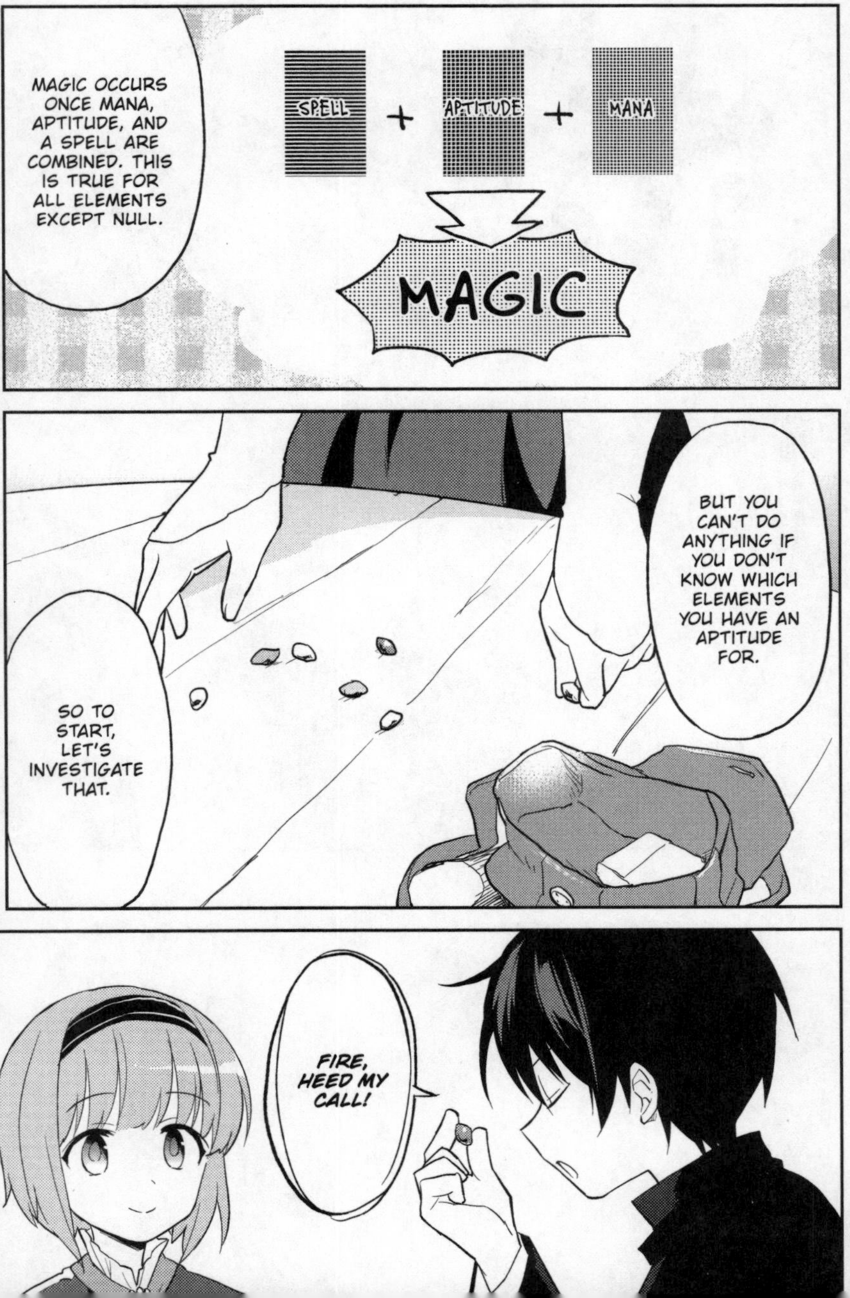
MAGIC OCCURS ONCE MANA, APTITUDE, AND A SPELL ARE COMBINED. THIS IS TRUE FOR ALL ELEMENTS EXCEPT NULL.
SPELL
+
APTITUDE
+
MANA
MAGIC
BUT YOU CAN'T DO ANYTHING IF YOU DON'T KNOW WHICH ELEMENTS YOU HAVE AN APTITUDE FOR.
SO TO START, LET'S INVESTIGATE THAT.
FIRE, HEED MY CALL!

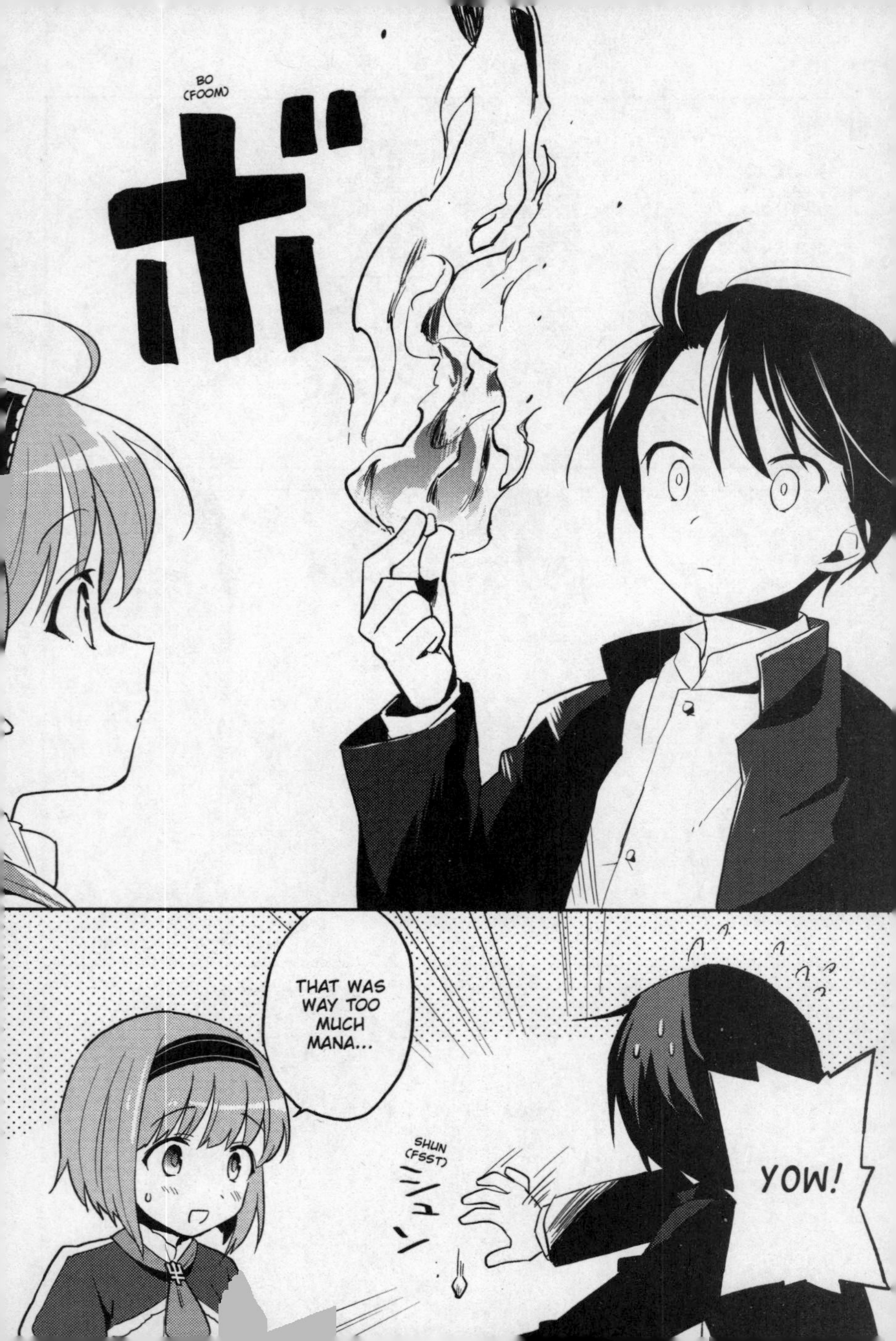
BO
(FOOM)
ボ
THAT WAS WAY TOO MUCH MANA...
YOW!
SHUN
(FSST)

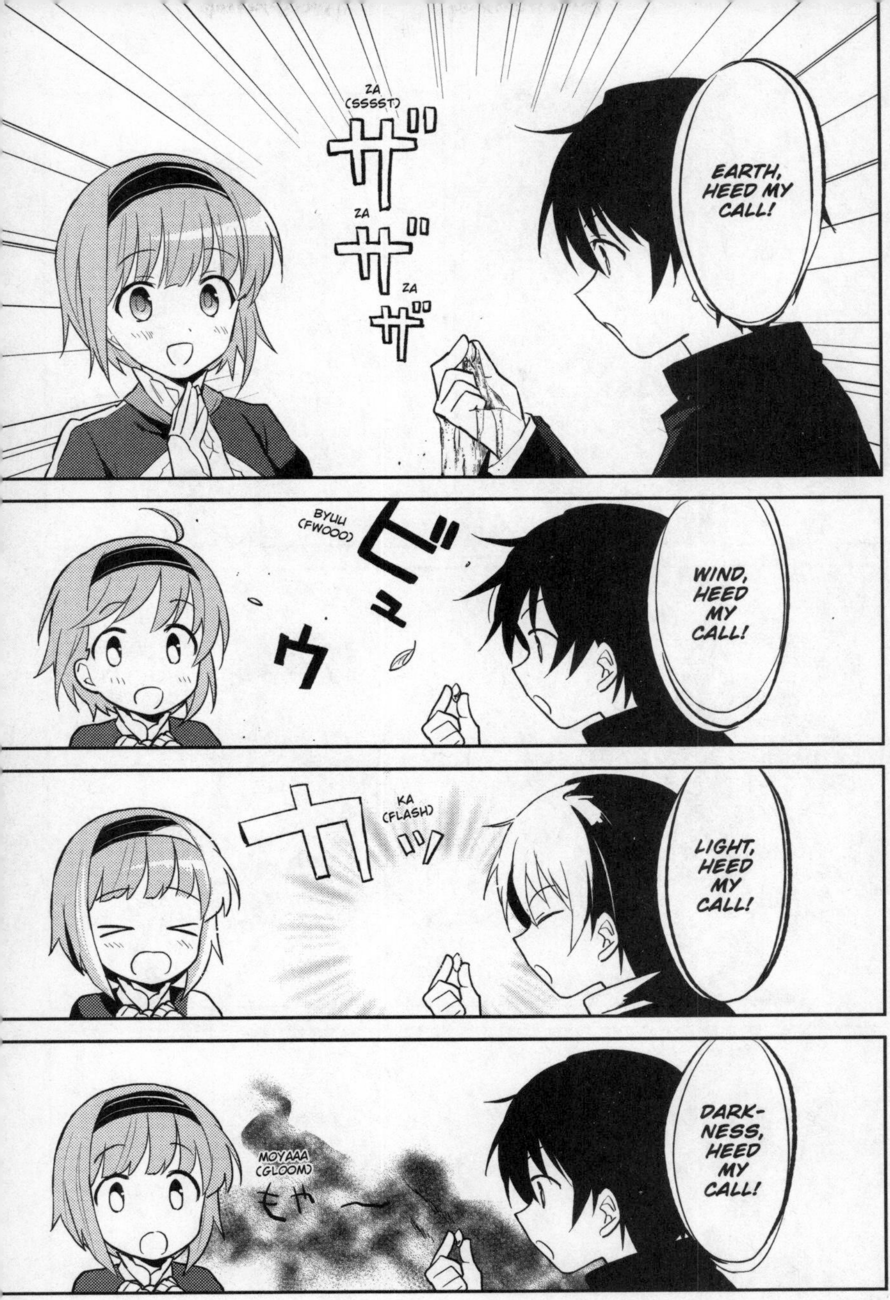

EARTH, HEED MY CALL!
ZA (SSSST)
ZA
ZA
WIND, HEED MY CALL!
BYUU (FWOOO)
LIGHT, HEED MY CALL!
KA (FLASH)
DARKNESS, HEED MY CALL!
MOYAAA (GLOOM)

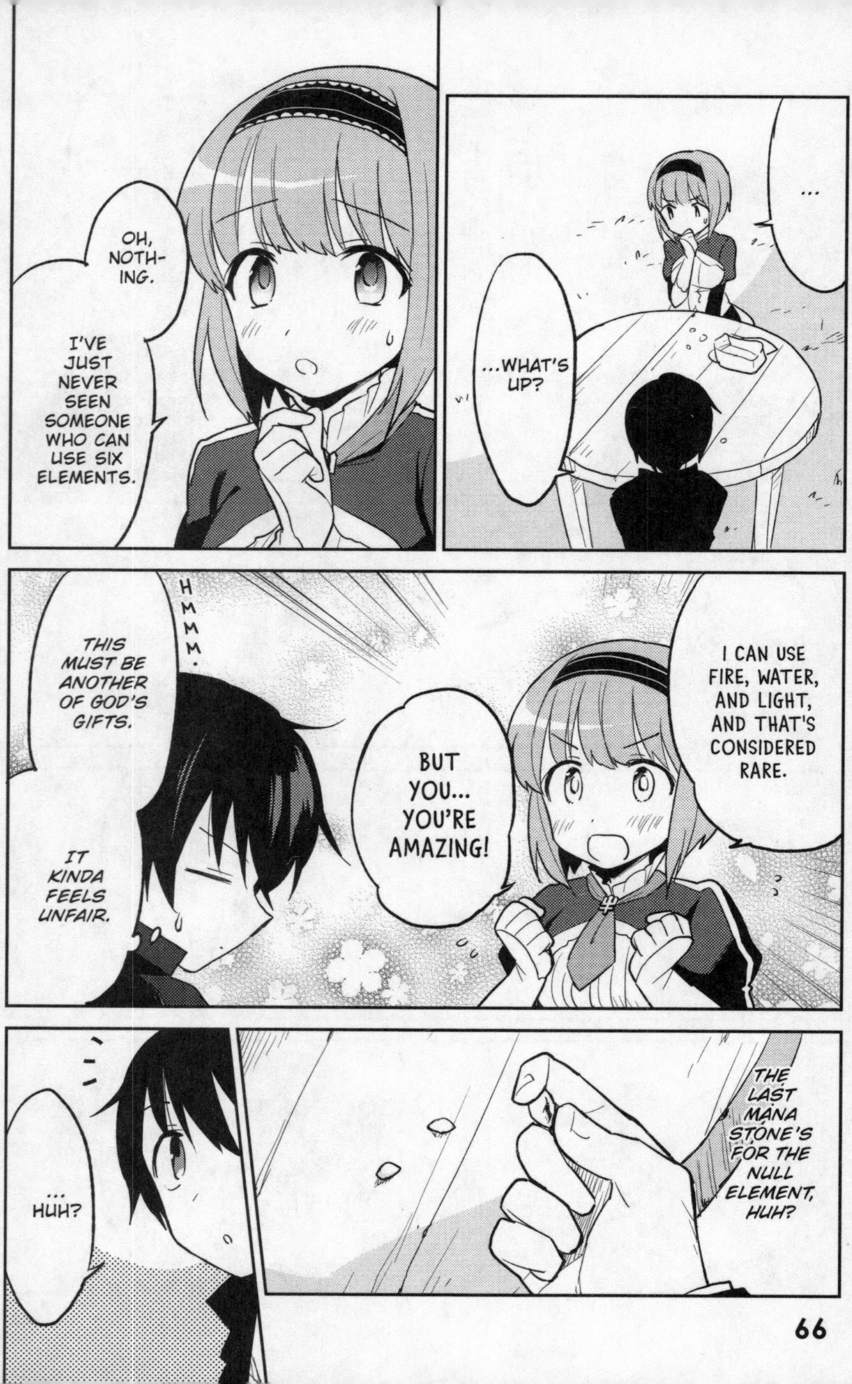
...
...WHAT'S UP?
OH, NOTHING.
I'VE JUST NEVER SEEN SOMEONE WHO CAN USE SIX ELEMENTS.
I CAN USE FIRE, WATER, AND LIGHT, AND THAT'S CONSIDERED RARE.
BUT YOU... YOU'RE AMAZING!
HMMM.
THIS MUST BE ANOTHER OF GOD'S GIFTS.
IT KINDA FEELS UNFAIR.
THE LAST MANA STONE'S FOR THE NULL ELEMENT, HUH?
... HUH?

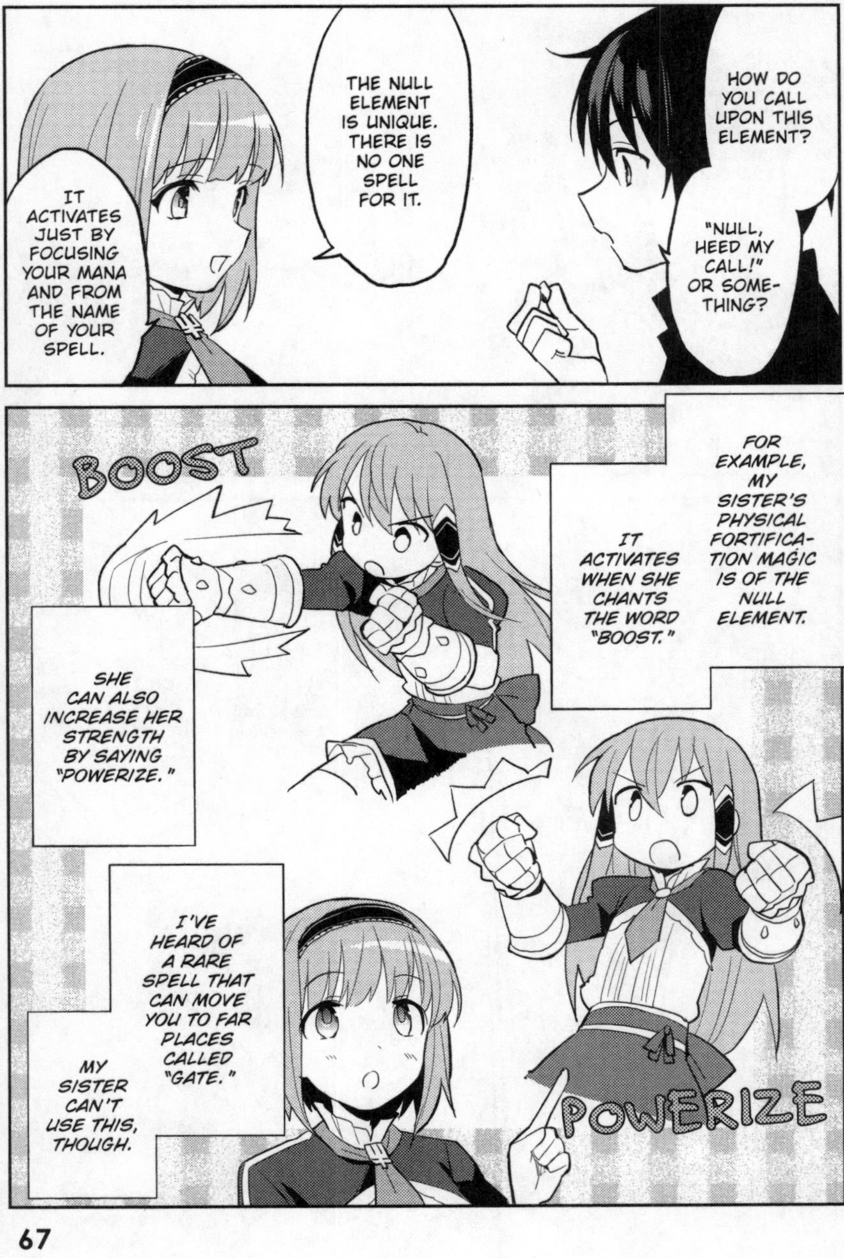
HOW DO YOU CALL UPON THIS ELEMENT?
"NULL, HEED MY CALL!" OR SOME-THING?
THE NULL ELEMENT IS UNIQUE. THERE IS NO ONE SPELL FOR IT.
IT ACTIVATES JUST BY FOCUSING YOUR MANA AND FROM THE NAME OF YOUR SPELL.
FOR EXAMPLE, MY SISTER'S PHYSICAL FORTIFICA-TION MAGIC IS OF THE NULL ELEMENT.
IT ACTIVATES WHEN SHE CHANTS THE WORD "BOOST."
BOOST
SHE CAN ALSO INCREASE HER STRENGTH BY SAYING "POWERIZE."
POWERIZE
I'VE HEARD OF A RARE SPELL THAT CAN MOVE YOU TO FAR PLACES CALLED "GATE."
MY SISTER CAN'T USE THIS, THOUGH.

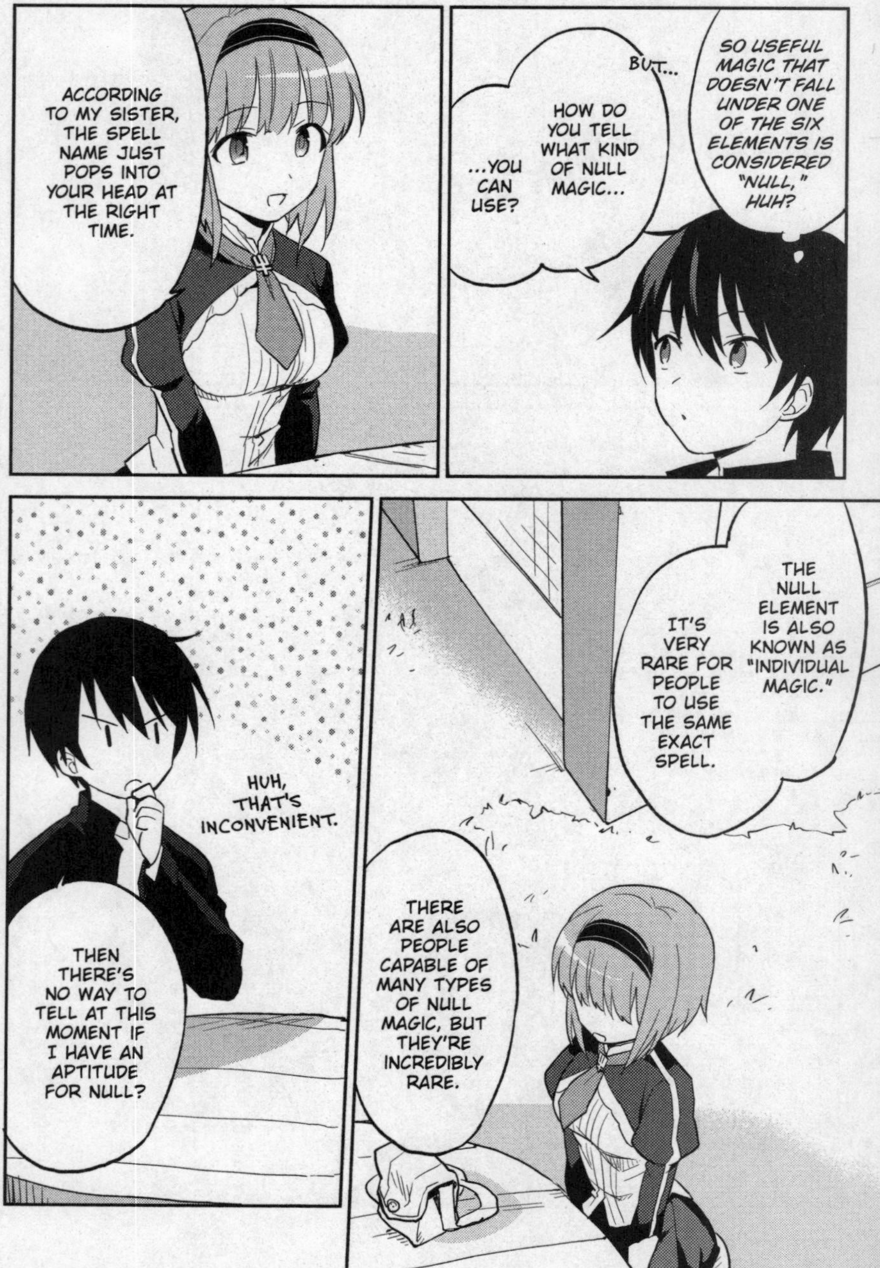
SO USEFUL MAGIC THAT DOESN'T FALL UNDER ONE OF THE SIX ELEMENTS IS CONSIDERED "NULL," HUH?
BUT...
HOW DO YOU TELL WHAT KIND OF NULL MAGIC...
...YOU CAN USE?
ACCORDING TO MY SISTER, THE SPELL NAME JUST POPS INTO YOUR HEAD AT THE RIGHT TIME.
THE NULL ELEMENT IS ALSO KNOWN AS "INDIVIDUAL MAGIC."
IT'S VERY RARE FOR PEOPLE TO USE THE SAME EXACT SPELL.
THERE ARE ALSO PEOPLE CAPABLE OF MANY TYPES OF NULL MAGIC, BUT THEY'RE INCREDIBLY RARE.
HUH, THAT'S INCONVENIENT.
THEN THERE'S NO WAY TO TELL AT THIS MOMENT IF I HAVE AN APTITUDE FOR NULL?

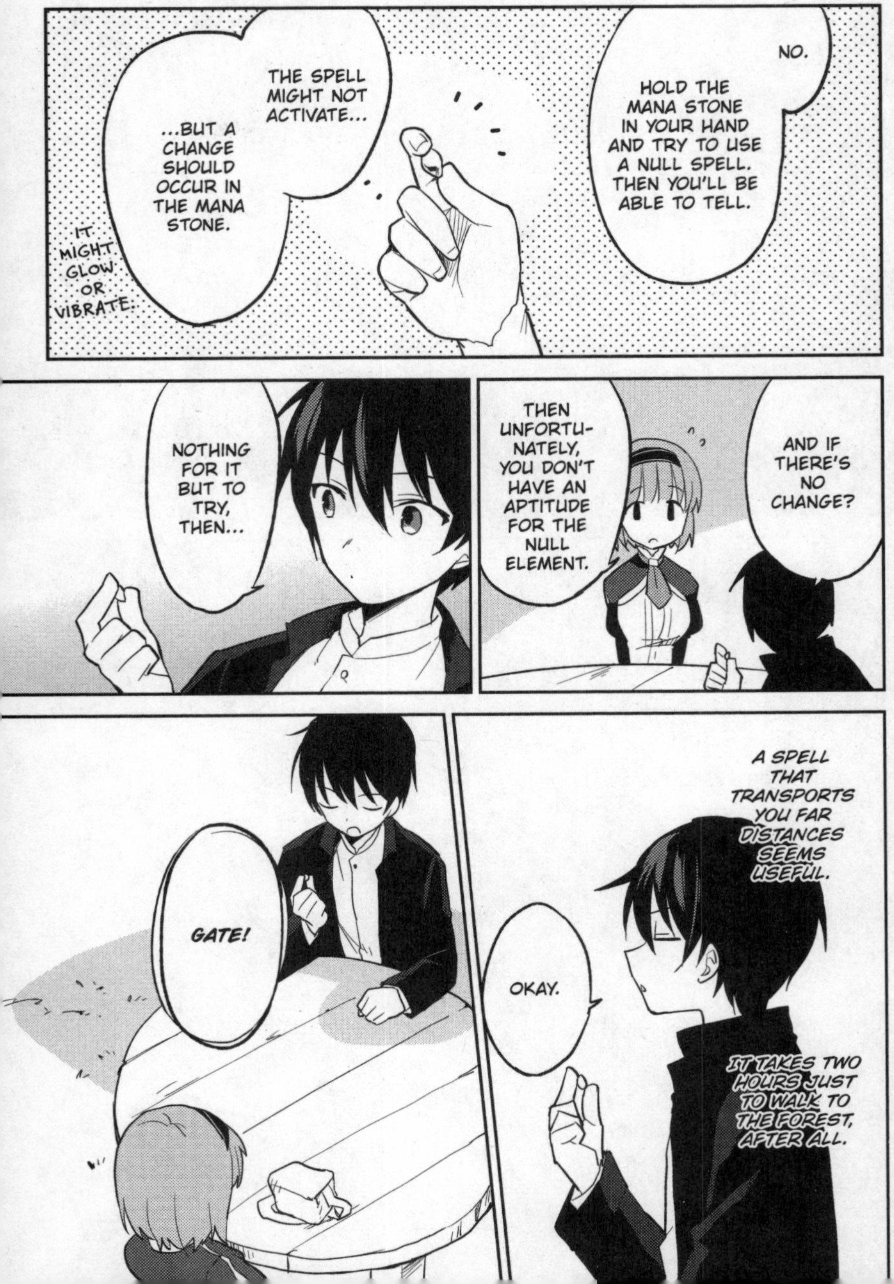
NO.
HOLD THE MANA STONE IN YOUR HAND AND TRY TO USE A NULL SPELL. THEN YOU'LL BE ABLE TO TELL.
THE SPELL MIGHT NOT ACTIVATE...
...BUT A CHANGE SHOULD OCCUR IN THE MANA STONE.
IT MIGHT GLOW OR VIBRATE.
AND IF THERE'S NO CHANGE?
THEN UNFORTUNATELY, YOU DON'T HAVE AN APTITUDE FOR THE NULL ELEMENT.
NOTHING FOR IT BUT TO TRY, THEN...
A SPELL THAT TRANSPORTS YOU FAR DISTANCES SEEMS USEFUL.
OKAY.
IT TAKES TWO HOURS JUST TO WALK TO THE FOREST, AFTER ALL.
GATE!

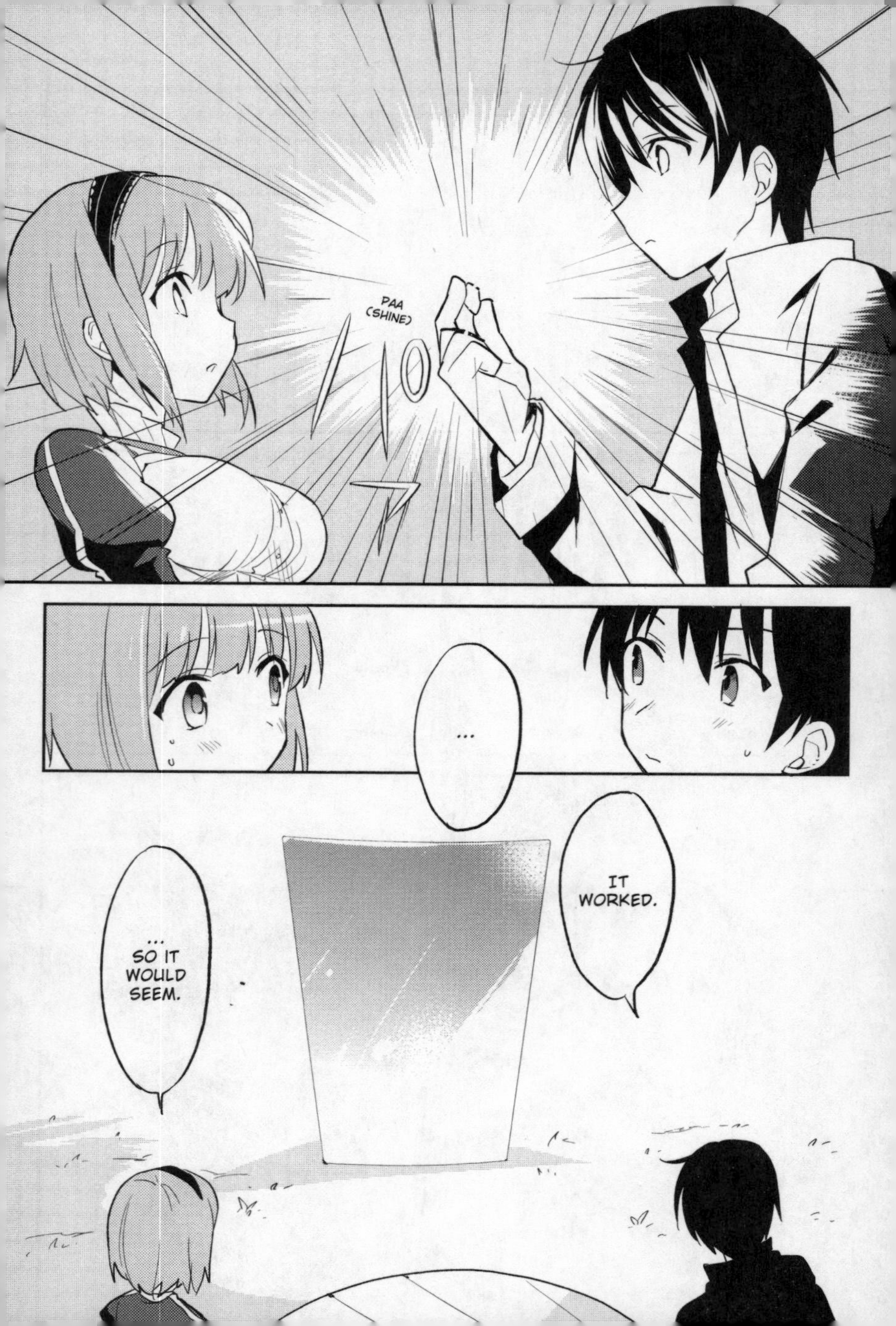
PAA (SHINE)
...
IT WORKED.
... SO IT WOULD SEEM.

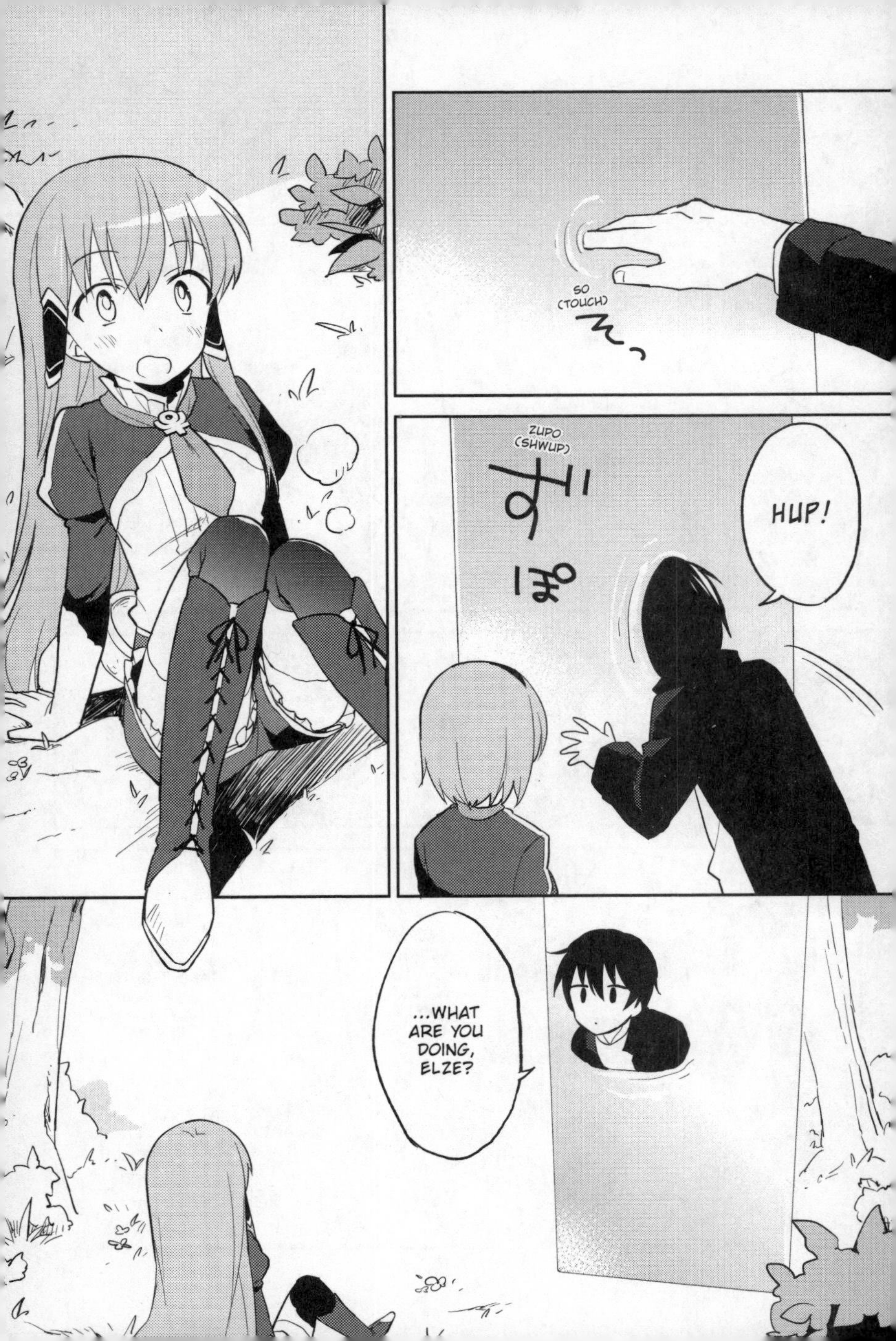
SO (TOUCH)
そっ
ZUPO (SHWUP)
ずぽ
HUP!
...WHAT ARE YOU DOING, ELZE?

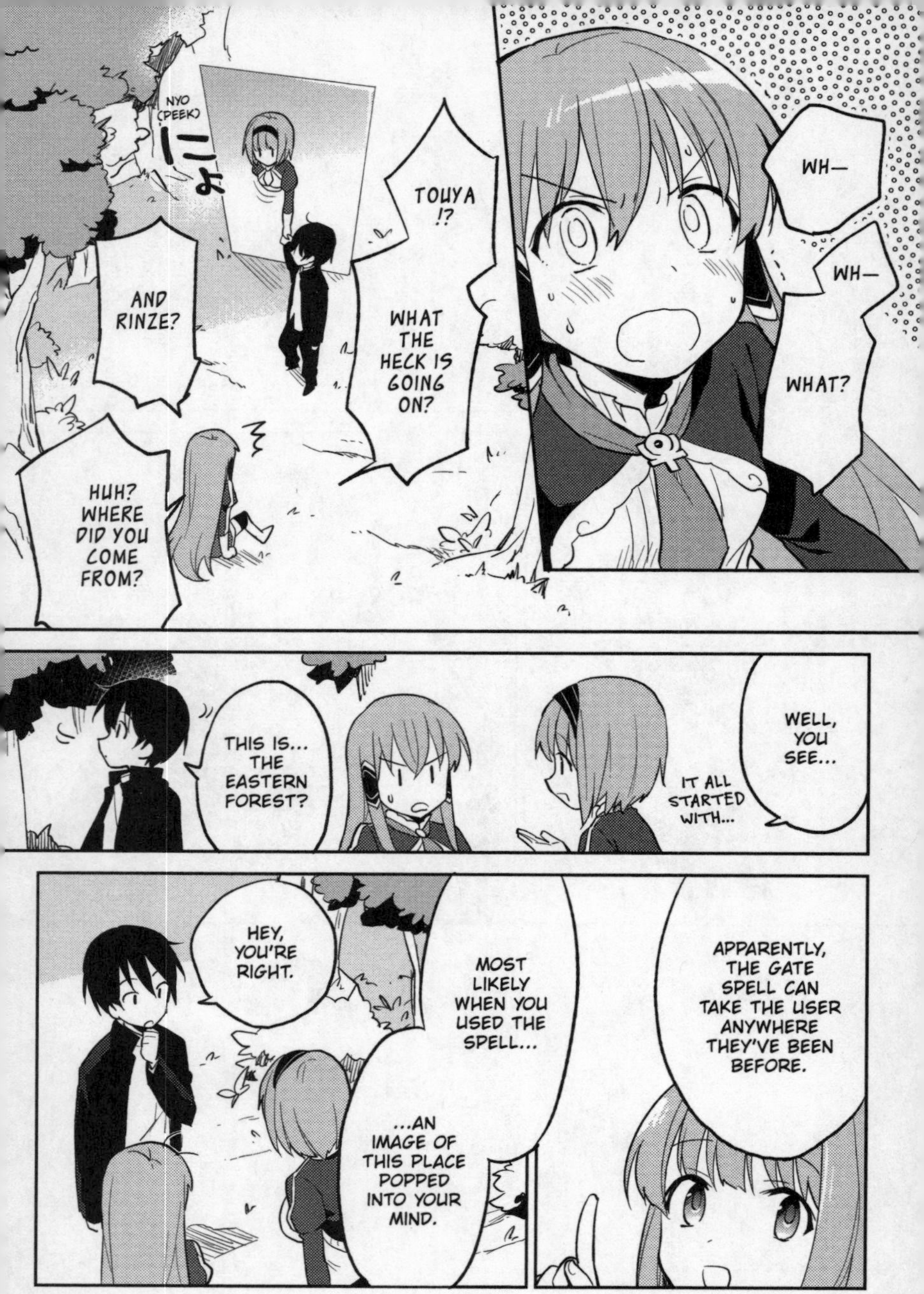
WH—
WH—
WHAT?
TOUYA !?
WHAT THE HECK IS GOING ON?
NYO (PEEK)
にょ
AND RINZE?
HUH? WHERE DID YOU COME FROM?
WELL, YOU SEE...
IT ALL STARTED WITH...
THIS IS... THE EASTERN FOREST?
APPARENTLY, THE GATE SPELL CAN TAKE THE USER ANYWHERE THEY'VE BEEN BEFORE.
MOST LIKELY WHEN YOU USED THE SPELL...
...AN IMAGE OF THIS PLACE POPPED INTO YOUR MIND.
HEY, YOU'RE RIGHT.

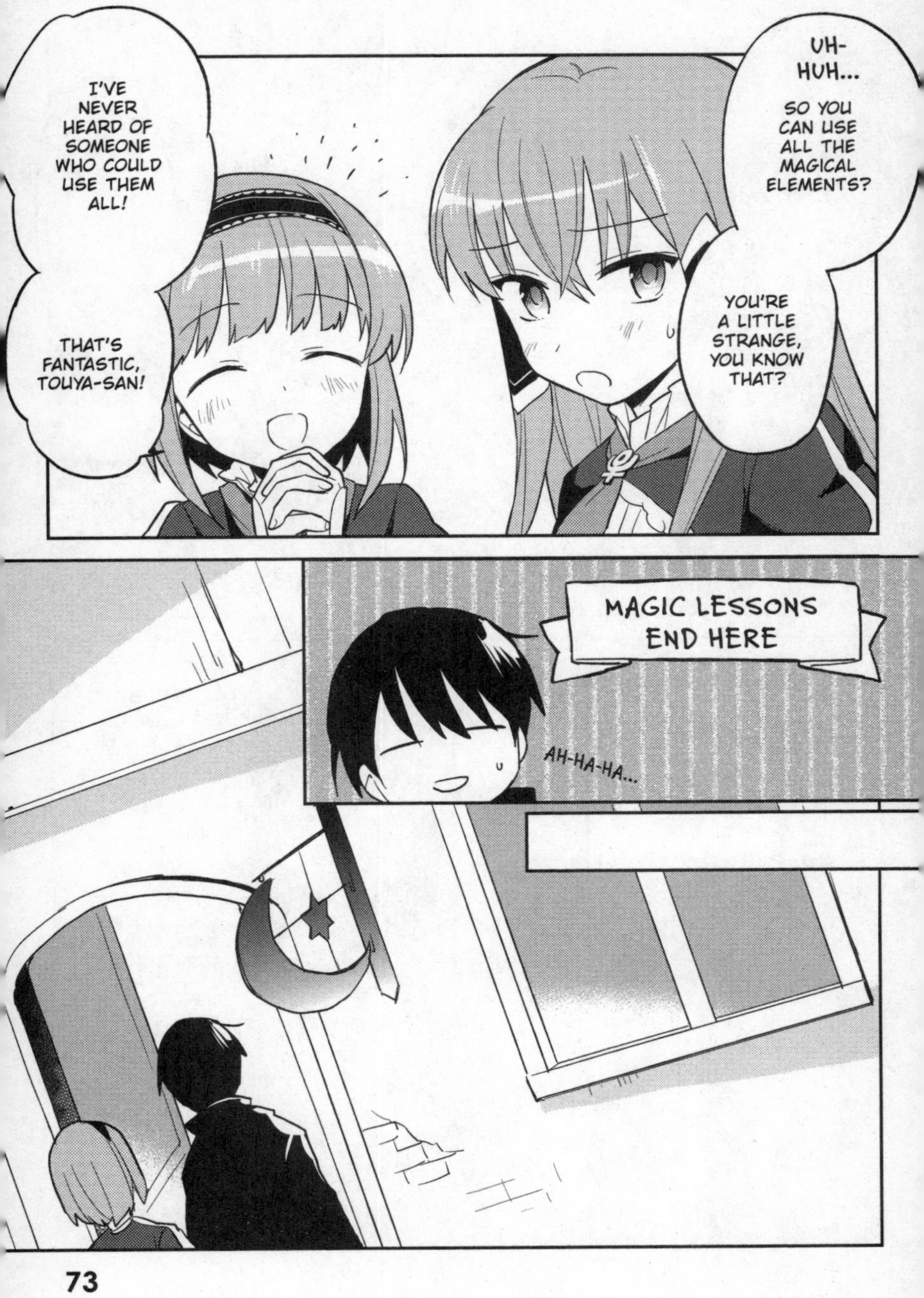
UH-HUH... SO YOU CAN USE ALL THE MAGICAL ELEMENTS?
I'VE NEVER HEARD OF SOMEONE WHO COULD USE THEM ALL!
YOU'RE A LITTLE STRANGE, YOU KNOW THAT?
THAT'S FANTASTIC, TOUYA-SAN!
MAGIC LESSONS END HERE
AH-HA-HA...

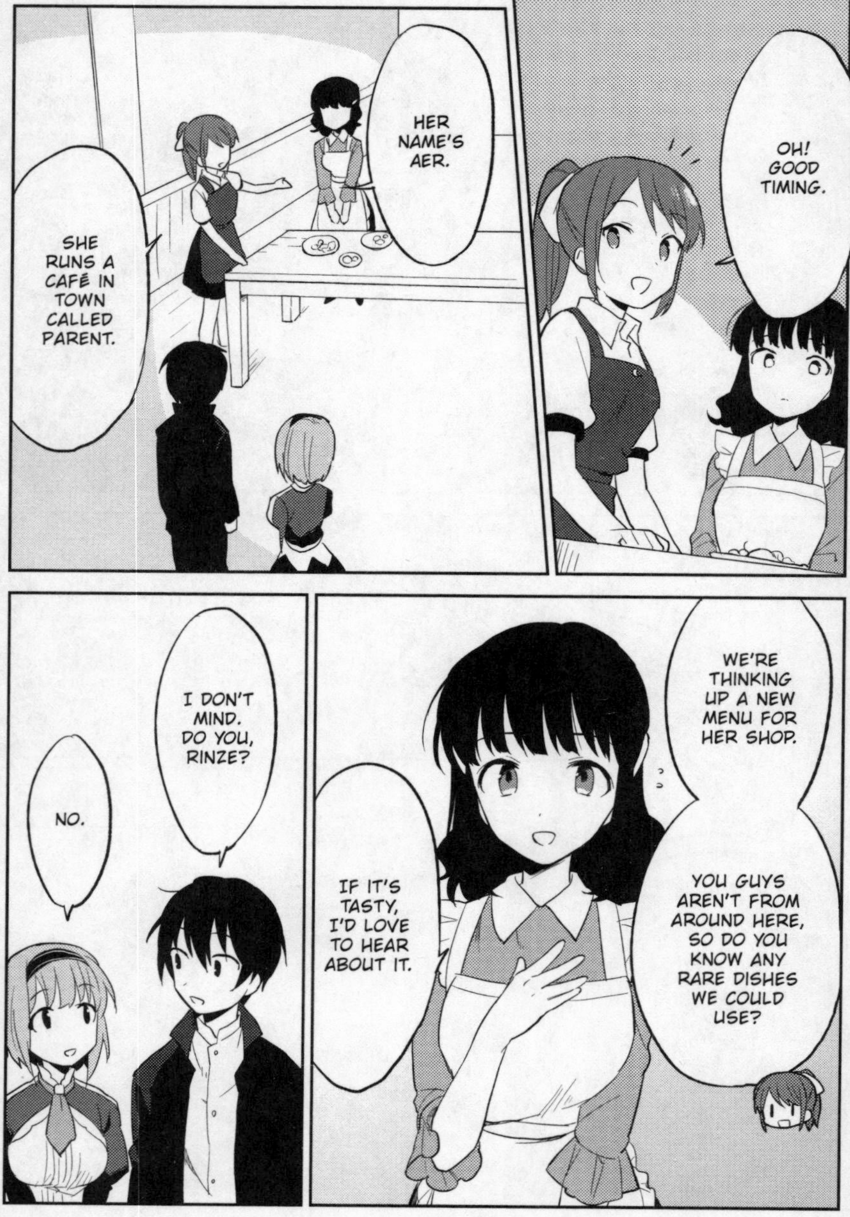
OH! GOOD TIMING.
HER NAME'S AER.
SHE RUNS A CAFÉ IN TOWN CALLED PARENT.
WE'RE THINKING UP A NEW MENU FOR HER SHOP.
YOU GUYS AREN'T FROM AROUND HERE, SO DO YOU KNOW ANY RARE DISHES WE COULD USE?
IF IT'S TASTY, I'D LOVE TO HEAR ABOUT IT.
I DON'T MIND. DO YOU, RINZE?
NO.

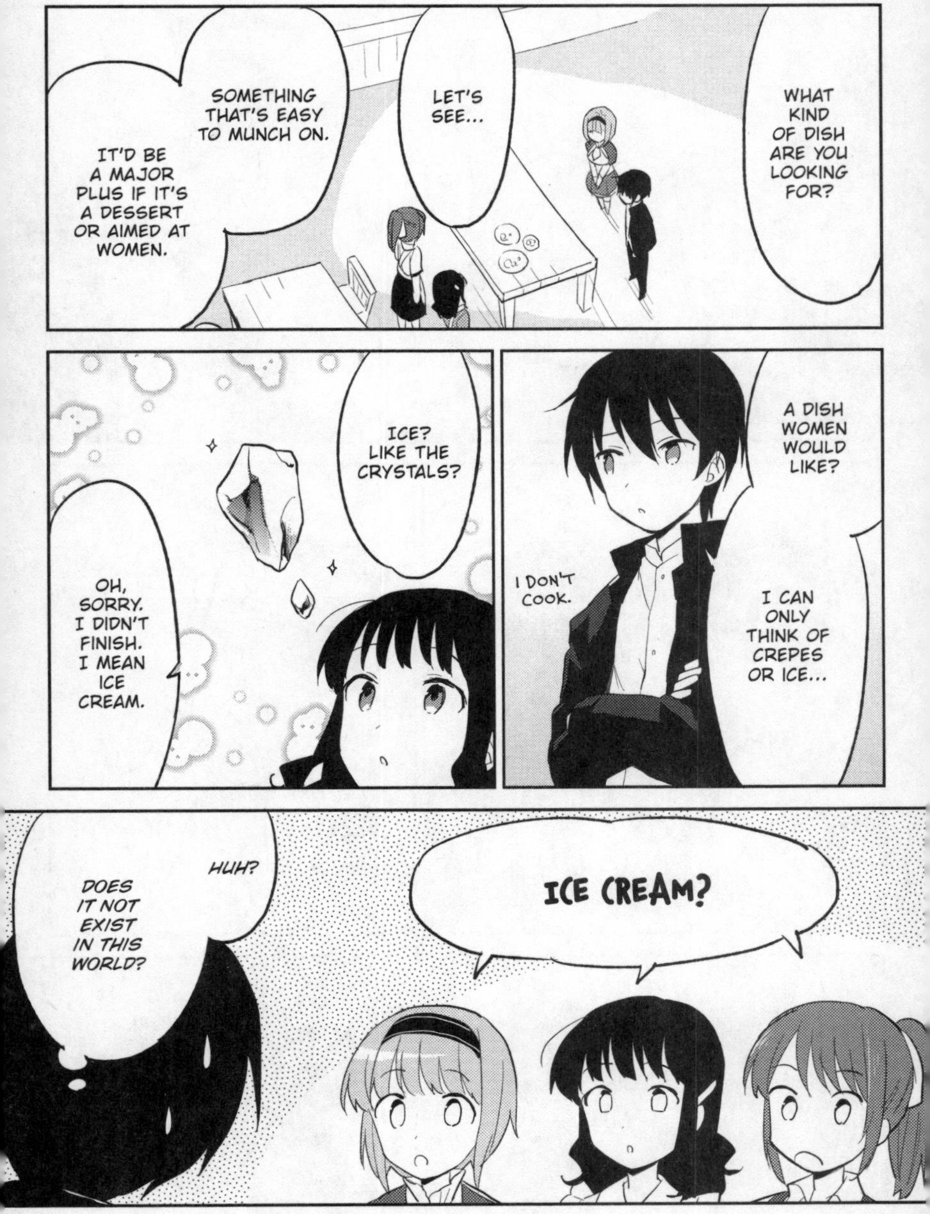
WHAT KIND OF DISH ARE YOU LOOKING FOR?
LET'S SEE...
SOMETHING THAT'S EASY TO MUNCH ON.
IT'D BE A MAJOR PLUS IF IT'S A DESSERT OR AIMED AT WOMEN.
A DISH WOMEN WOULD LIKE?
I CAN ONLY THINK OF CREPES OR ICE...
I DON'T COOK.
ICE? LIKE THE CRYSTALS?
OH, SORRY. I DIDN'T FINISH. I MEAN ICE CREAM.
ICE CREAM?
HUH?
DOES IT NOT EXIST IN THIS WORLD?

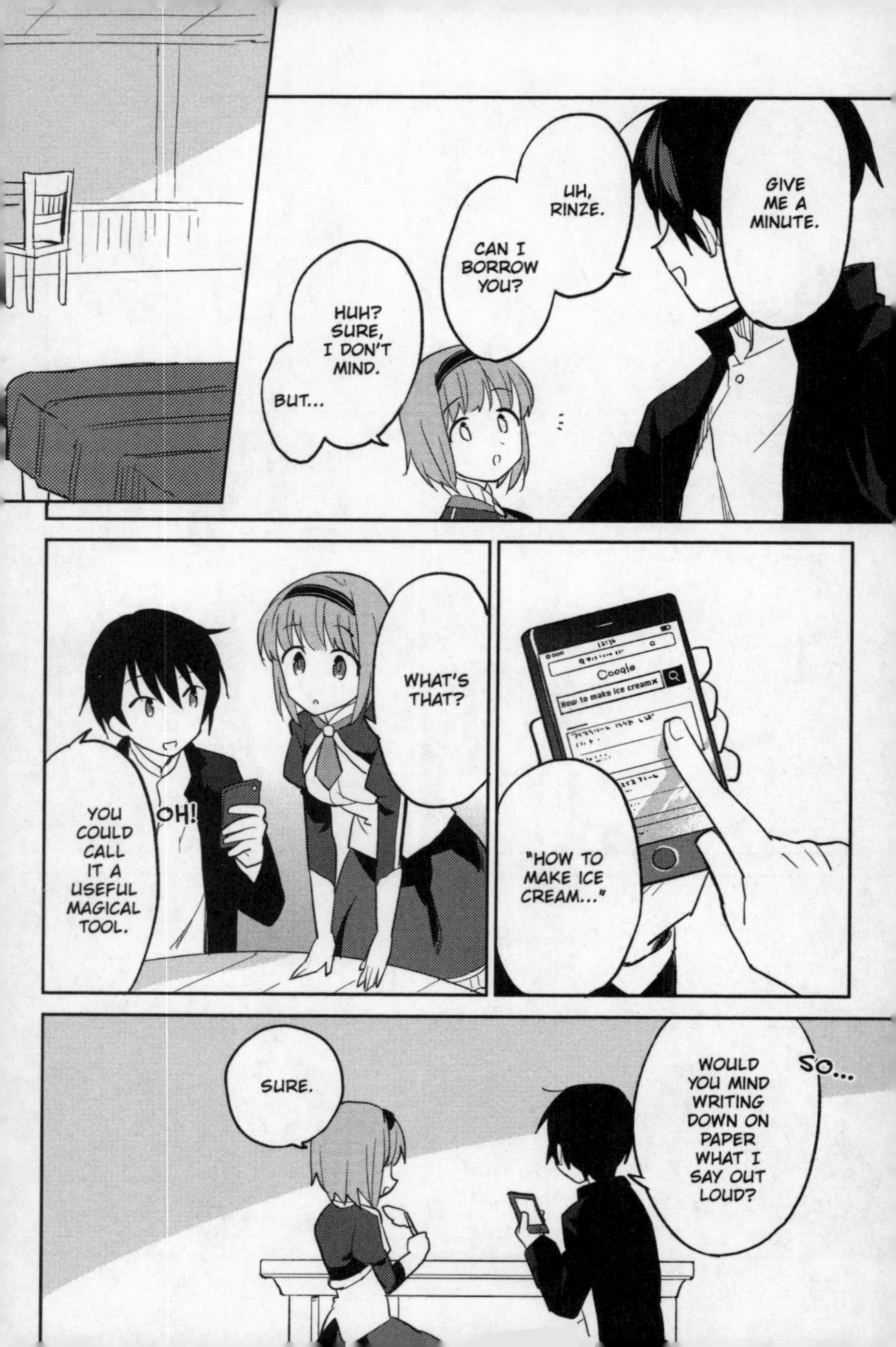
GIVE ME A MINUTE.
UH, RINZE.
CAN I BORROW YOU?
HUH? SURE, I DON'T MIND.
BUT...
Coogle
How to make ice creamx
"HOW TO MAKE ICE CREAM..."
WHAT'S THAT?
OH!
YOU COULD CALL IT A USEFUL MAGICAL TOOL.
SO...
WOULD YOU MIND WRITING DOWN ON PAPER WHAT I SAY OUT LOUD?
SURE.

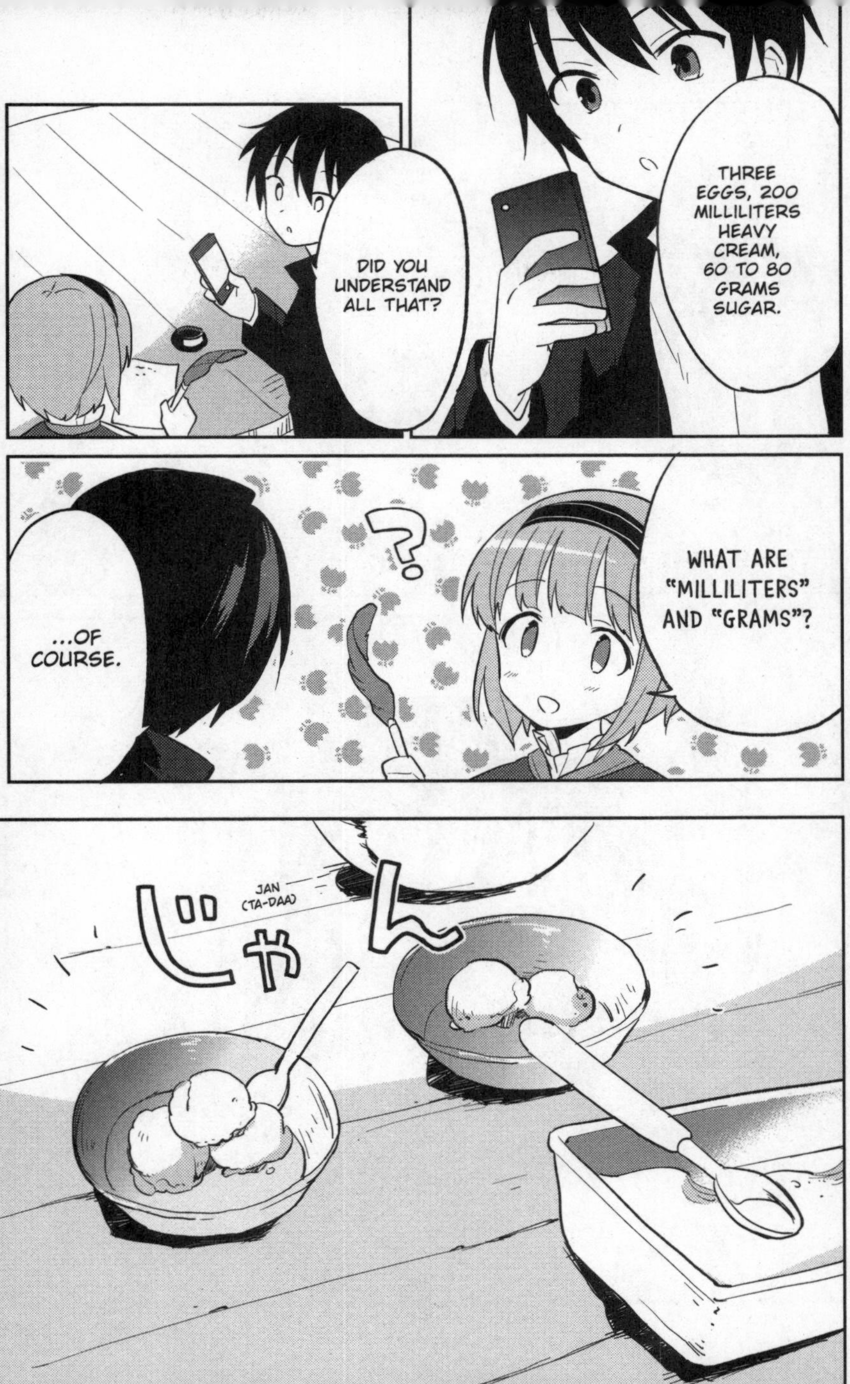
THREE EGGS, 200 MILLILITERS HEAVY CREAM, 60 TO 80 GRAMS SUGAR.
DID YOU UNDERSTAND ALL THAT?
WHAT ARE "MILLILITERS" AND "GRAMS"?
?
...OF COURSE.
じゃん
JAN (TA-DAA)

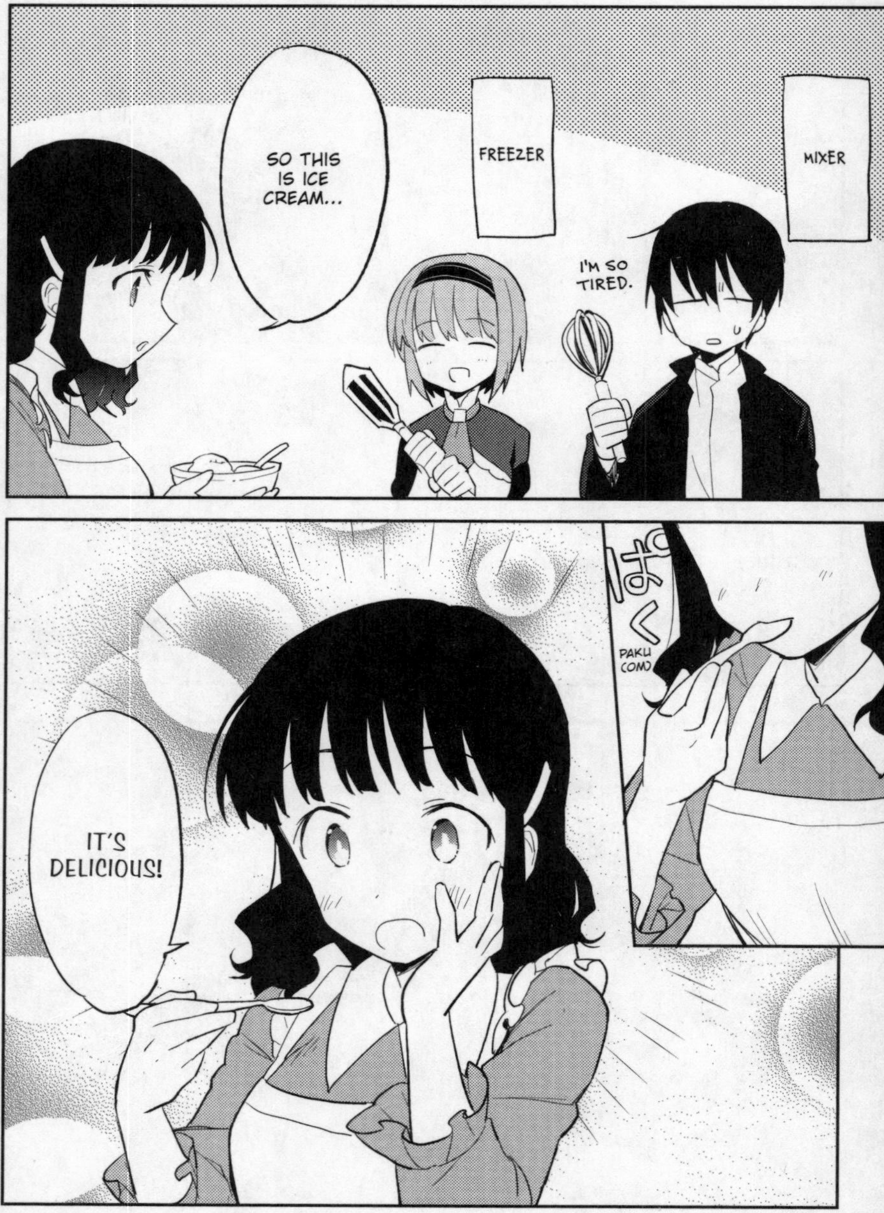
MIXER
FREEZER
SO THIS IS ICE CREAM...
I'M SO TIRED.
ぱく
PAKU (OM)
IT'S DELICIOUS!

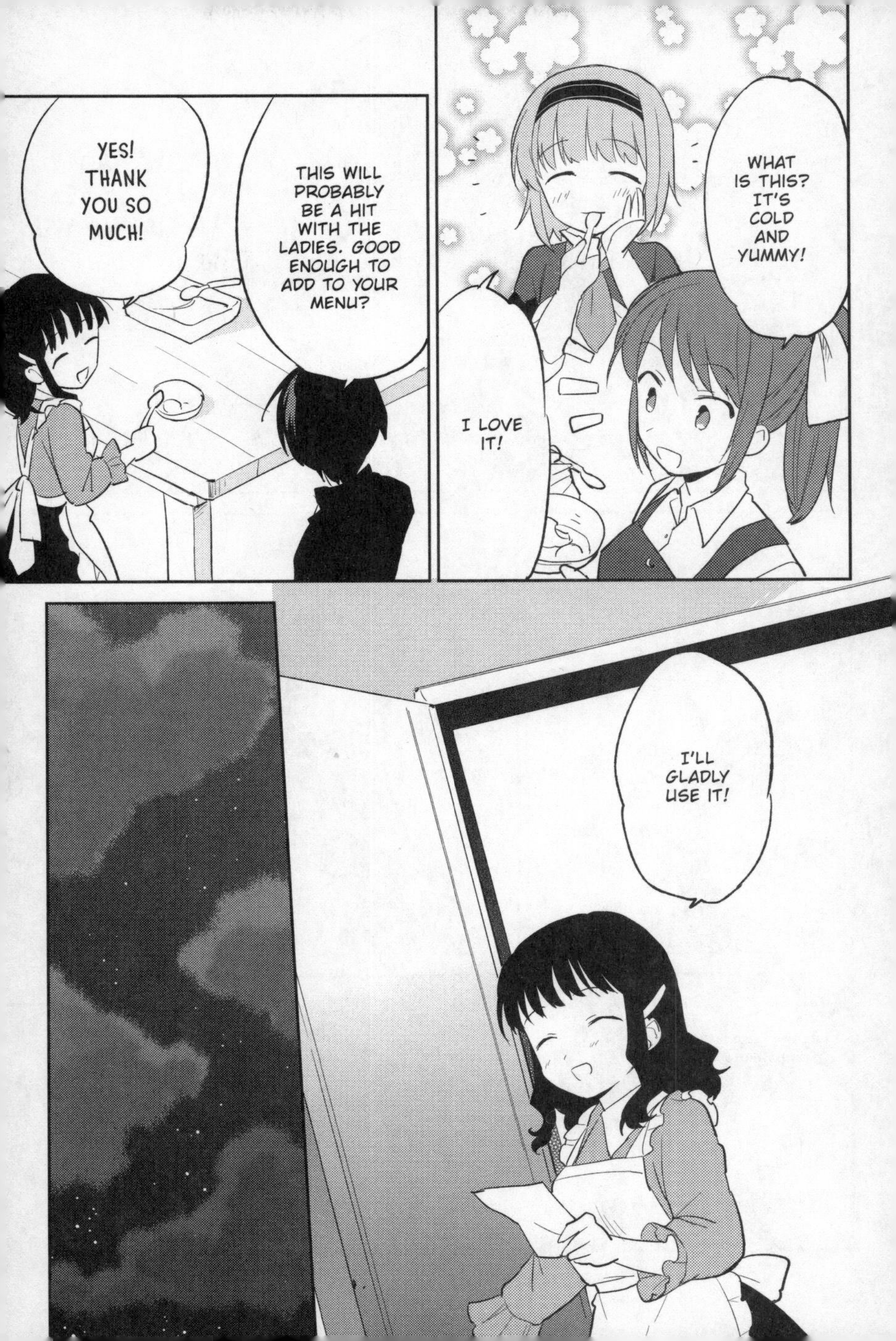
WHAT IS THIS? IT'S COLD AND YUMMY!
I LOVE IT!
THIS WILL PROBABLY BE A HIT WITH THE LADIES. GOOD ENOUGH TO ADD TO YOUR MENU?
YES! THANK YOU SO MUCH!
I'LL GLADLY USE IT!

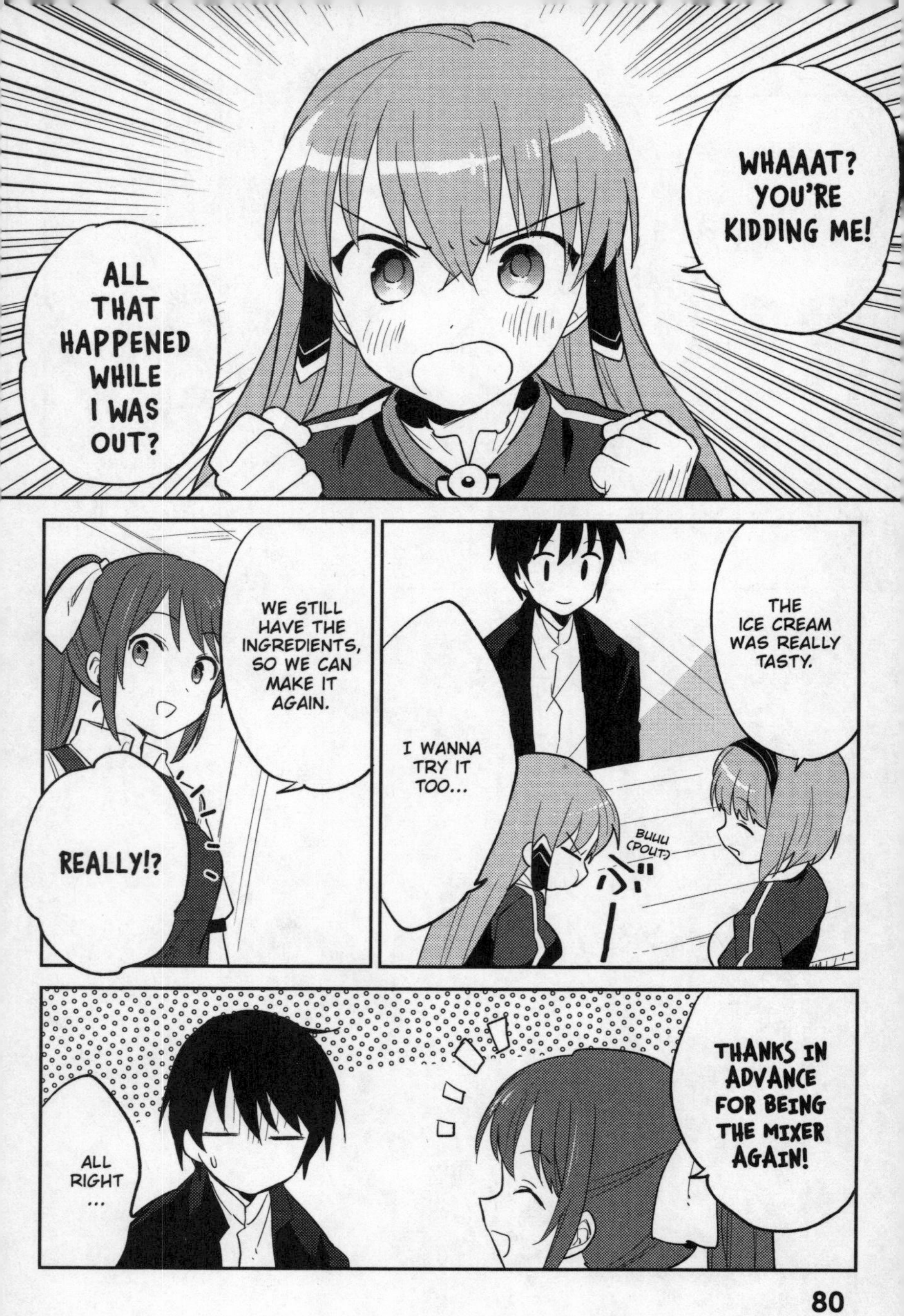
WHAAAT? YOU'RE KIDDING ME!
ALL THAT HAPPENED WHILE I WAS OUT?
THE ICE CREAM WAS REALLY TASTY.
I WANNA TRY IT TOO...
BUUU (POUT)
WE STILL HAVE THE INGREDIENTS, SO WE CAN MAKE IT AGAIN.
REALLY!?
THANKS IN ADVANCE FOR BEING THE MIXER AGAIN!
ALL RIGHT...

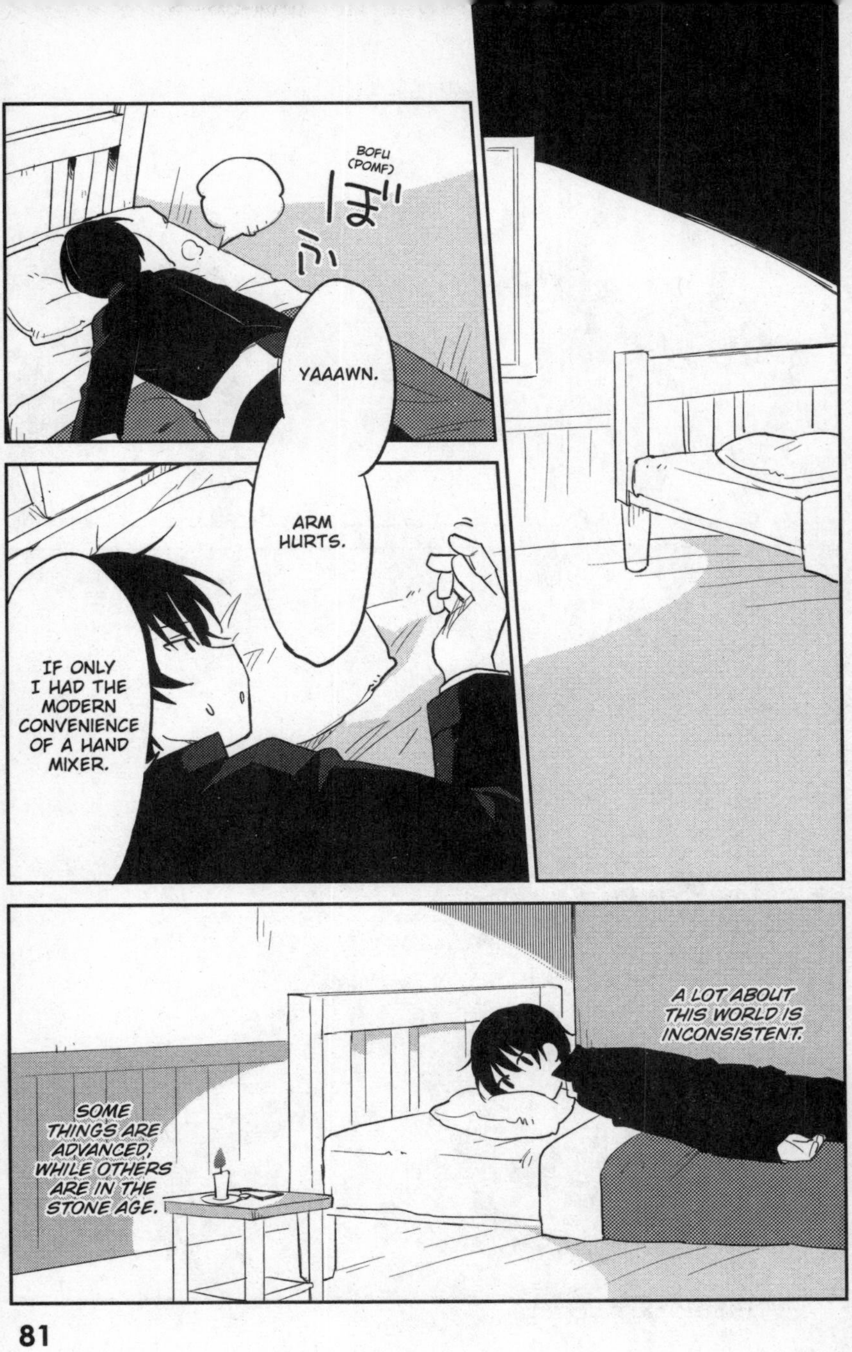
BOFU (POMF)
ぼふ
YAAAWN.
ARM HURTS.
IF ONLY I HAD THE MODERN CONVENIENCE OF A HAND MIXER.
A LOT ABOUT THIS WORLD IS INCONSISTENT.
SOME THINGS ARE ADVANCED, WHILE OTHERS ARE IN THE STONE AGE.

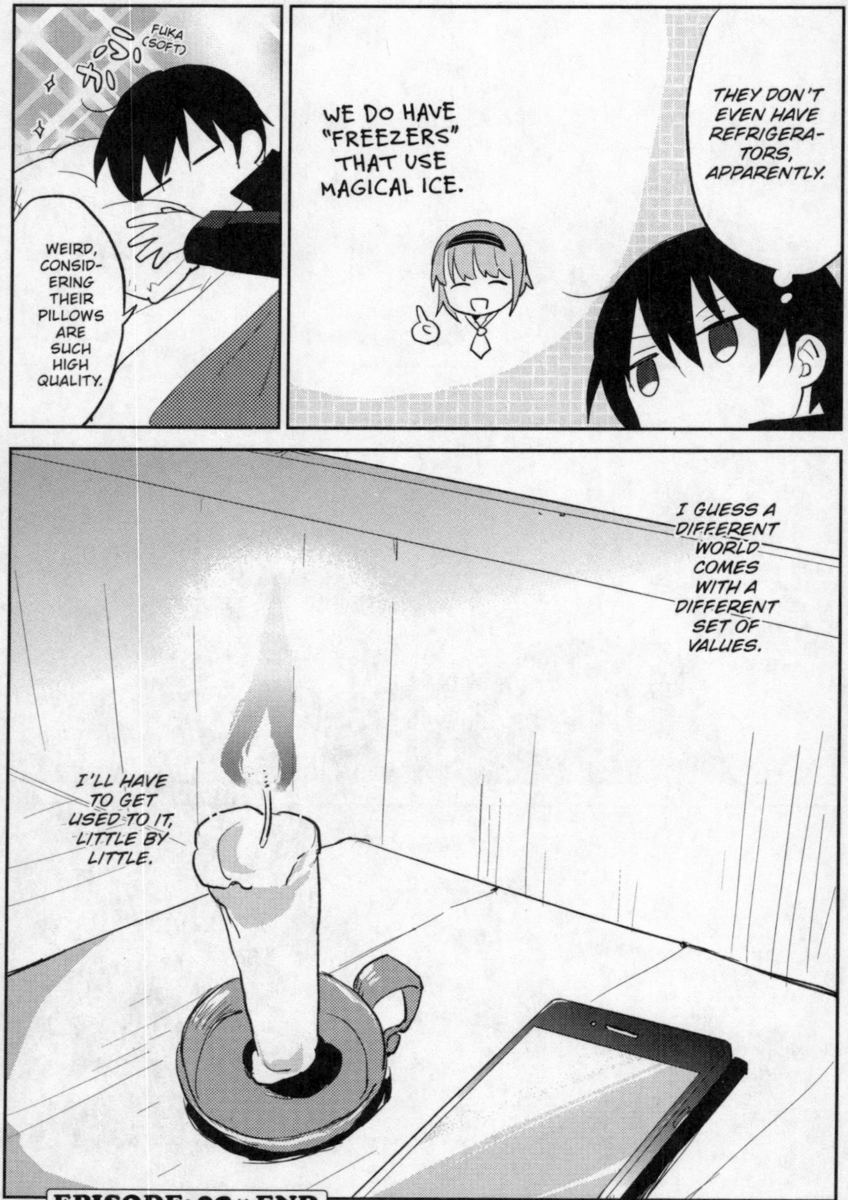
THEY DON'T EVEN HAVE REFRIGERATORS, APPARENTLY.
WE DO HAVE "FREEZERS" THAT USE MAGICAL ICE.
FUKA (SOFT)
WEIRD, CONSIDERING THEIR PILLOWS ARE SUCH HIGH QUALITY.
I GUESS A DIFFERENT WORLD COMES WITH A DIFFERENT SET OF VALUES.
I'LL HAVE TO GET USED TO IT, LITTLE BY LITTLE.

EPISODE: 02 » END

In Another World With
My Smartphone

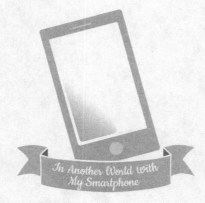

In Another World with My Smartphone

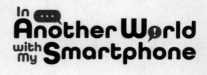

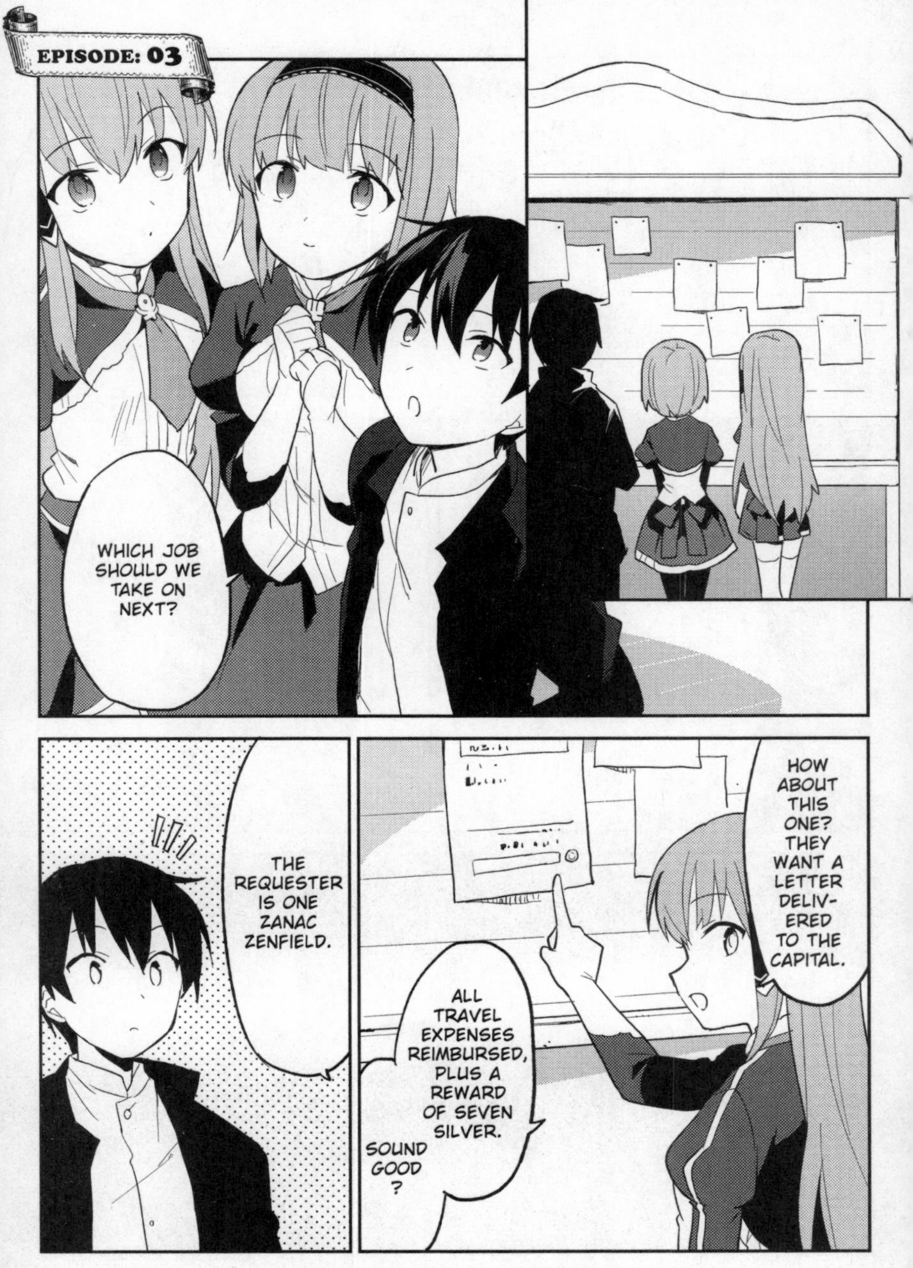
EPISODE: 03
WHICH JOB SHOULD WE TAKE ON NEXT?
HOW ABOUT THIS ONE? THEY WANT A LETTER DELIV-ERED TO THE CAPITAL.
ALL TRAVEL EXPENSES REIMBURSED, PLUS A REWARD OF SEVEN SILVER.
SOUND GOOD?
THE REQUESTER IS ONE ZANAC ZENFIELD.

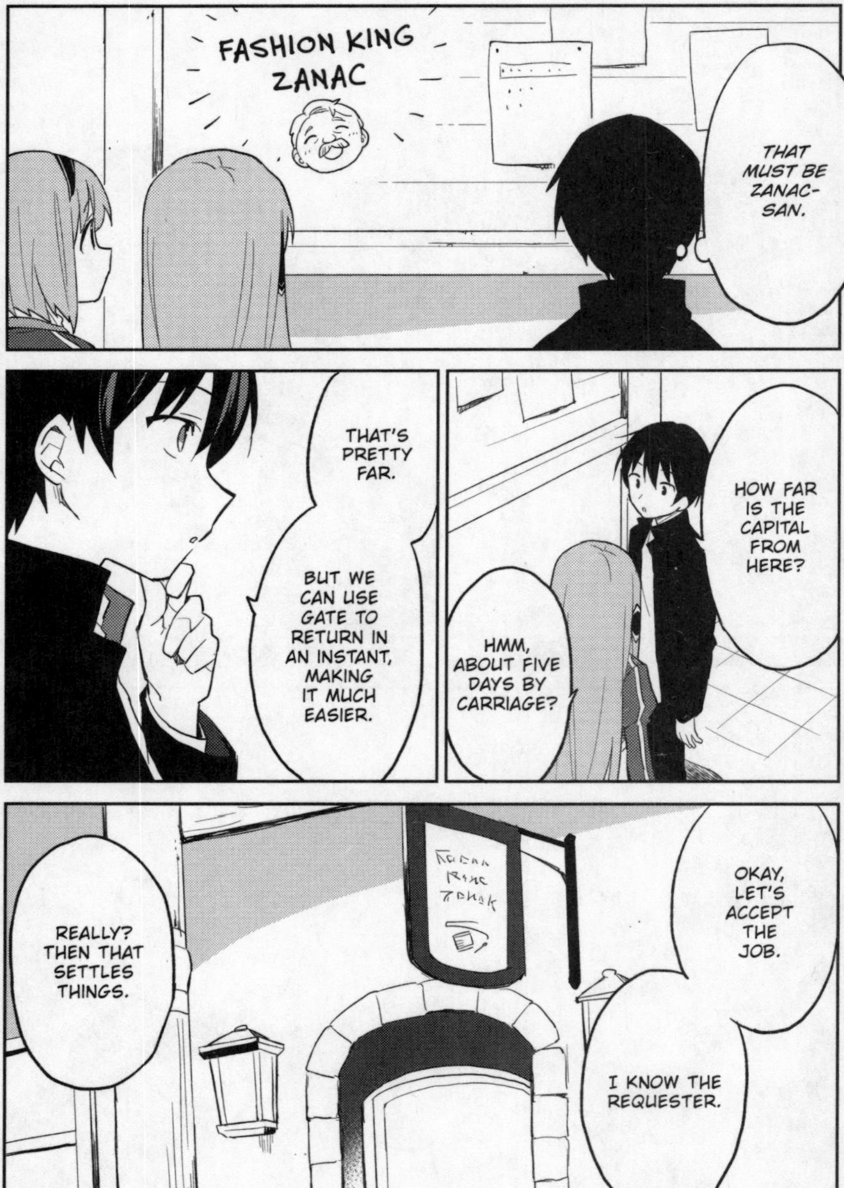
THAT MUST BE ZANAC-SAN.
FASHION KING ZANAC
HOW FAR IS THE CAPITAL FROM HERE?
HMM, ABOUT FIVE DAYS BY CARRIAGE?
THAT'S PRETTY FAR.
BUT WE CAN USE GATE TO RETURN IN AN INSTANT, MAKING IT MUCH EASIER.
OKAY, LET'S ACCEPT THE JOB.
I KNOW THE REQUESTER.
REALLY? THEN THAT SETTLES THINGS.

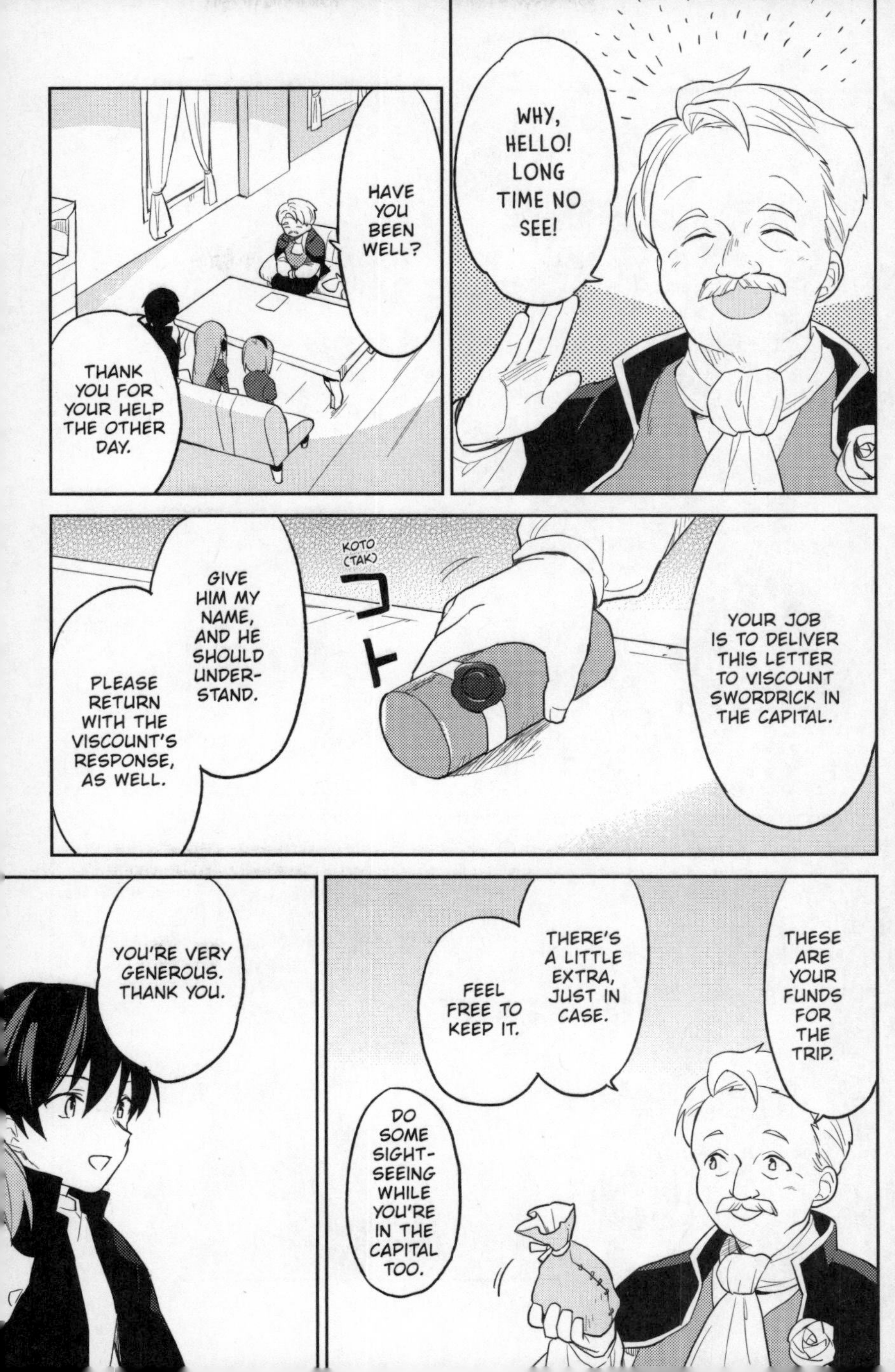
WHY, HELLO! LONG TIME NO SEE!
HAVE YOU BEEN WELL?
THANK YOU FOR YOUR HELP THE OTHER DAY.
YOUR JOB IS TO DELIVER THIS LETTER TO VISCOUNT SWORDRICK IN THE CAPITAL.
KOTO (TAK)
GIVE HIM MY NAME, AND HE SHOULD UNDERSTAND.
PLEASE RETURN WITH THE VISCOUNT'S RESPONSE, AS WELL.
THESE ARE YOUR FUNDS FOR THE TRIP.
THERE'S A LITTLE EXTRA, JUST IN CASE.
FEEL FREE TO KEEP IT.
DO SOME SIGHT-SEEING WHILE YOU'RE IN THE CAPITAL TOO.
YOU'RE VERY GENEROUS. THANK YOU.

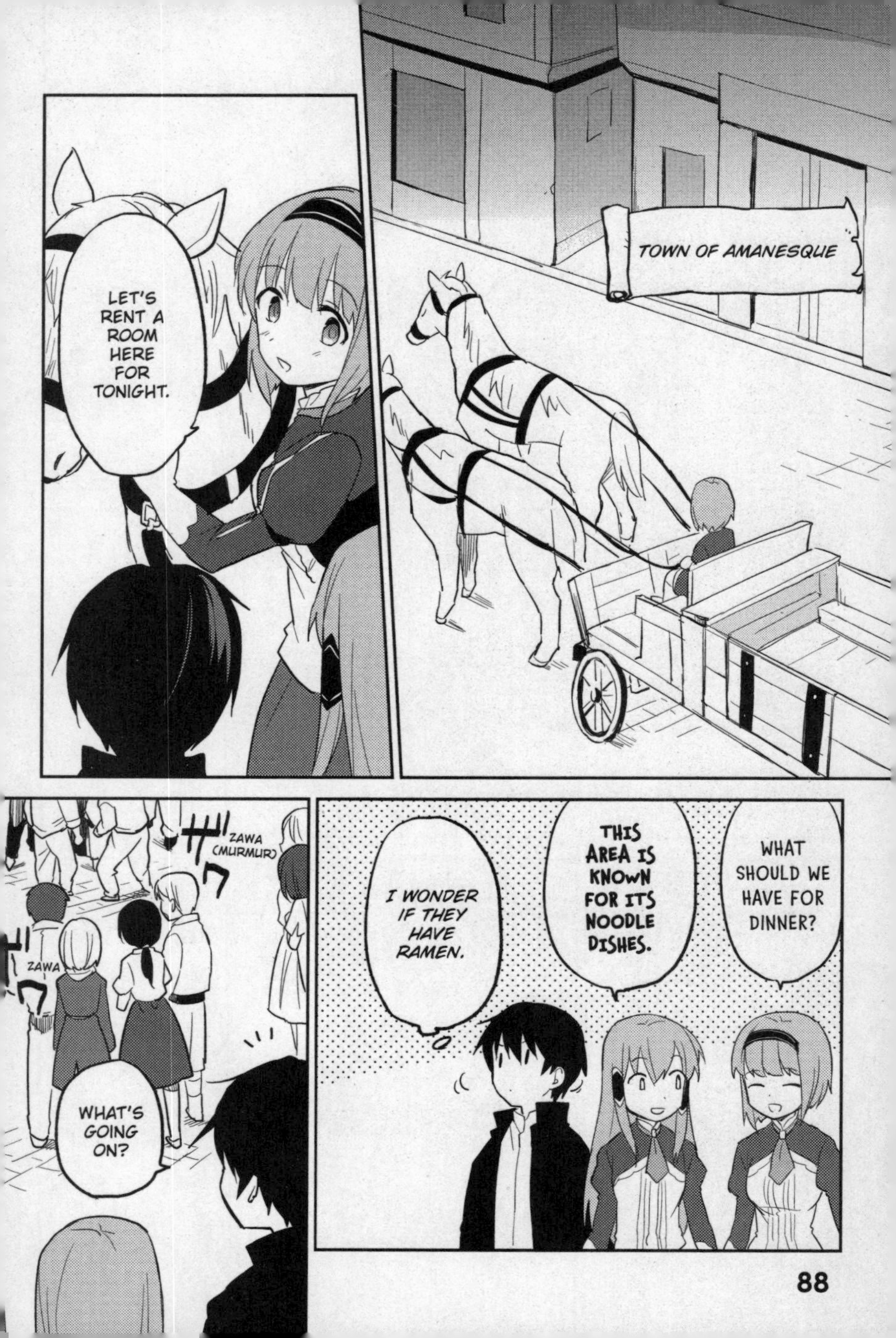
TOWN OF AMANESQUE
LET'S RENT A ROOM HERE FOR TONIGHT.
WHAT SHOULD WE HAVE FOR DINNER?
THIS AREA IS KNOWN FOR ITS NOODLE DISHES.
I WONDER IF THEY HAVE RAMEN.
ZAWA (MURMUR)
ZAWA
WHAT'S GOING ON?

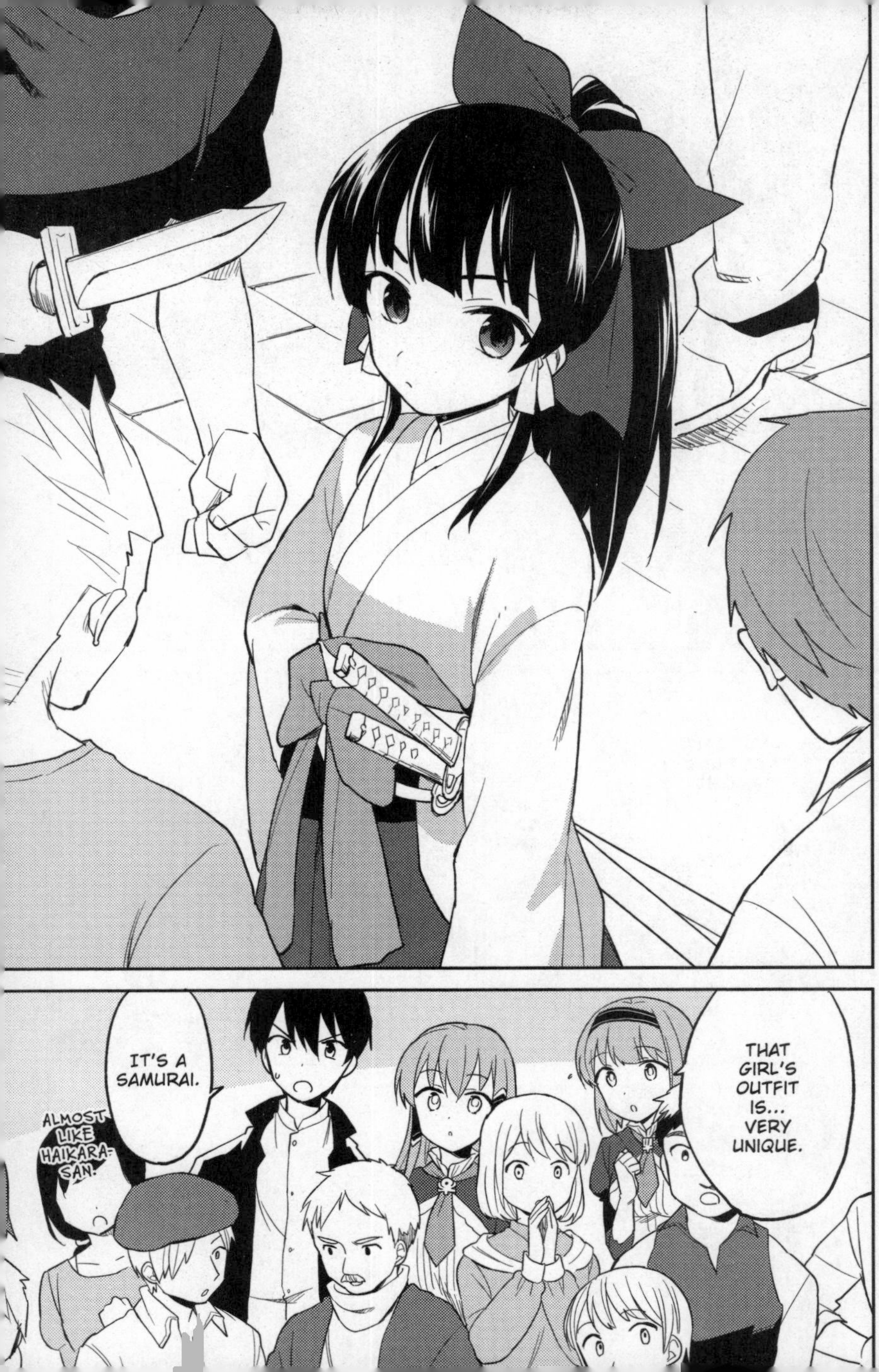
THAT GIRL'S OUTFIT IS... VERY UNIQUE.
IT'S A SAMURAI.
ALMOST LIKE HAIKARA-SAN.

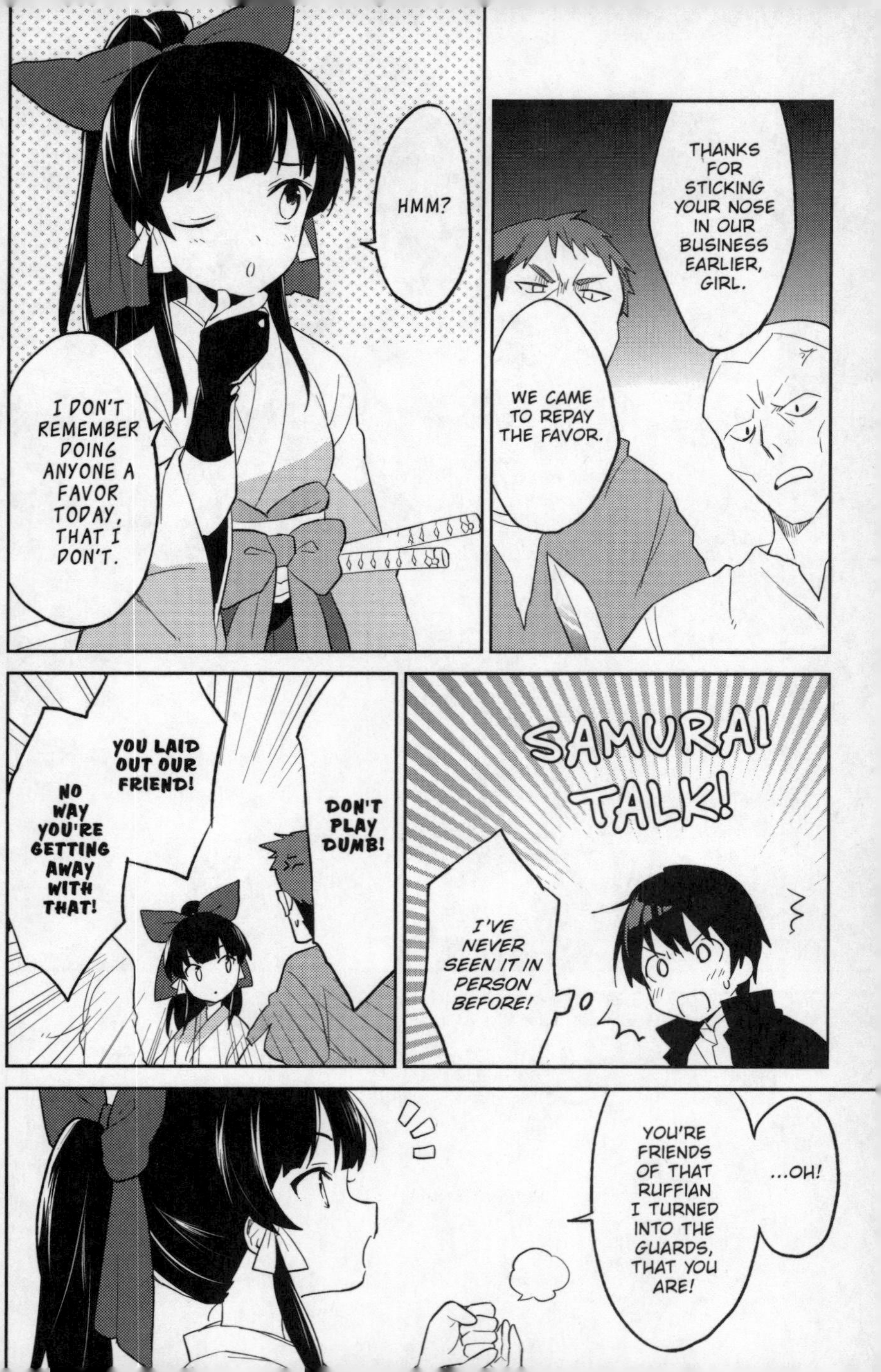
THANKS FOR STICKING YOUR NOSE IN OUR BUSINESS EARLIER, GIRL.
WE CAME TO REPAY THE FAVOR.
HMM?
I DON'T REMEMBER DOING ANYONE A FAVOR TODAY, THAT I DON'T.
SAMURAI TALK!
I'VE NEVER SEEN IT IN PERSON BEFORE!
DON'T PLAY DUMB!
YOU LAID OUT OUR FRIEND!
NO WAY YOU'RE GETTING AWAY WITH THAT!
...OH!
YOU'RE FRIENDS OF THAT RUFFIAN I TURNED INTO THE GUARDS, THAT YOU ARE!

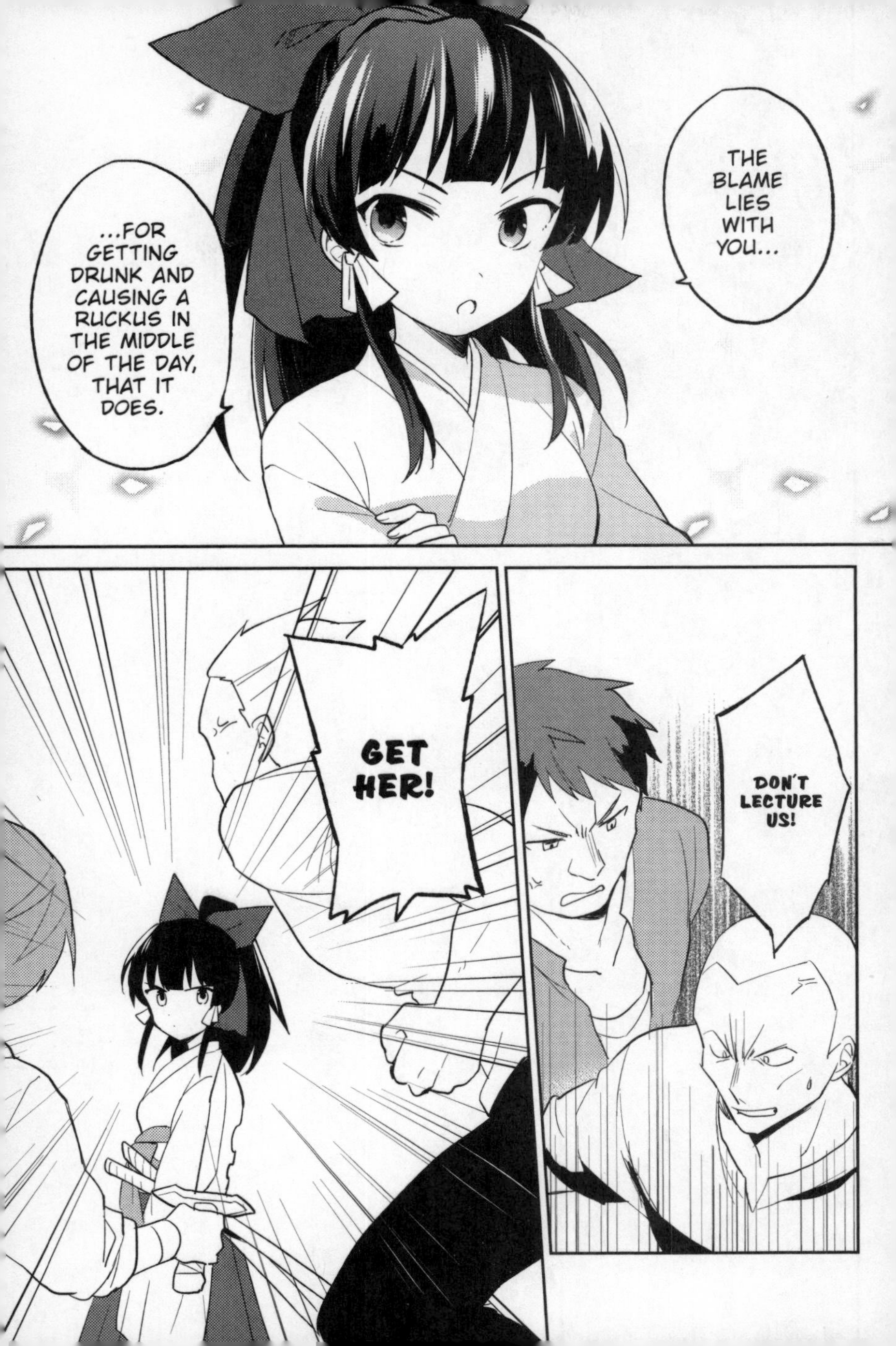
THE BLAME LIES WITH YOU...
...FOR GETTING DRUNK AND CAUSING A RUCKUS IN THE MIDDLE OF THE DAY, THAT IT DOES.
DON'T LECTURE US!
GET HER!

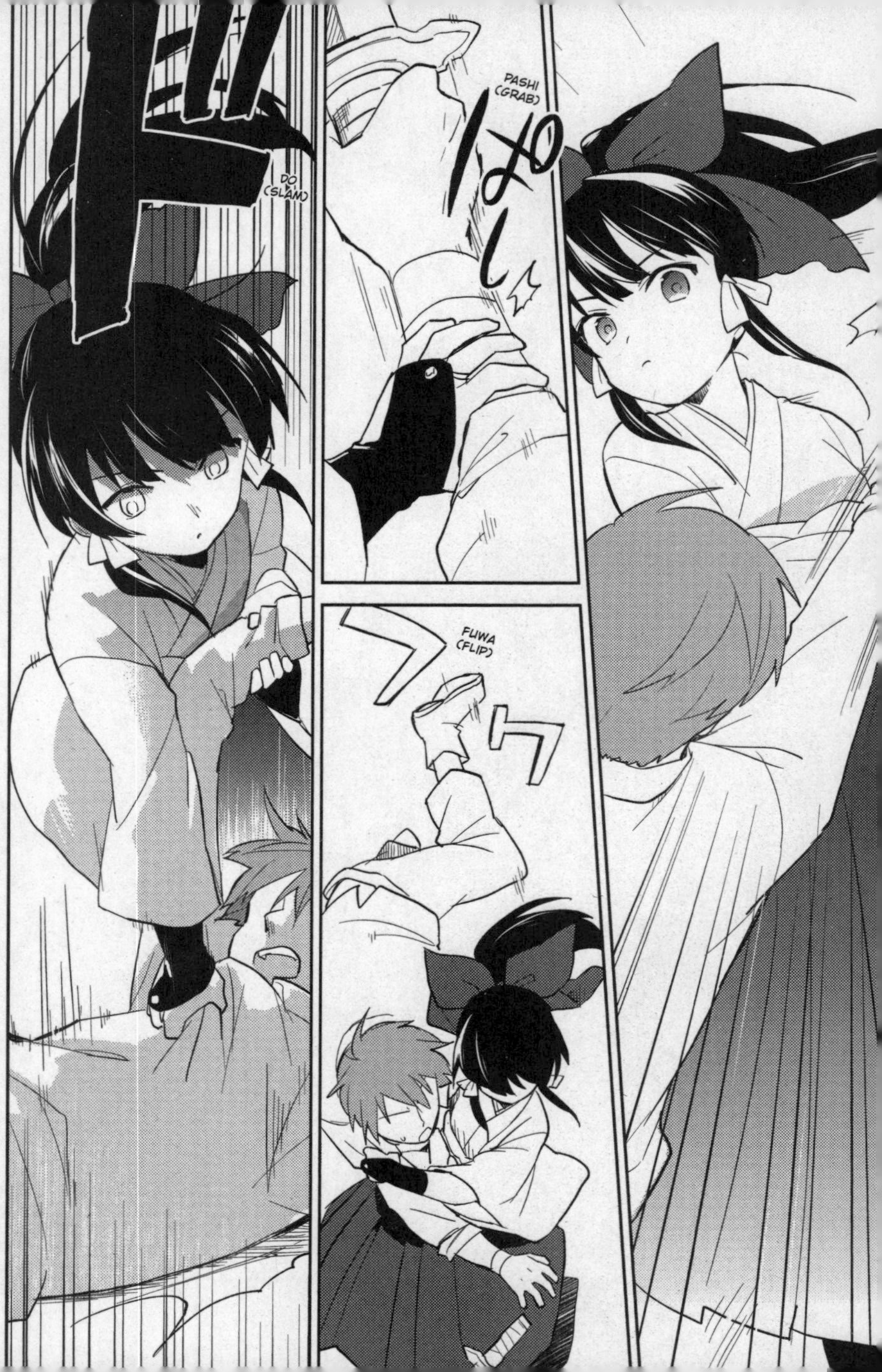
PASHI (GRAB)
ぱし
FUWA (FLIP)
DO (SLAM)

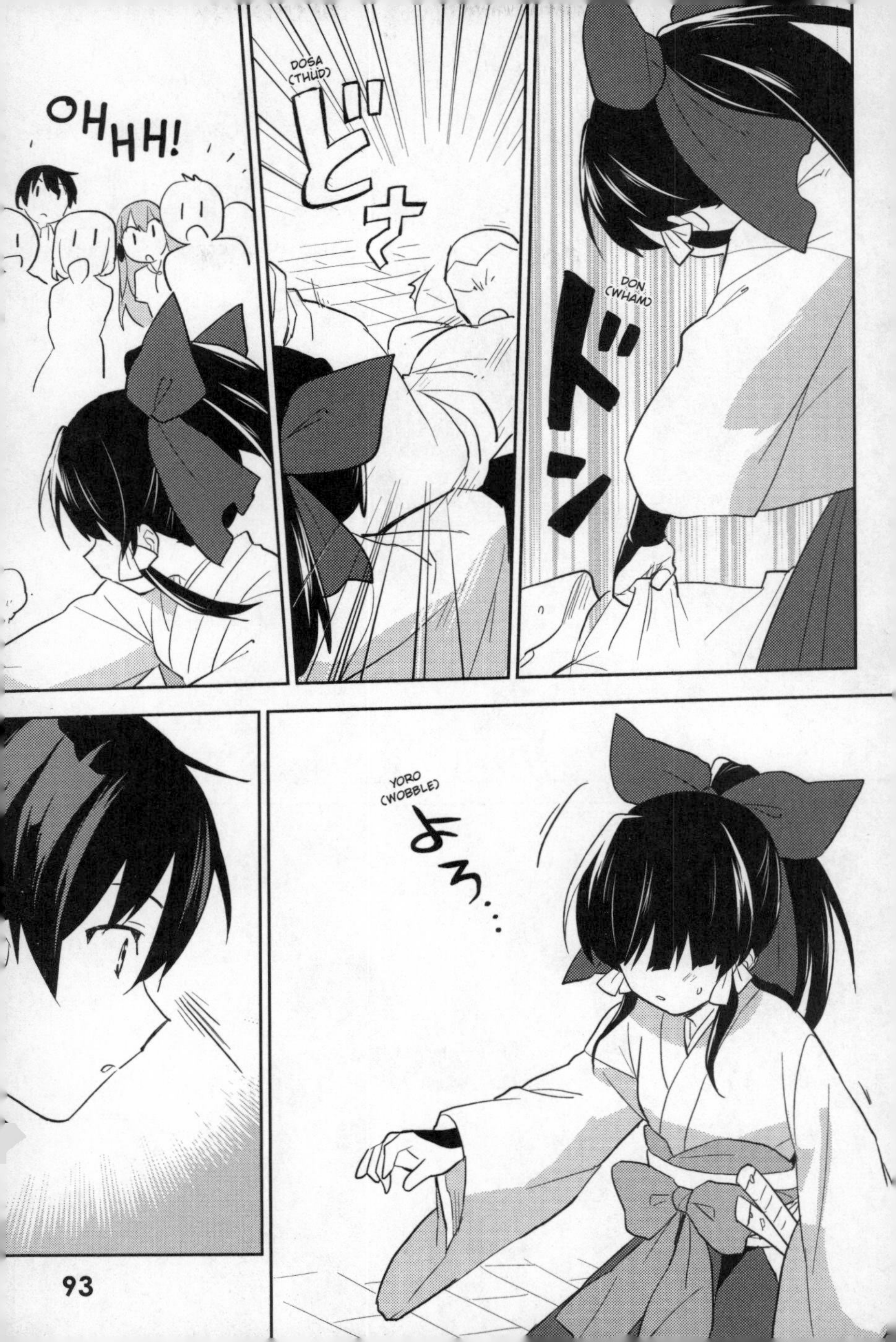
DON
(WHAM)
ドン
DOSA
(THUD)
どさ
OHHH!
YORO
(WOBBLE)
よろ…

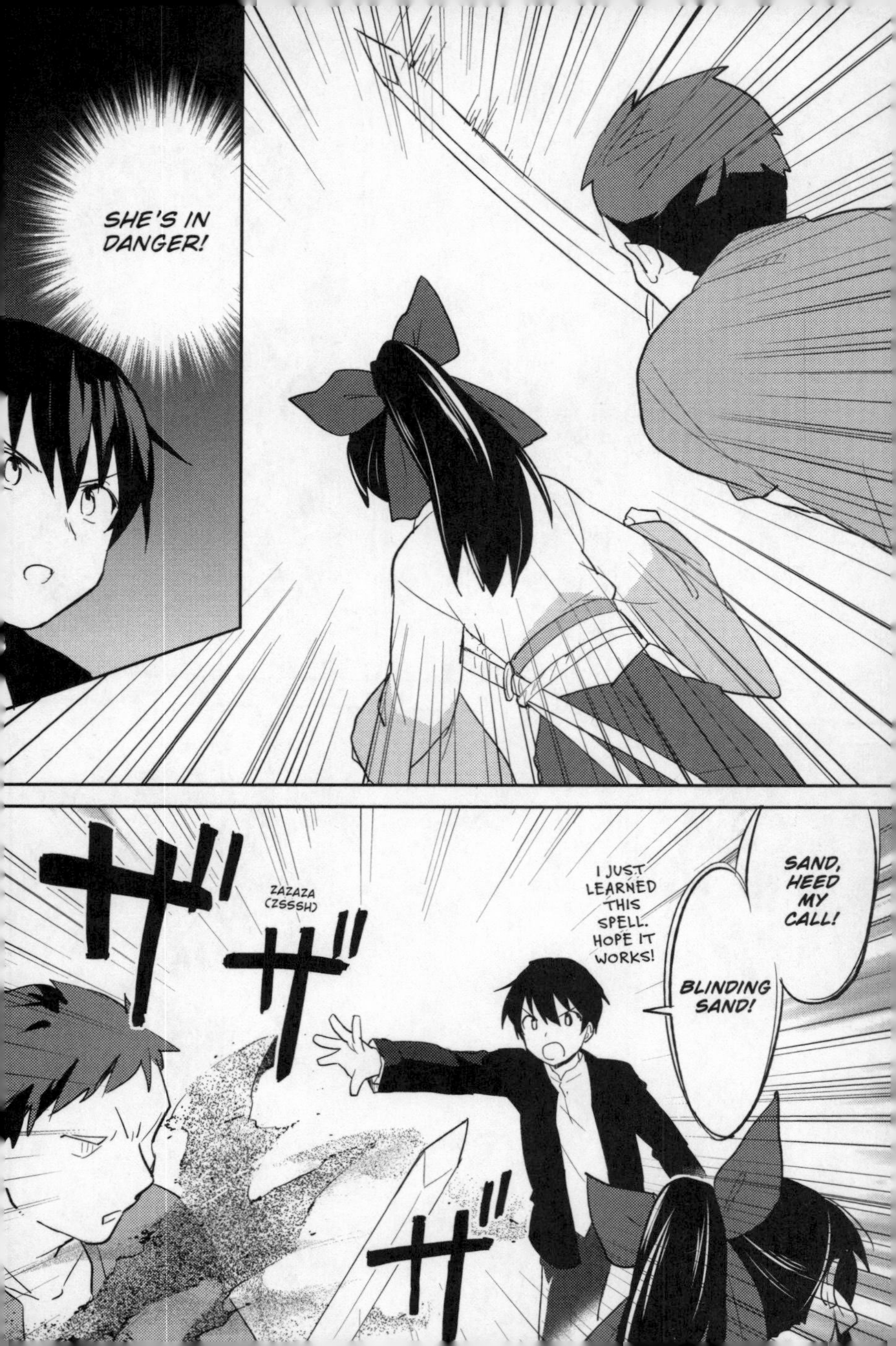
SHE'S IN DANGER!
SAND, HEED MY CALL!
BLINDING SAND!
I JUST LEARNED THIS SPELL. HOPE IT WORKS!
ザザザ
ZAZAZA (ZSSSH)

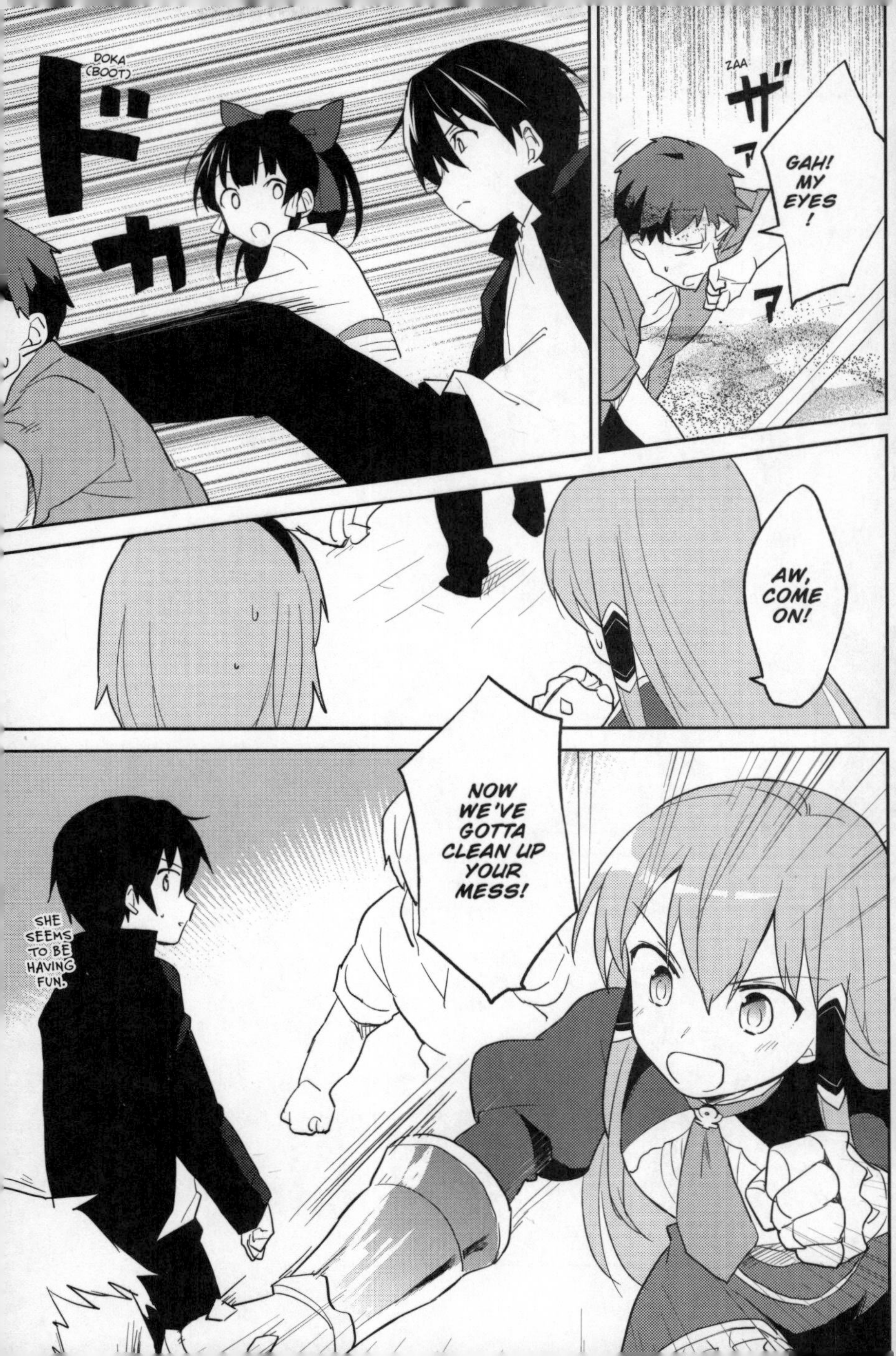
ZAA
ザァァ
GAH! MY EYES!
DOKA (BOOT)
ドカ
AW, COME ON!
NOW WE'VE GOTTA CLEAN UP YOUR MESS!
SHE SEEMS TO BE HAVING FUN.

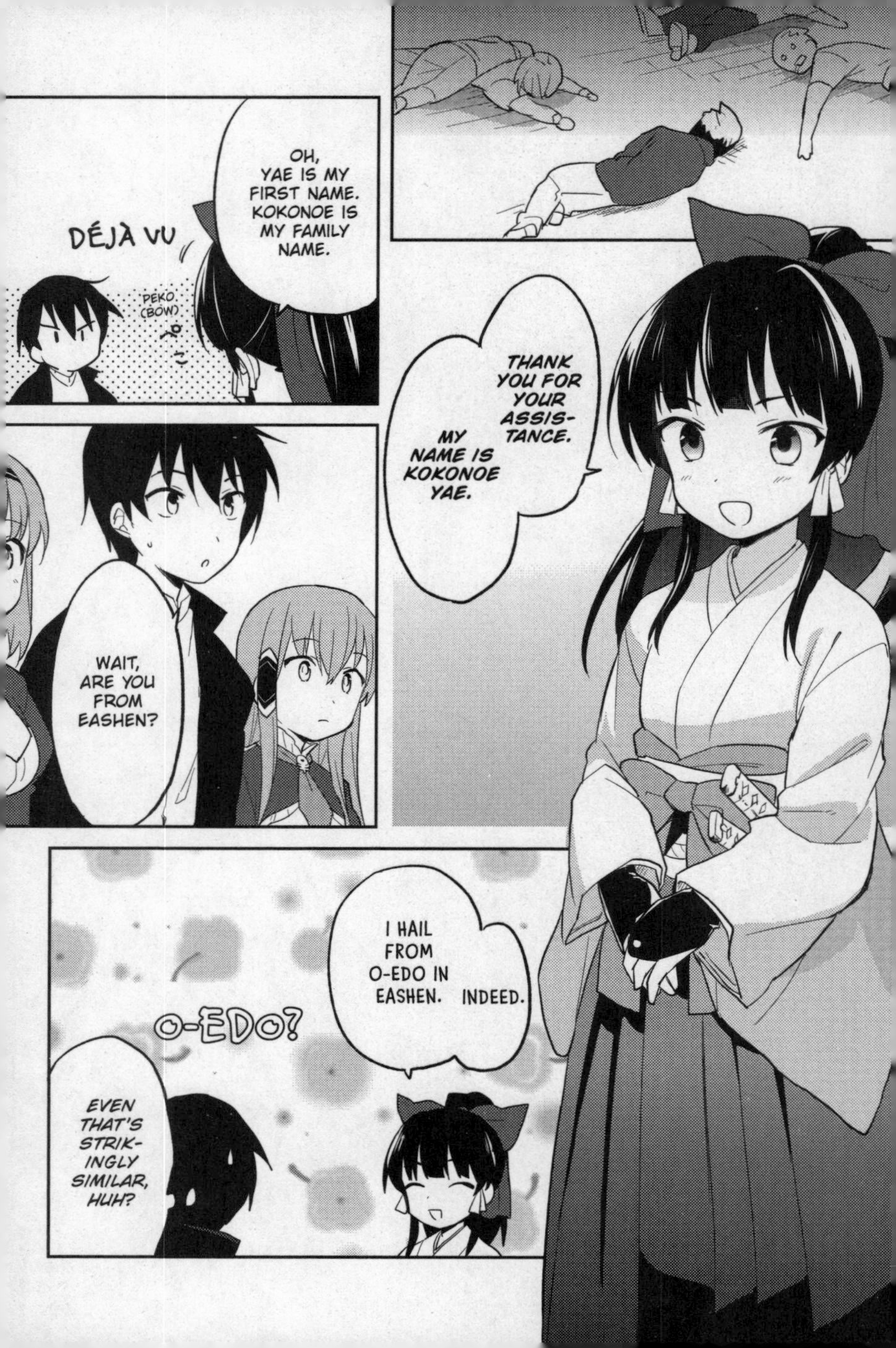
THANK YOU FOR YOUR ASSISTANCE.
MY NAME IS KOKONOE YAE.
OH, YAE IS MY FIRST NAME. KOKONOE IS MY FAMILY NAME.
PEKO (BOW)
DÉJÀ VU
WAIT, ARE YOU FROM EASHEN?
I HAIL FROM O-EDO IN EASHEN.
INDEED.
O-EDO?
EVEN THAT'S STRIKINGLY SIMILAR, HUH?

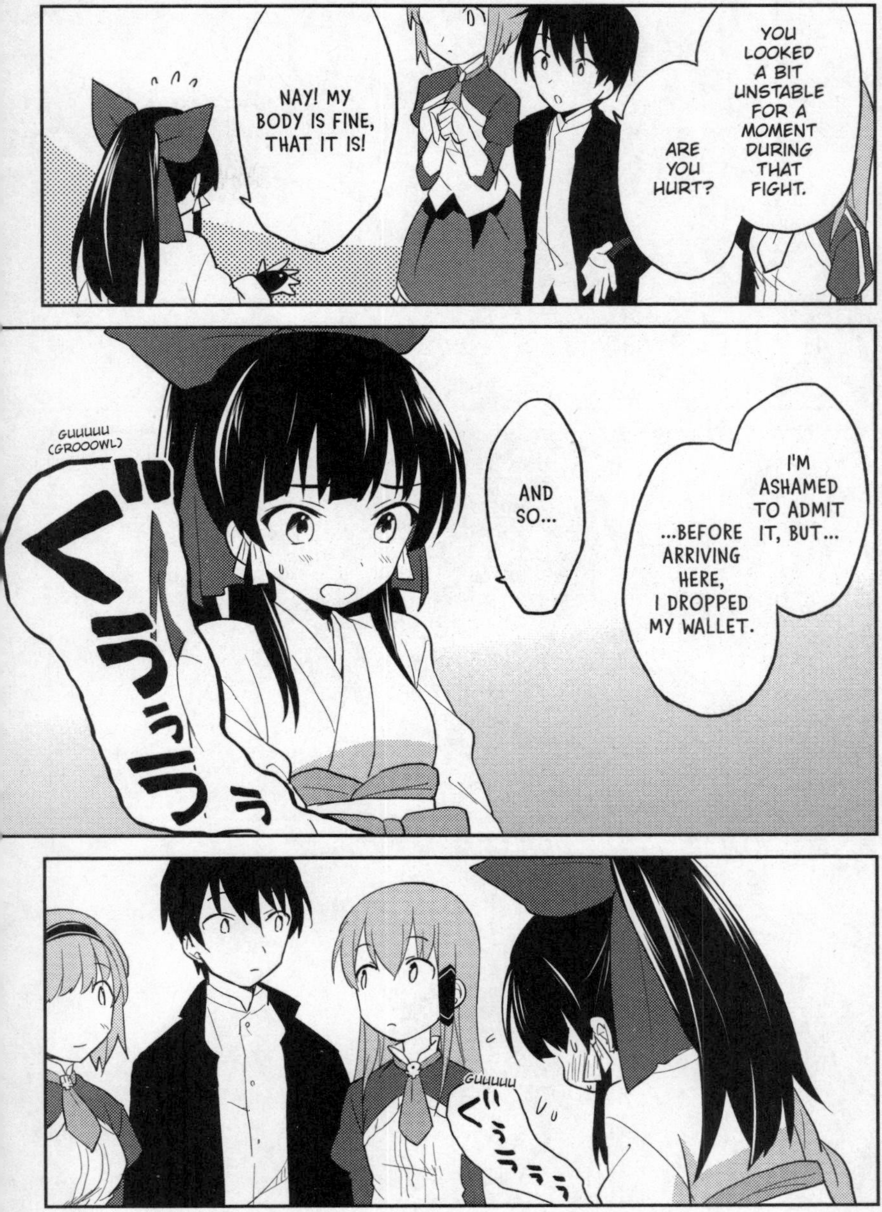
YOU LOOKED A BIT UNSTABLE FOR A MOMENT DURING THAT FIGHT.
ARE YOU HURT?
NAY! MY BODY IS FINE, THAT IT IS!
I'M ASHAMED TO ADMIT IT, BUT...
...BEFORE ARRIVING HERE, I DROPPED MY WALLET.
AND SO...
GUUUUU (GROOOWL)
GUUUUU

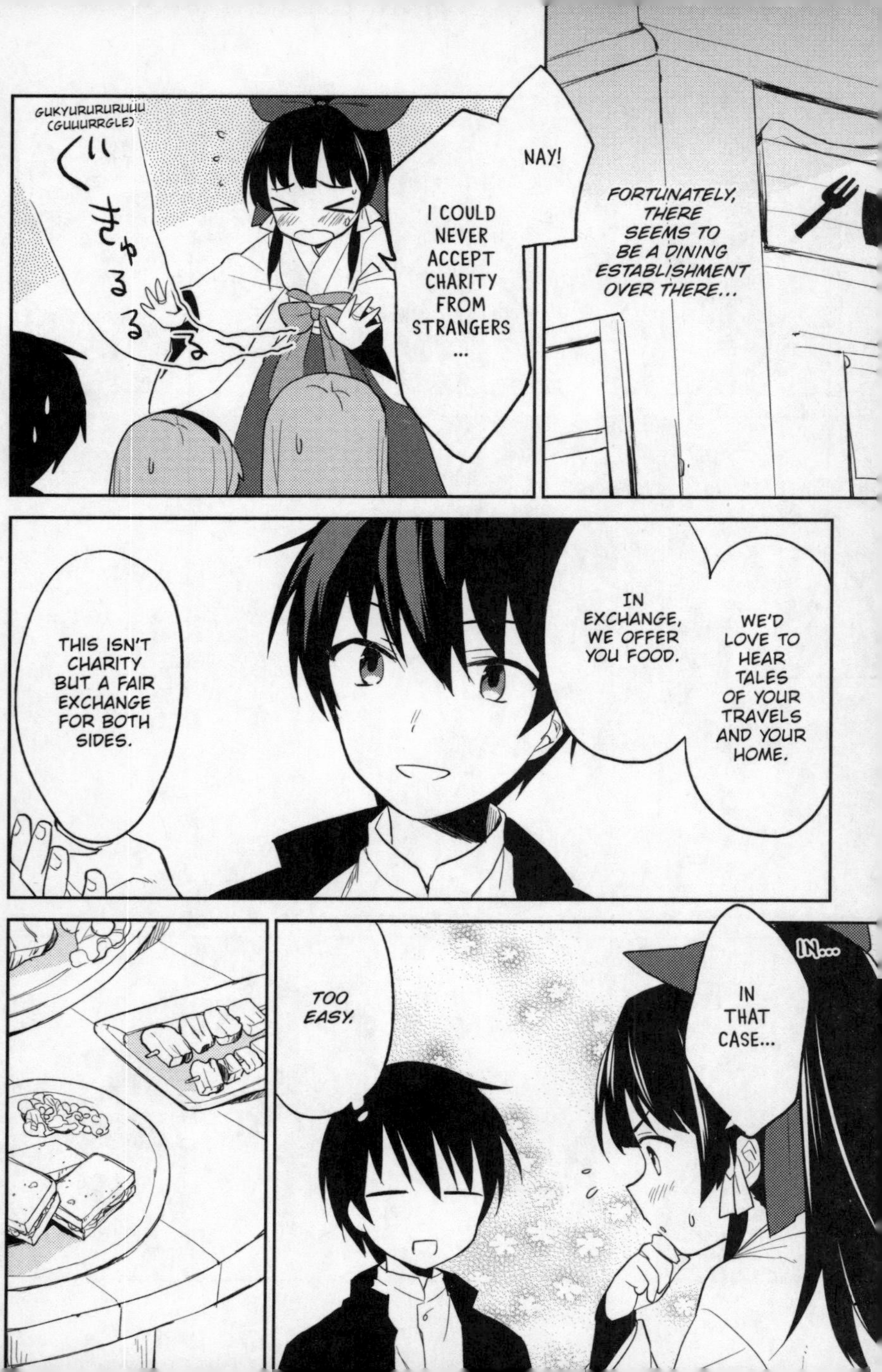

FORTUNATELY, THERE SEEMS TO BE A DINING ESTABLISHMENT OVER THERE...
NAY!
I COULD NEVER ACCEPT CHARITY FROM STRANGERS...
GUKYURURURUUU (GUUURRGLE)
ぐきゅるるる
WE'D LOVE TO HEAR TALES OF YOUR TRAVELS AND YOUR HOME.
IN EXCHANGE, WE OFFER YOU FOOD.
THIS ISN'T CHARITY BUT A FAIR EXCHANGE FOR BOTH SIDES.
IN...
IN THAT CASE...
TOO EASY.

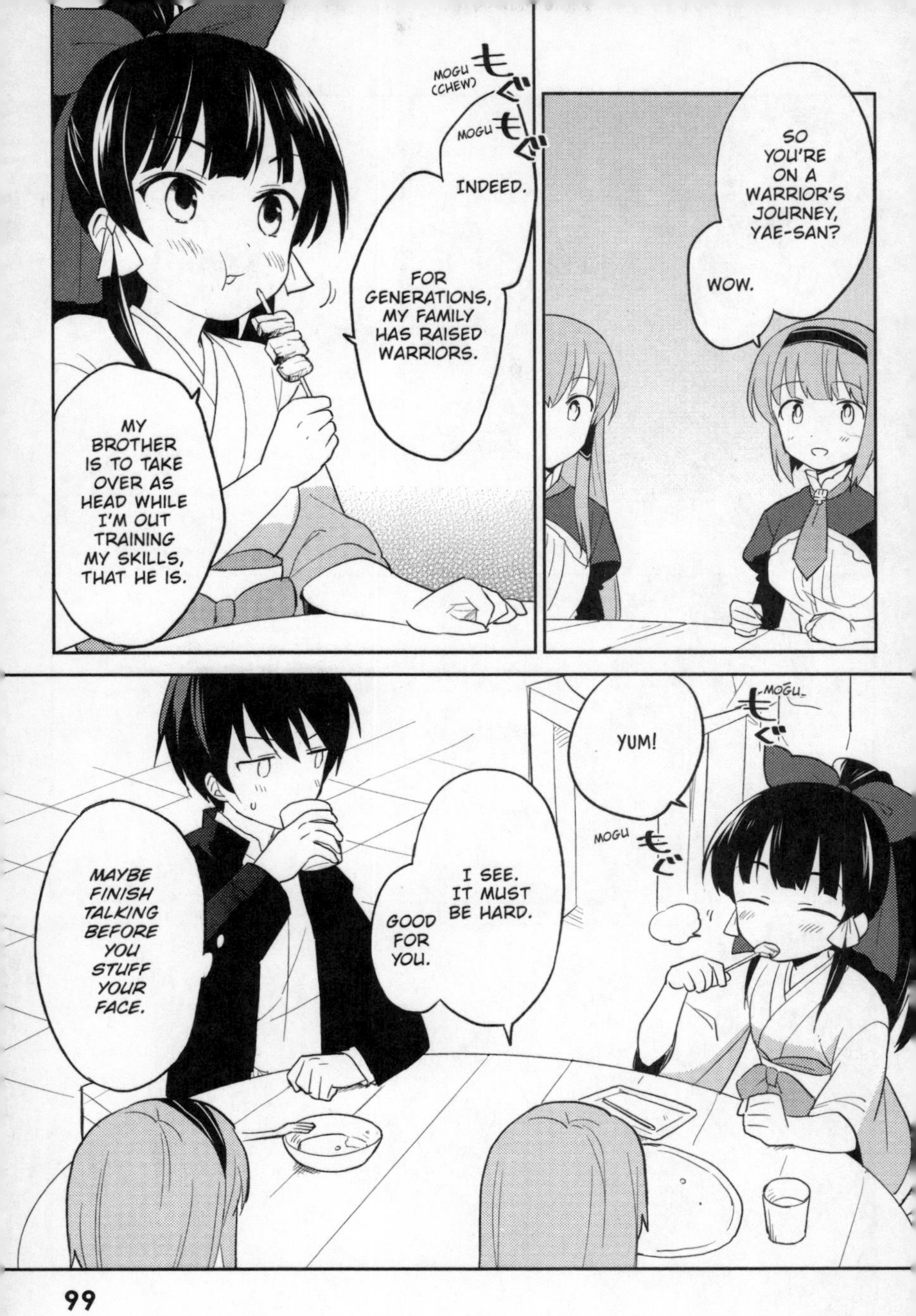
SO YOU'RE ON A WARRIOR'S JOURNEY, YAE-SAN?
WOW.
MOGU (CHEW) もぐ
MOGU もぐ
INDEED.
FOR GENERATIONS, MY FAMILY HAS RAISED WARRIORS.
MY BROTHER IS TO TAKE OVER AS HEAD WHILE I'M OUT TRAINING MY SKILLS, THAT HE IS.
MOGU もぐ
YUM!
MOGU もぐ
I SEE. IT MUST BE HARD.
GOOD FOR YOU.
MAYBE FINISH TALKING BEFORE YOU STUFF YOUR FACE.

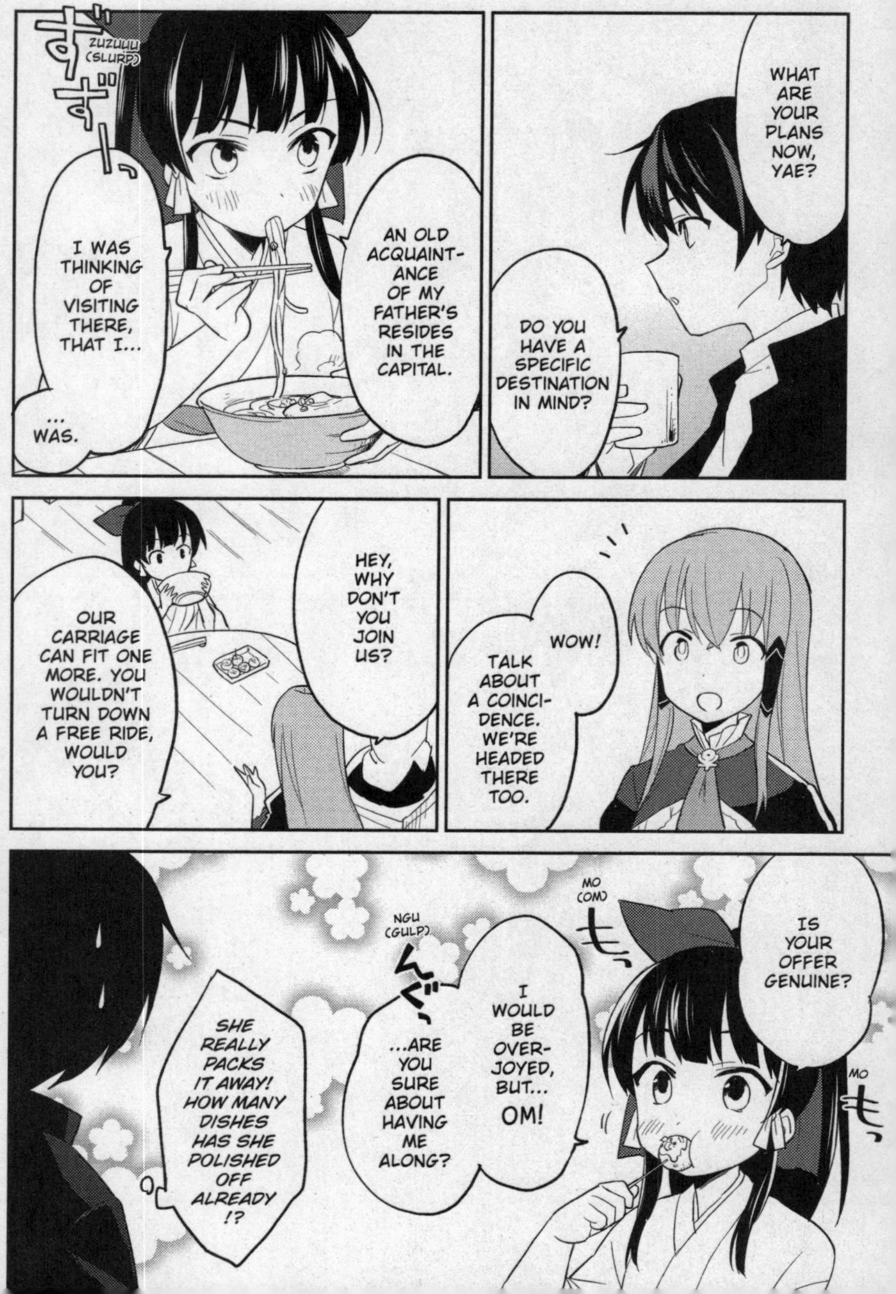
WHAT ARE YOUR PLANS NOW, YAE?
DO YOU HAVE A SPECIFIC DESTINATION IN MIND?
ZUZUUU (SLURP)
AN OLD ACQUAINT-ANCE OF MY FATHER'S RESIDES IN THE CAPITAL.
I WAS THINKING OF VISITING THERE, THAT I...
...WAS.
WOW!
TALK ABOUT A COINCI-DENCE. WE'RE HEADED THERE TOO.
HEY, WHY DON'T YOU JOIN US?
OUR CARRIAGE CAN FIT ONE MORE. YOU WOULDN'T TURN DOWN A FREE RIDE, WOULD YOU?
IS YOUR OFFER GENUINE?
MO (OM)
MO
I WOULD BE OVER-JOYED, BUT... OM!
NGU (GULP)
...ARE YOU SURE ABOUT HAVING ME ALONG?
SHE REALLY PACKS IT AWAY! HOW MANY DISHES HAS SHE POLISHED OFF ALREADY!?

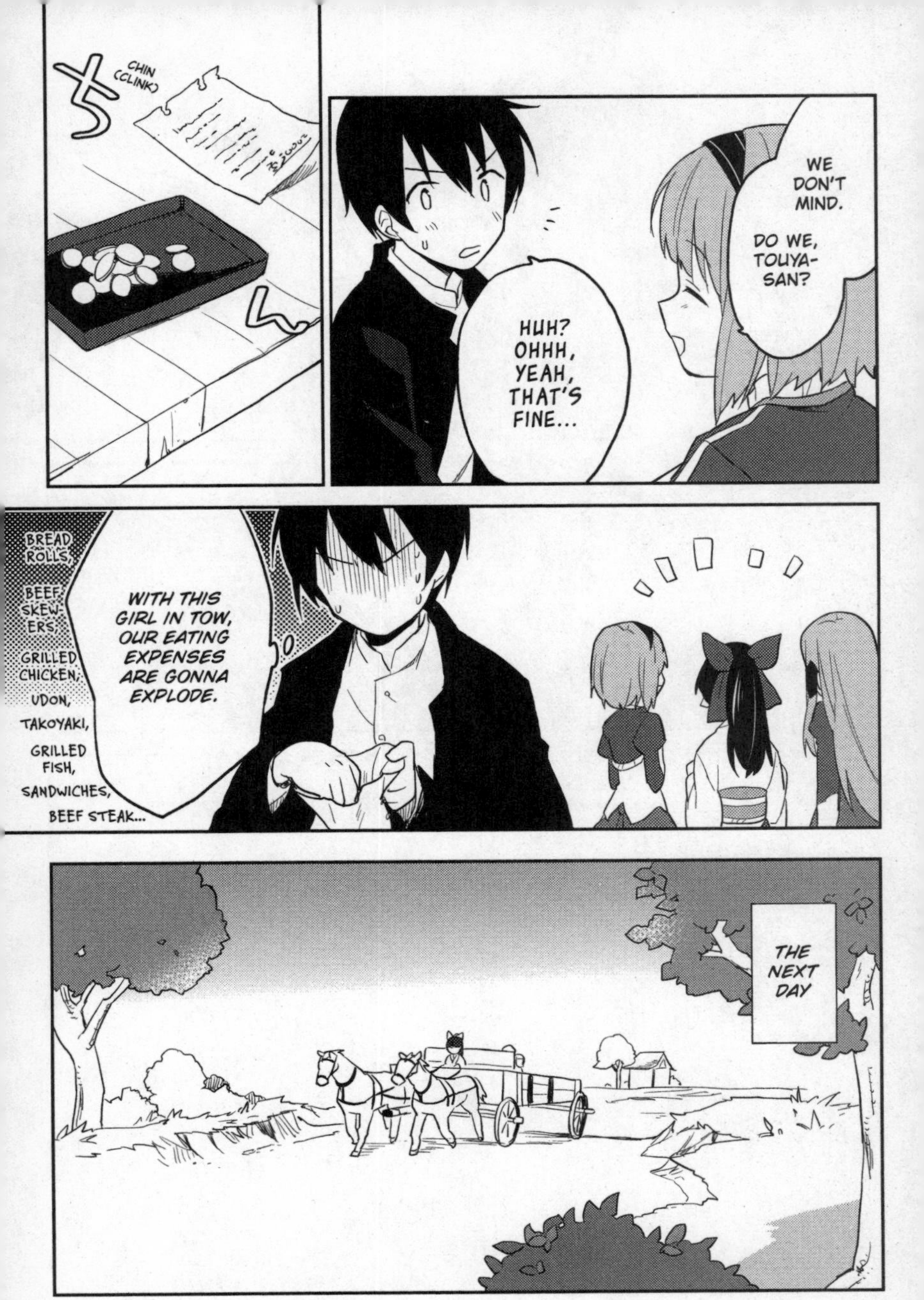
WE DON'T MIND.
DO WE, TOUYA-SAN?
HUH? OHHH, YEAH, THAT'S FINE...
CHIN (CLINK)
WITH THIS GIRL IN TOW, OUR EATING EXPENSES ARE GONNA EXPLODE.
BREAD ROLLS, BEEF SKEWERS, GRILLED CHICKEN, UDON, TAKOYAKI, GRILLED FISH, SANDWICHES, BEEF STEAK...
THE NEXT DAY

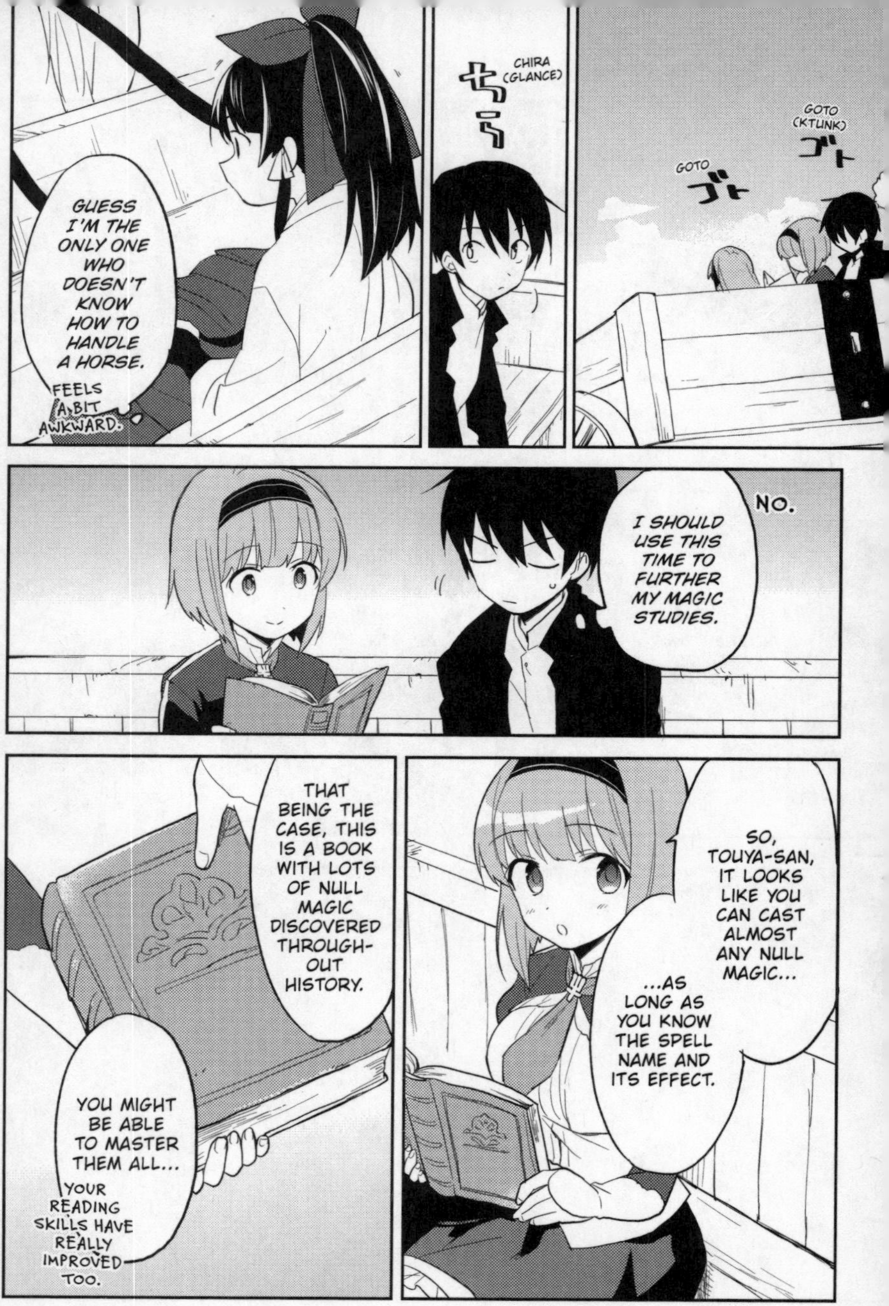
GOTO (KTUNK)
ゴト
GOTO
ゴト
CHIRA (GLANCE)
ちら
GUESS I'M THE ONLY ONE WHO DOESN'T KNOW HOW TO HANDLE A HORSE.
FEELS A BIT AWKWARD.
NO.
I SHOULD USE THIS TIME TO FURTHER MY MAGIC STUDIES.
SO, TOUYA-SAN, IT LOOKS LIKE YOU CAN CAST ALMOST ANY NULL MAGIC...
...AS LONG AS YOU KNOW THE SPELL NAME AND ITS EFFECT.
THAT BEING THE CASE, THIS IS A BOOK WITH LOTS OF NULL MAGIC DISCOVERED THROUGH-OUT HISTORY.
YOU MIGHT BE ABLE TO MASTER THEM ALL...
YOUR READING SKILLS HAVE REALLY IMPROVED TOO.

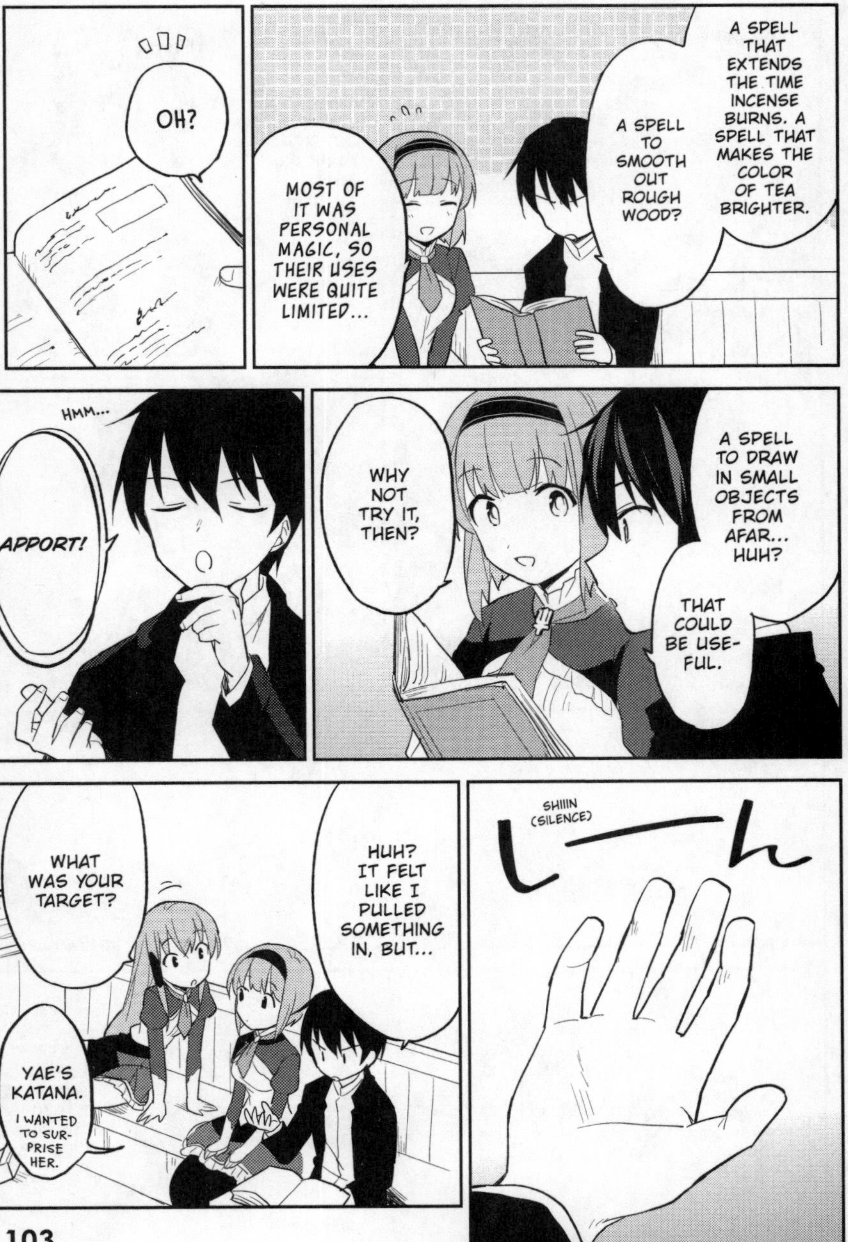
A SPELL THAT EXTENDS THE TIME INCENSE BURNS. A SPELL THAT MAKES THE COLOR OF TEA BRIGHTER.
A SPELL TO SMOOTH OUT ROUGH WOOD?
MOST OF IT WAS PERSONAL MAGIC, SO THEIR USES WERE QUITE LIMITED...
OH?
A SPELL TO DRAW IN SMALL OBJECTS FROM AFAR... HUH?
THAT COULD BE USE-FUL.
WHY NOT TRY IT, THEN?
HMM...
APPORT!
SHIIIN (SILENCE)
しーん
HUH? IT FELT LIKE I PULLED SOMETHING IN, BUT...
WHAT WAS YOUR TARGET?
YAE'S KATANA.
I WANTED TO SUR-PRISE HER.

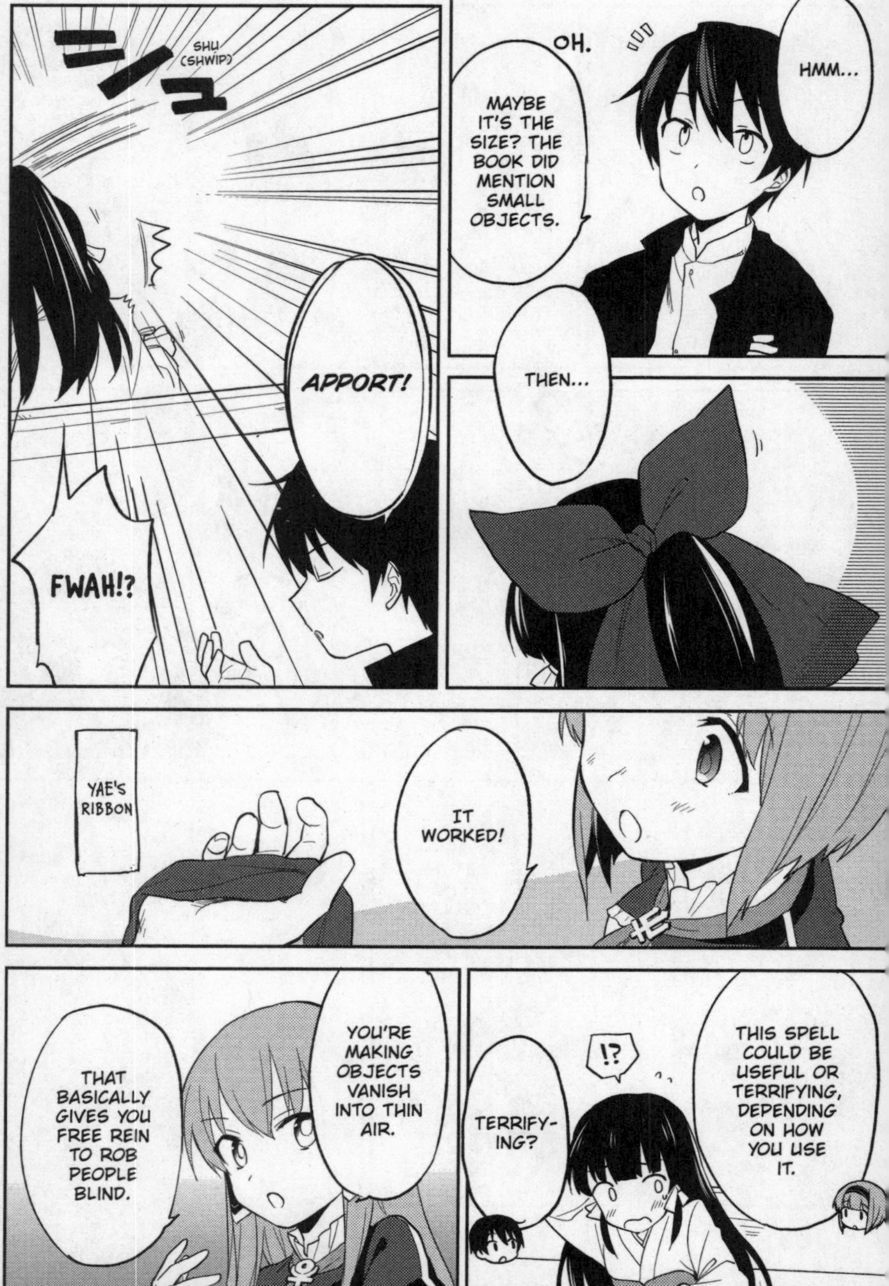
HMM...
OH.
MAYBE IT'S THE SIZE? THE BOOK DID MENTION SMALL OBJECTS.
THEN...
SHU (SHWIP)
APPORT!
FWAH!?
IT WORKED!
YAE'S RIBBON
THIS SPELL COULD BE USEFUL OR TERRIFYING, DEPENDING ON HOW YOU USE IT.
!?
TERRIFY-ING?
YOU'RE MAKING OBJECTS VANISH INTO THIN AIR.
THAT BASICALLY GIVES YOU FREE REIN TO ROB PEOPLE BLIND.

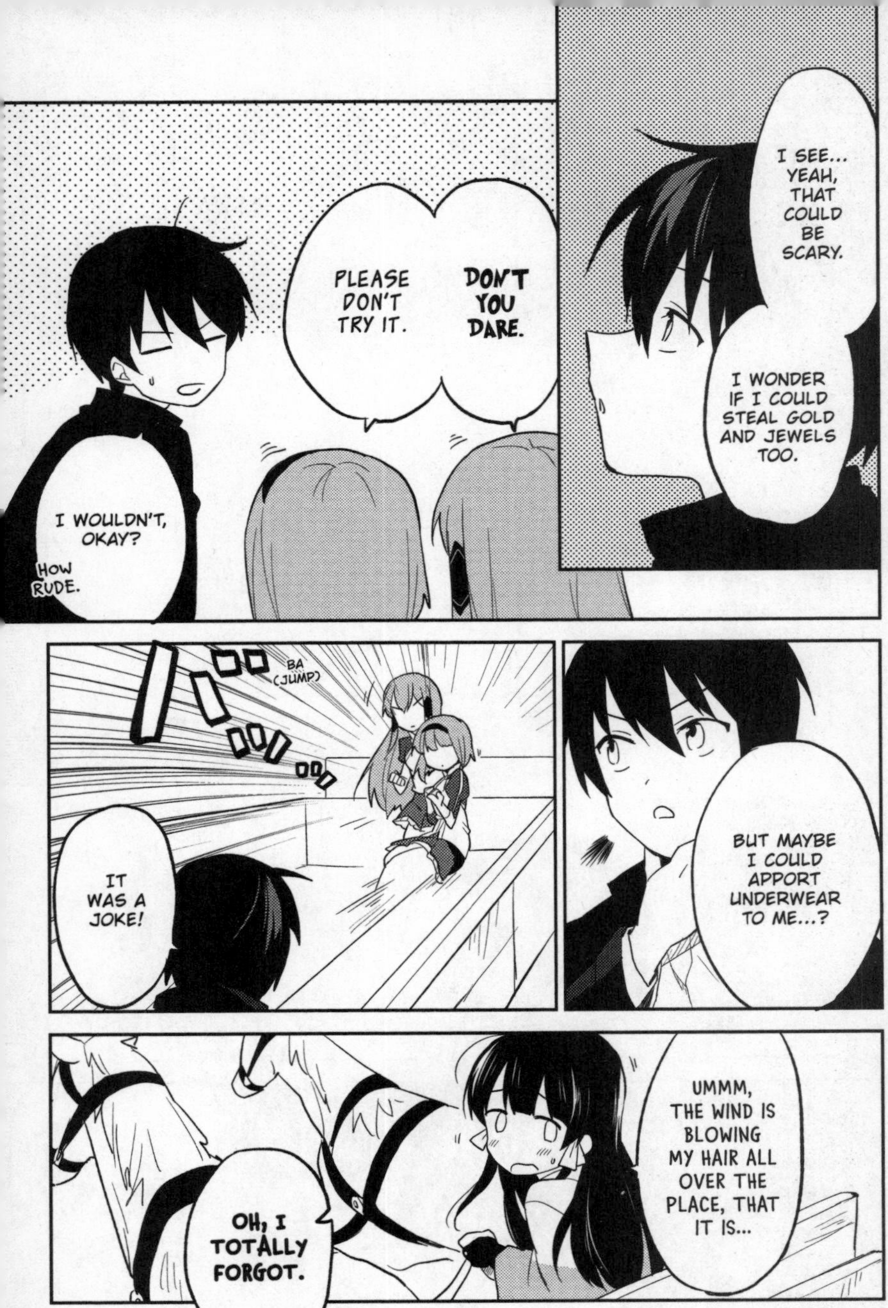
I SEE... YEAH, THAT COULD BE SCARY.
I WONDER IF I COULD STEAL GOLD AND JEWELS TOO.
DON'T YOU DARE.
PLEASE DON'T TRY IT.
I WOULDN'T, OKAY?
HOW RUDE.
BUT MAYBE I COULD APPORT UNDERWEAR TO ME...?
BA (JUMP)
IT WAS A JOKE!
UMMM, THE WIND IS BLOWING MY HAIR ALL OVER THE PLACE, THAT IT IS...
OH, I TOTALLY FORGOT.

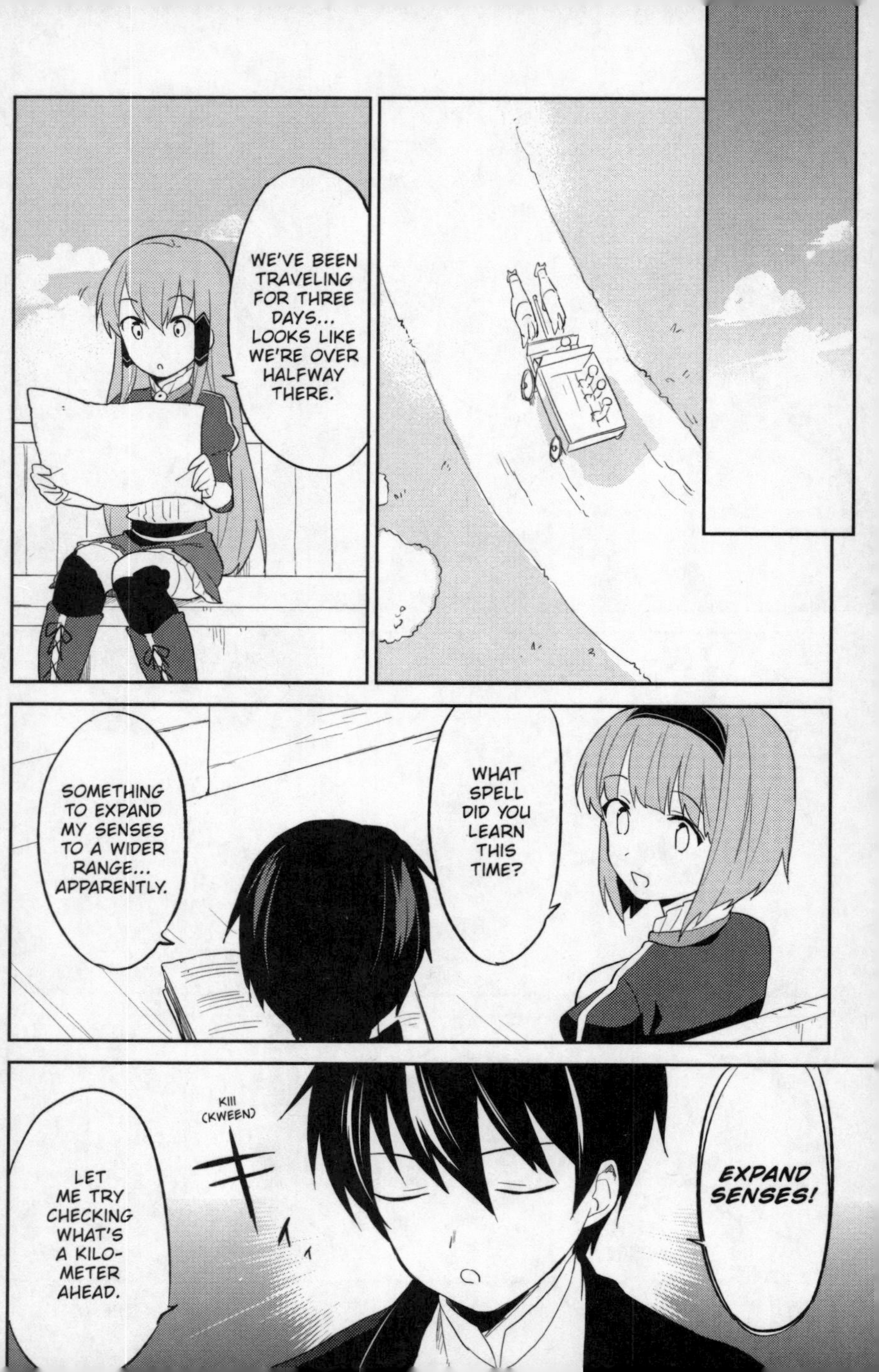
WE'VE BEEN TRAVELING FOR THREE DAYS... LOOKS LIKE WE'RE OVER HALFWAY THERE.
WHAT SPELL DID YOU LEARN THIS TIME?
SOMETHING TO EXPAND MY SENSES TO A WIDER RANGE... APPARENTLY.
EXPAND SENSES!
KIII (KWEEN)
LET ME TRY CHECKING WHAT'S A KILO-METER AHEAD.

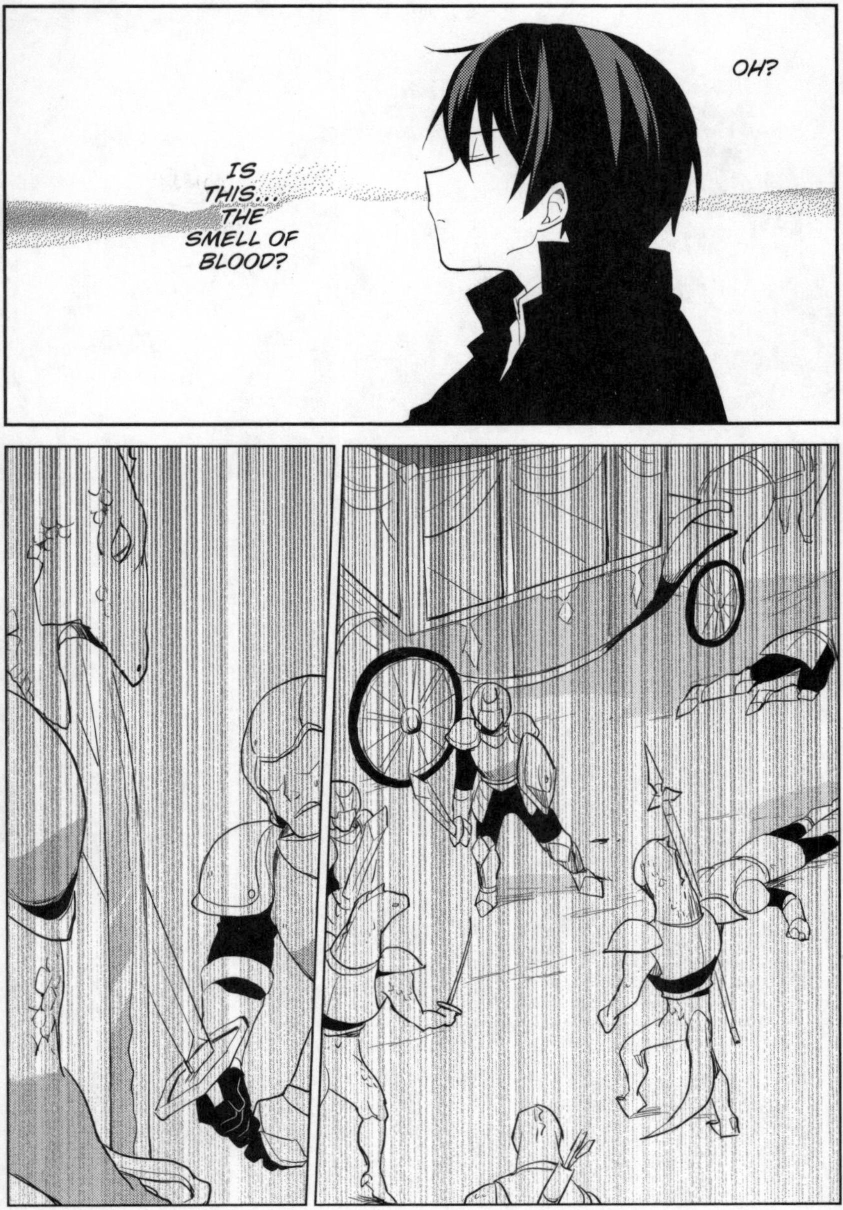
OH?
IS THIS... THE SMELL OF BLOOD?

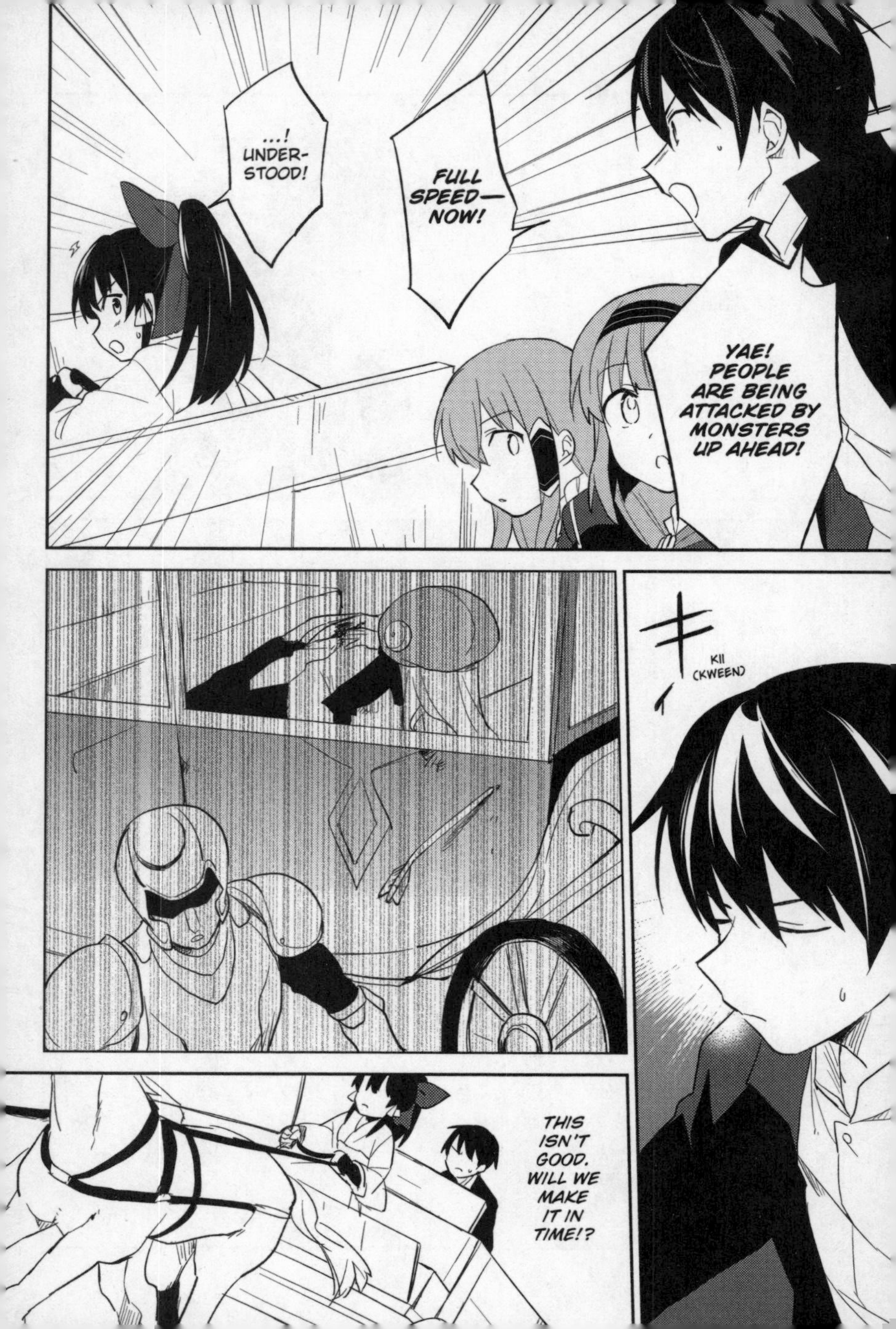
YAE! PEOPLE ARE BEING ATTACKED BY MONSTERS UP AHEAD!
FULL SPEED—NOW!
...! UNDER-STOOD!
KII (KWEEN)
THIS ISN'T GOOD. WILL WE MAKE IT IN TIME!?

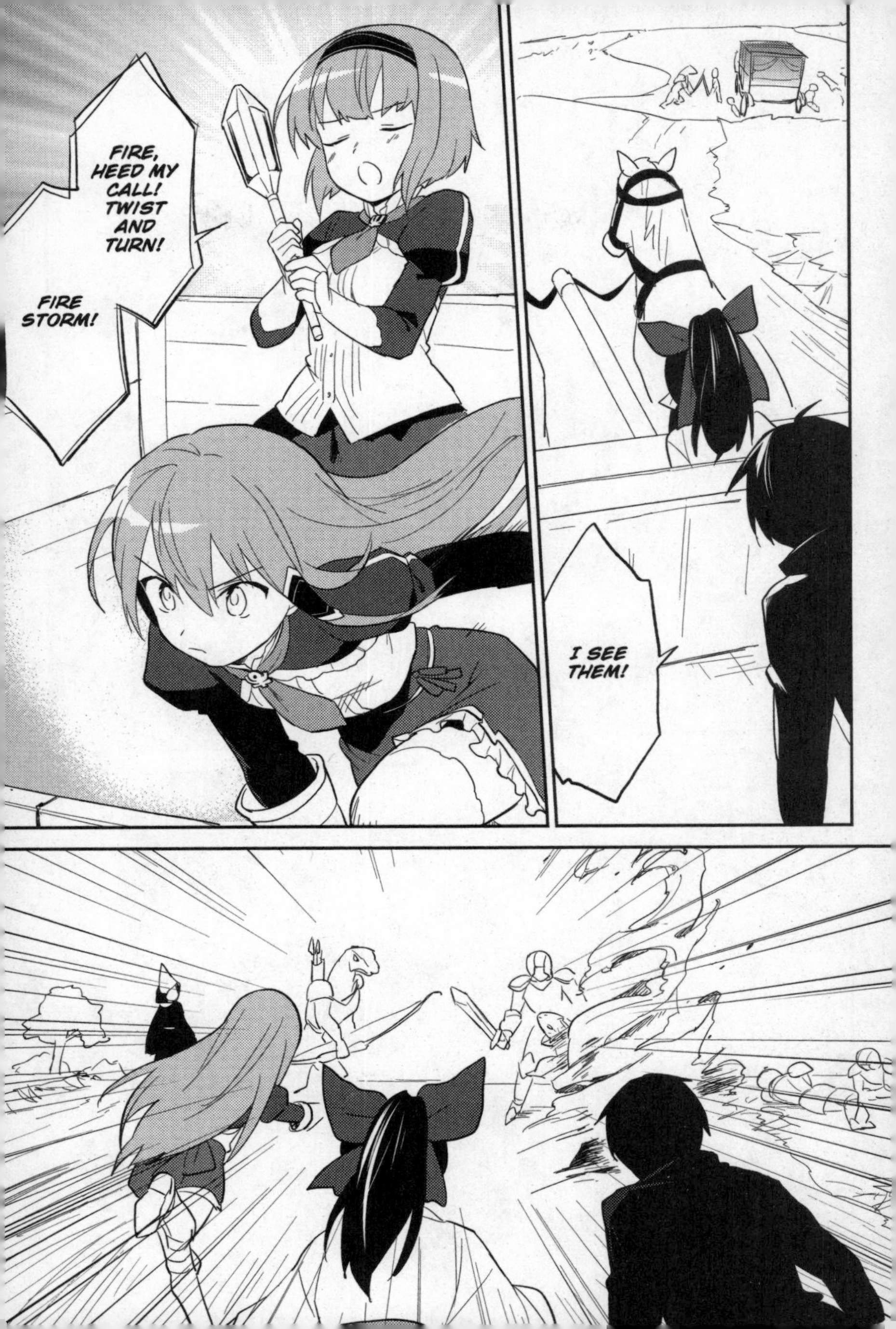
I SEE THEM!
FIRE, HEED MY CALL! TWIST AND TURN!
FIRE STORM!

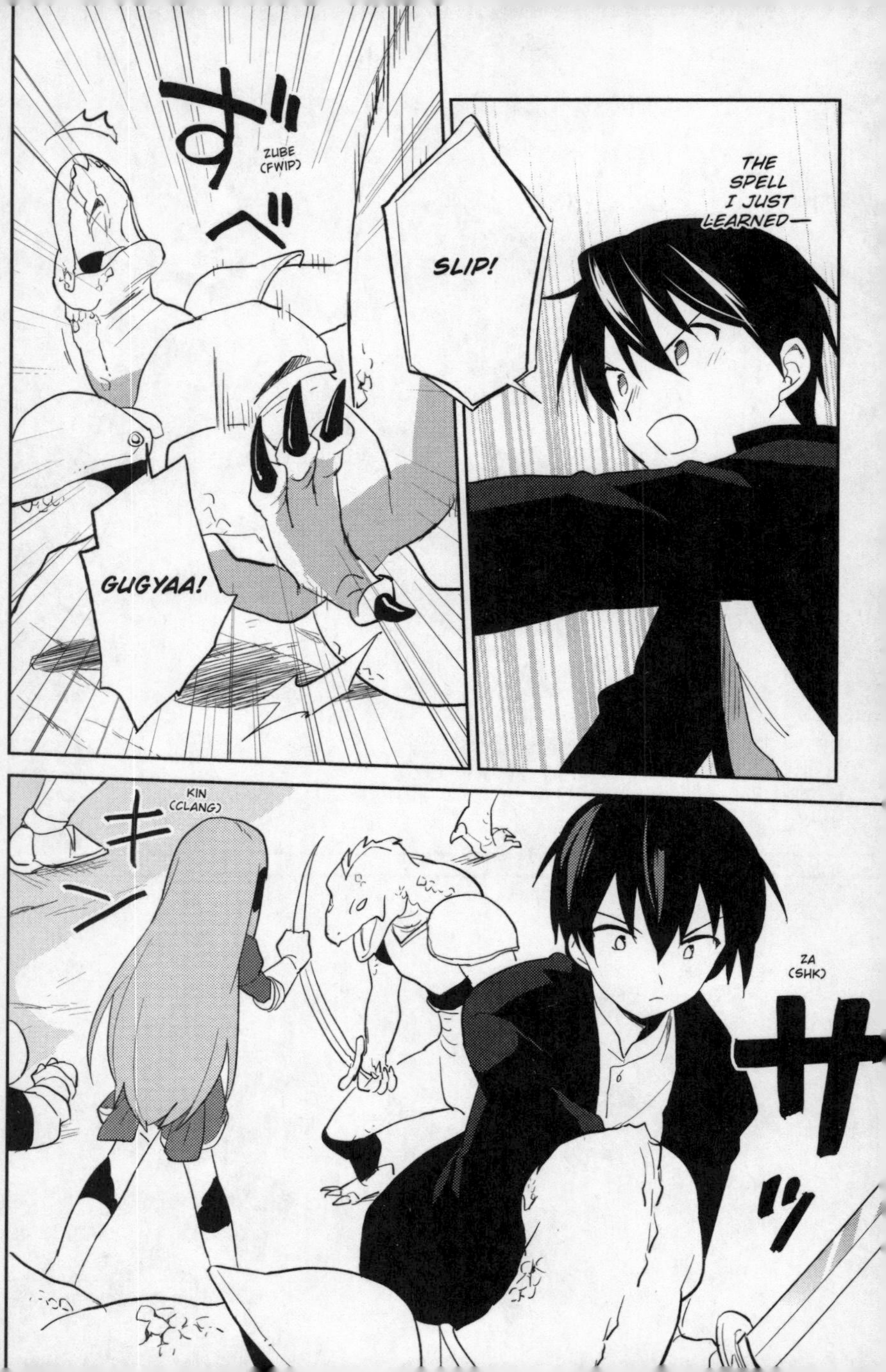
THE SPELL I JUST LEARNED—
SLIP!
ZUBE (FWIP)
GUGYAA!
ZA (SHK)
KIN (CLANG)

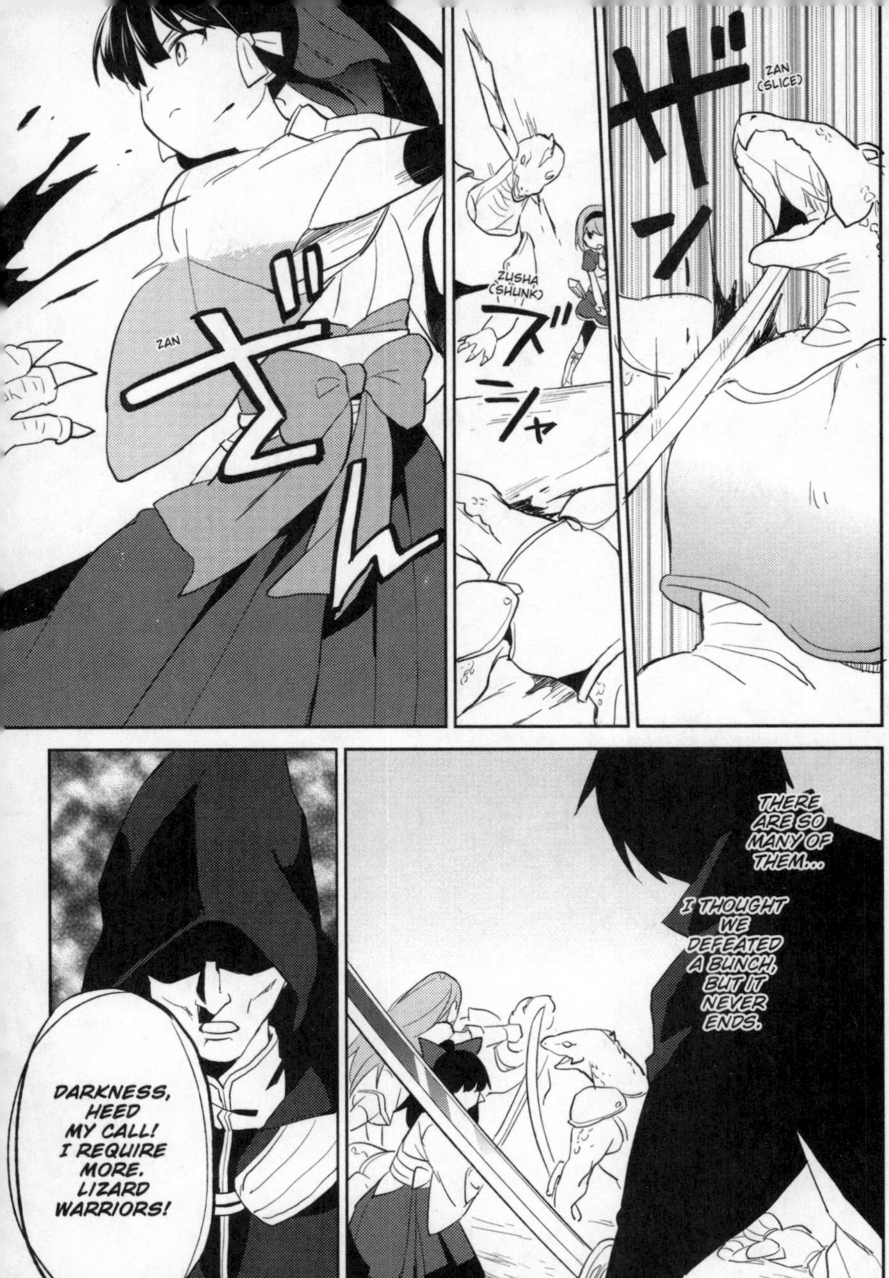
ザン
ZAN (SLICE)
ズシャ
ZUSHA (SHUNK)
ザン
ZAN
THERE ARE SO MANY OF THEM...
I THOUGHT WE DEFEATED A BUNCH, BUT IT NEVER ENDS.
DARKNESS, HEED MY CALL! I REQUIRE MORE. LIZARD WARRIORS!

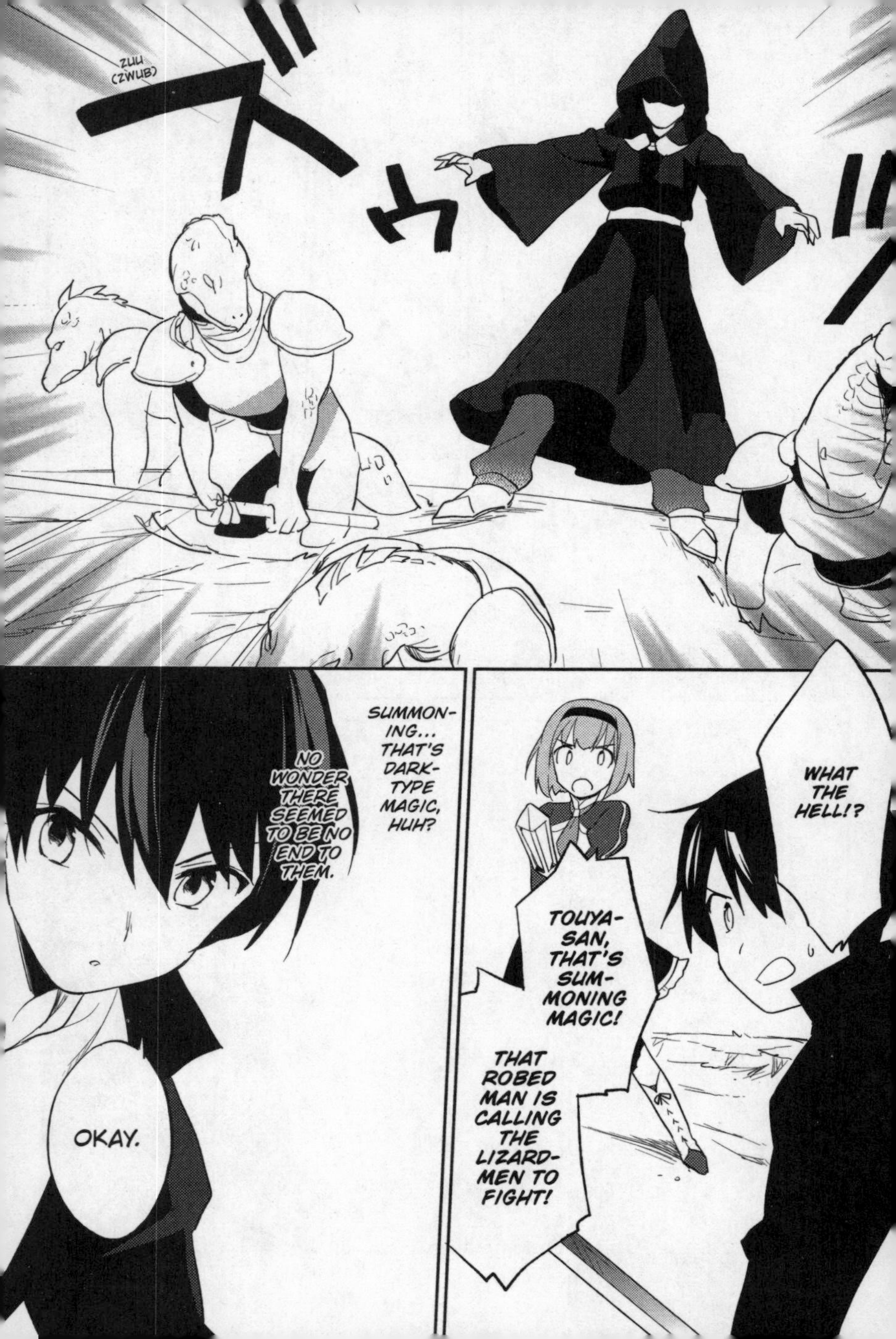
ZUU (ZWUB)
WHAT THE HELL!?
TOUYA-SAN, THAT'S SUMMONING MAGIC!
THAT ROBED MAN IS CALLING THE LIZARDMEN TO FIGHT!
SUMMONING... THAT'S DARK-TYPE MAGIC, HUH?
NO WONDER THERE SEEMED TO BE NO END TO THEM.
OKAY.

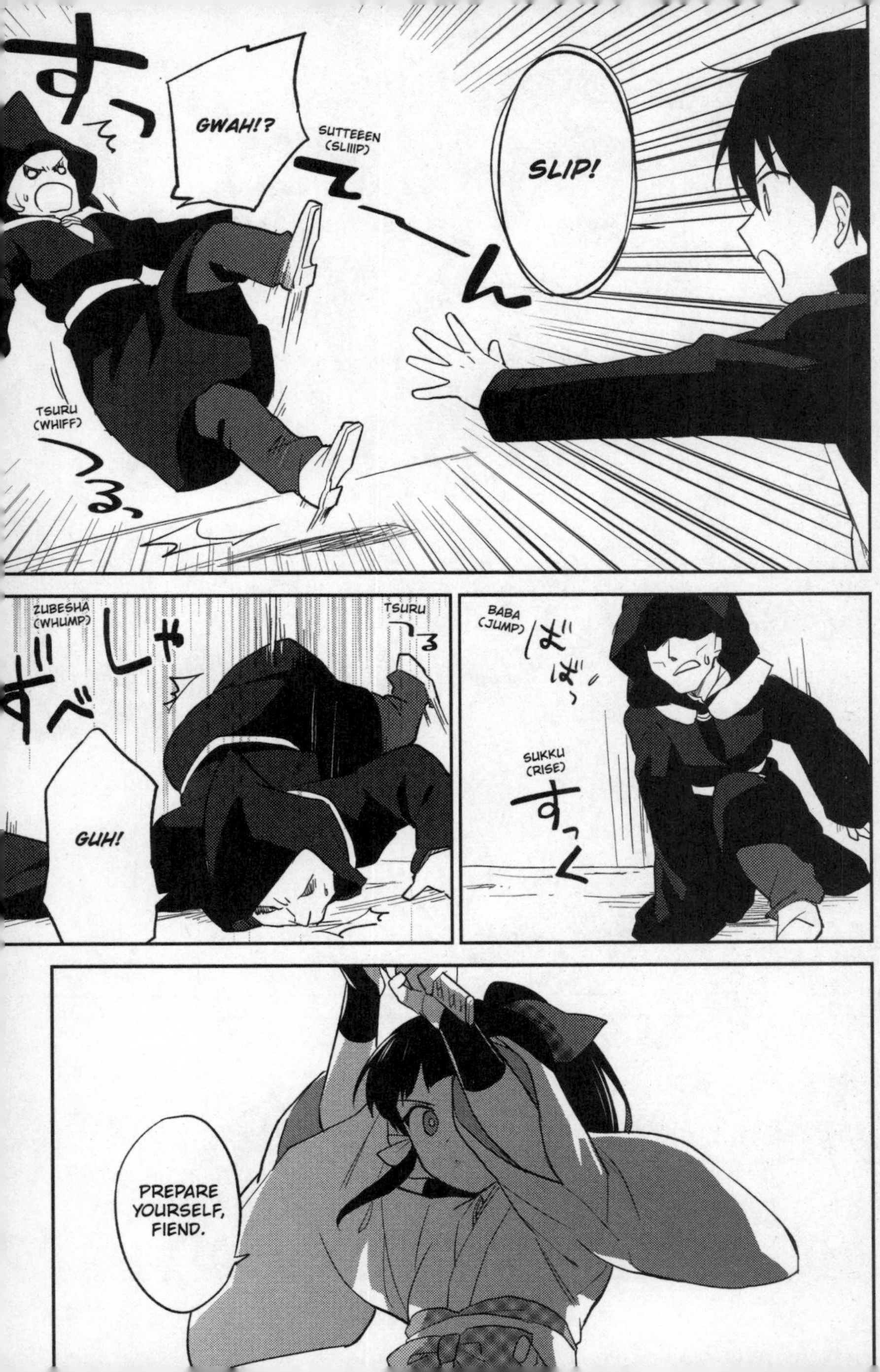

SLIP!
SUTTEEEN (SLIIIP)
すってーん
GWAH!?
TSURU (WHIFF)
つるっ
BABA (JUMP)
ばばっ
SUKKU (RISE)
すっく
TSURU
つる
ZUBESHA (WHUMP)
ずべしゃ
GUH!
PREPARE YOURSELF, FIEND.

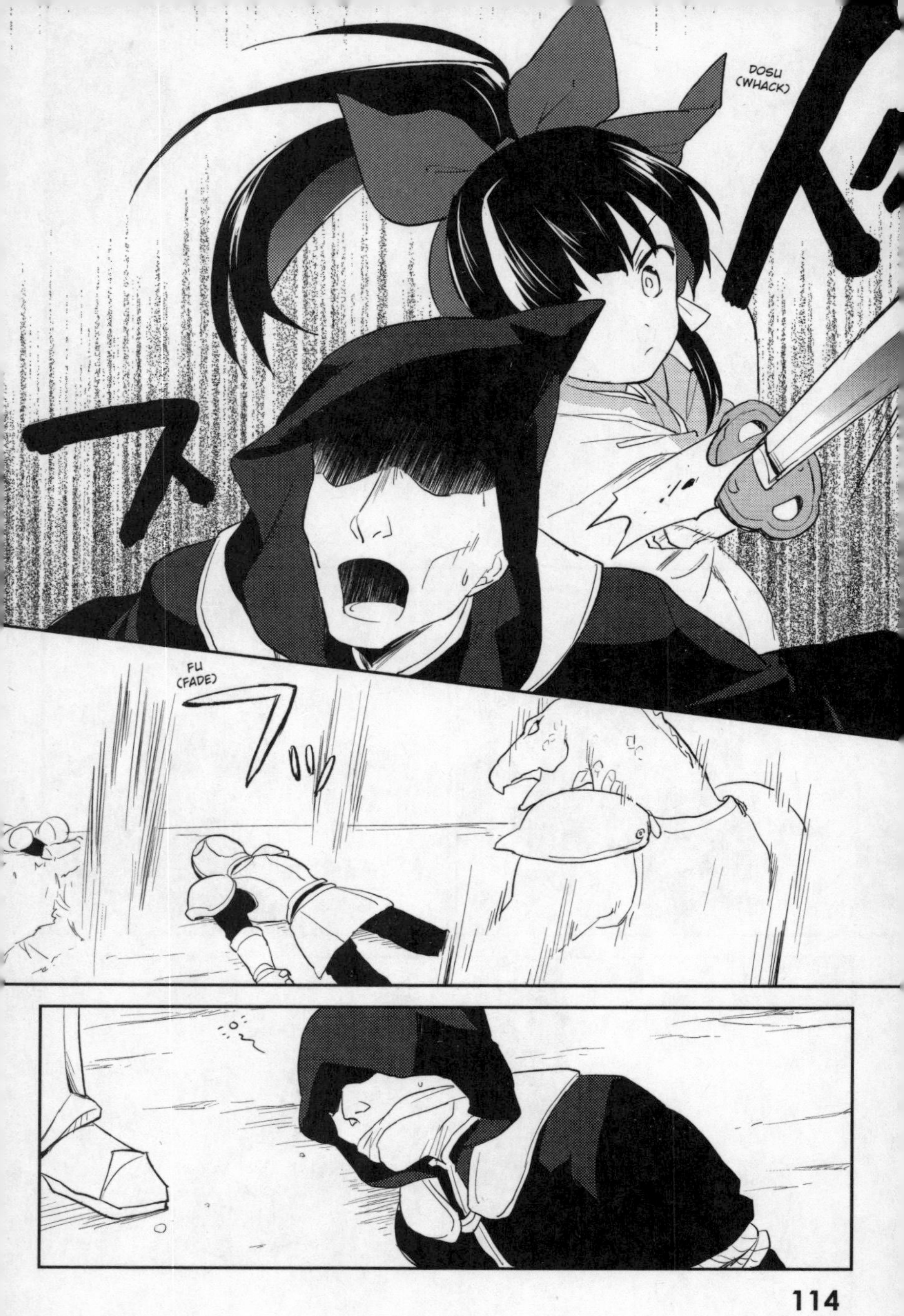
DOSU
(WHACK)
FU
(FADE)

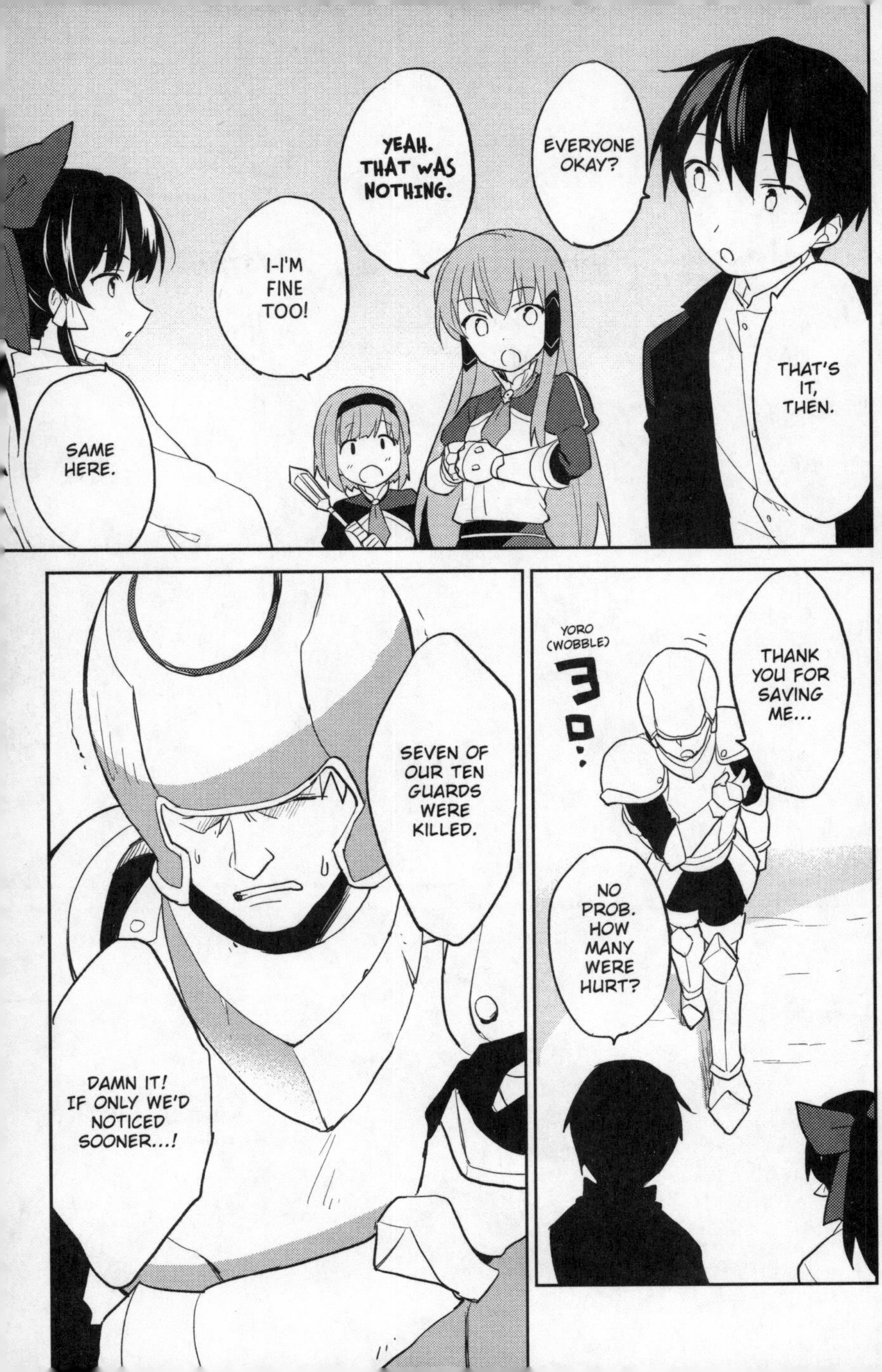
EVERYONE OKAY?
YEAH. THAT wAS NOTHING.
I-I'M FINE TOO!
SAME HERE.
THAT'S IT, THEN.
YORO (WOBBLE)
THANK YOU FOR SAVING ME...
NO PROB. HOW MANY WERE HURT?
SEVEN OF OUR TEN GUARDS WERE KILLED.
DAMN IT! IF ONLY WE'D NOTICED SOONER...!

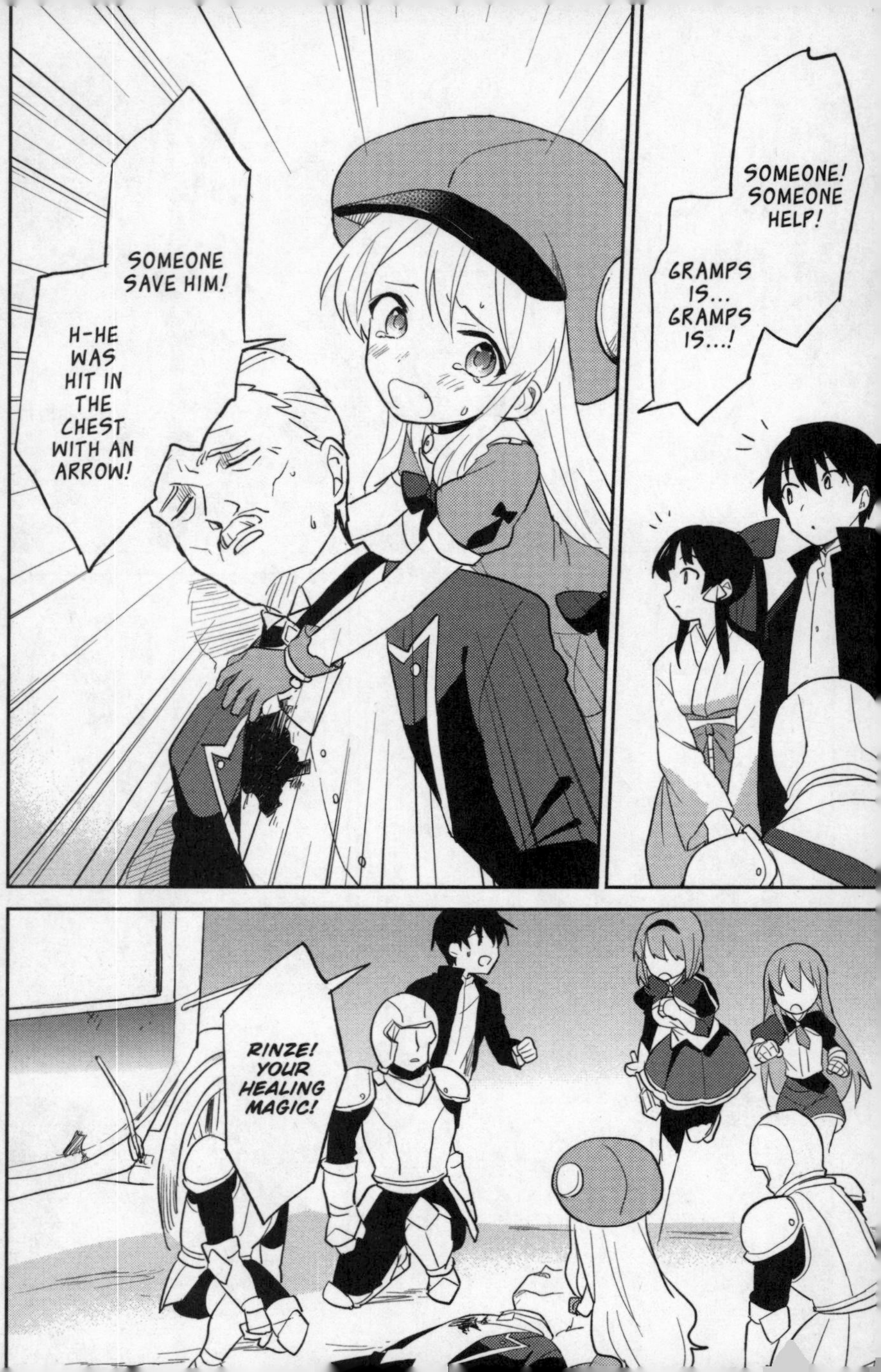
SOMEONE! SOMEONE HELP!
GRAMPS IS... GRAMPS IS...!
SOMEONE SAVE HIM!
H-HE WAS HIT IN THE CHEST WITH AN ARROW!
RINZE! YOUR HEALING MAGIC!

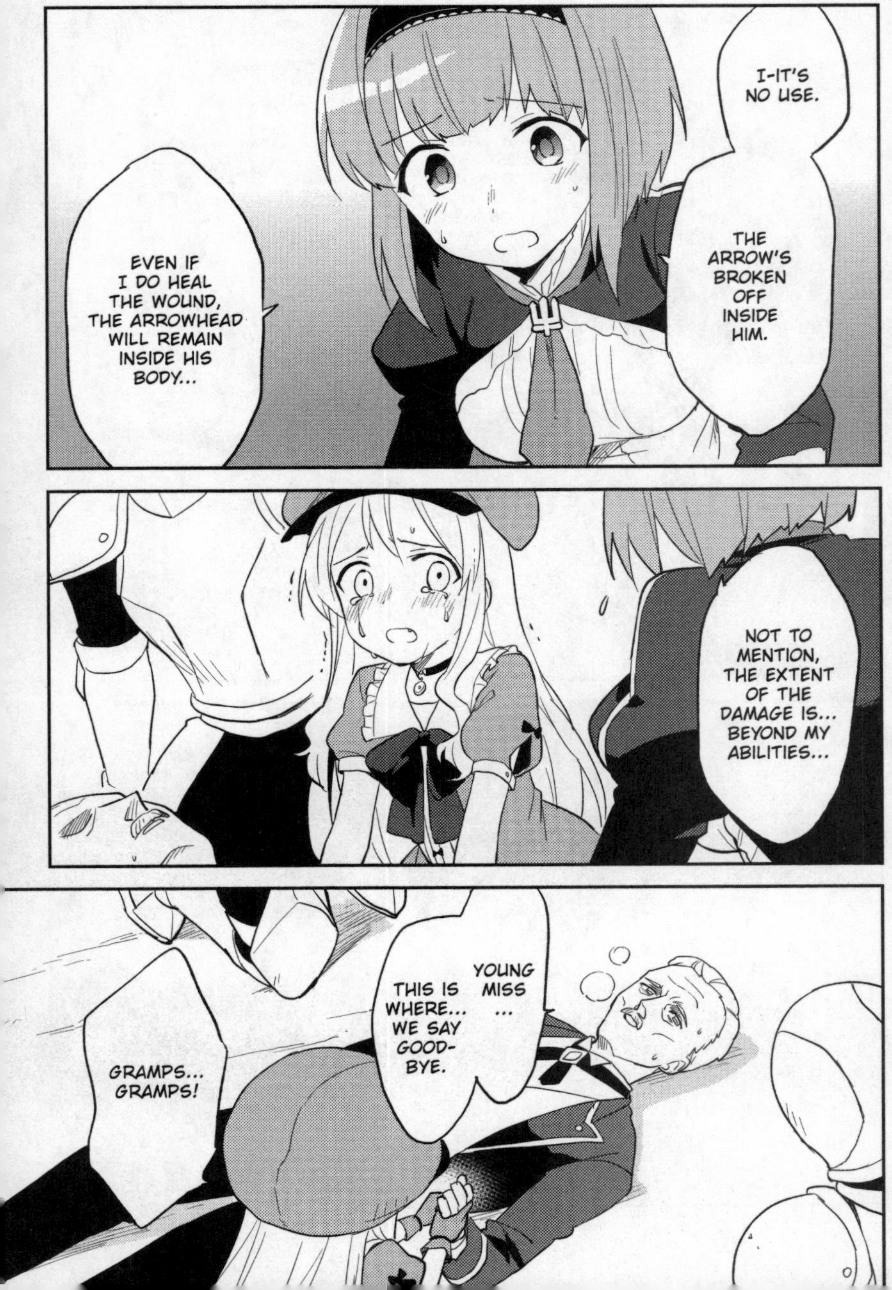
I-IT'S NO USE.
THE ARROW'S BROKEN OFF INSIDE HIM.
EVEN IF I DO HEAL THE WOUND, THE ARROWHEAD WILL REMAIN INSIDE HIS BODY...
NOT TO MENTION, THE EXTENT OF THE DAMAGE IS... BEYOND MY ABILITIES...
YOUNG MISS ...
THIS IS WHERE... WE SAY GOOD-BYE.
GRAMPS... GRAMPS!

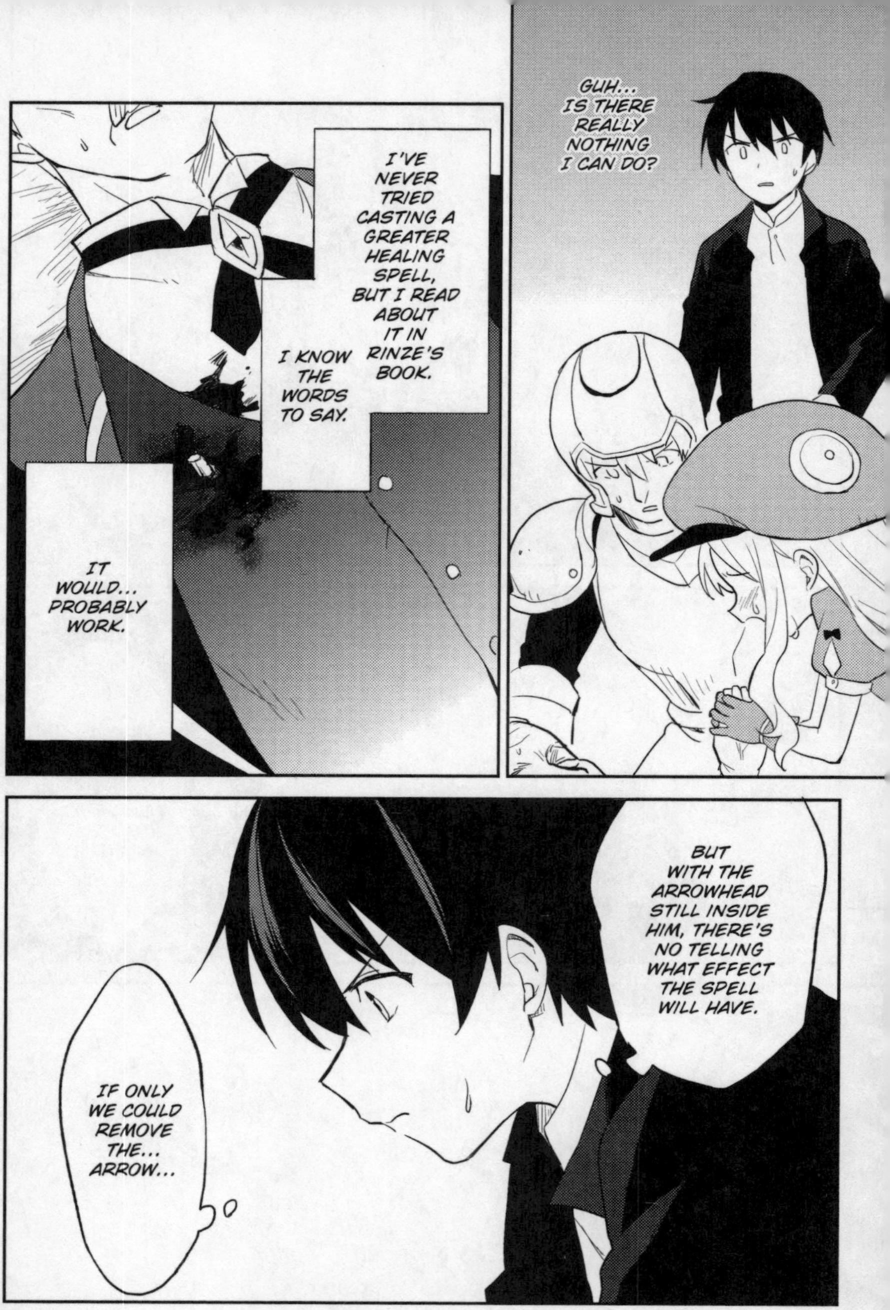
GUH... IS THERE REALLY NOTHING I CAN DO?
I'VE NEVER TRIED CASTING A GREATER HEALING SPELL, BUT I READ ABOUT IT IN RINZE'S BOOK.
I KNOW THE WORDS TO SAY.
IT WOULD... PROBABLY WORK.
BUT WITH THE ARROWHEAD STILL INSIDE HIM, THERE'S NO TELLING WHAT EFFECT THE SPELL WILL HAVE.
IF ONLY WE COULD REMOVE THE... ARROW...

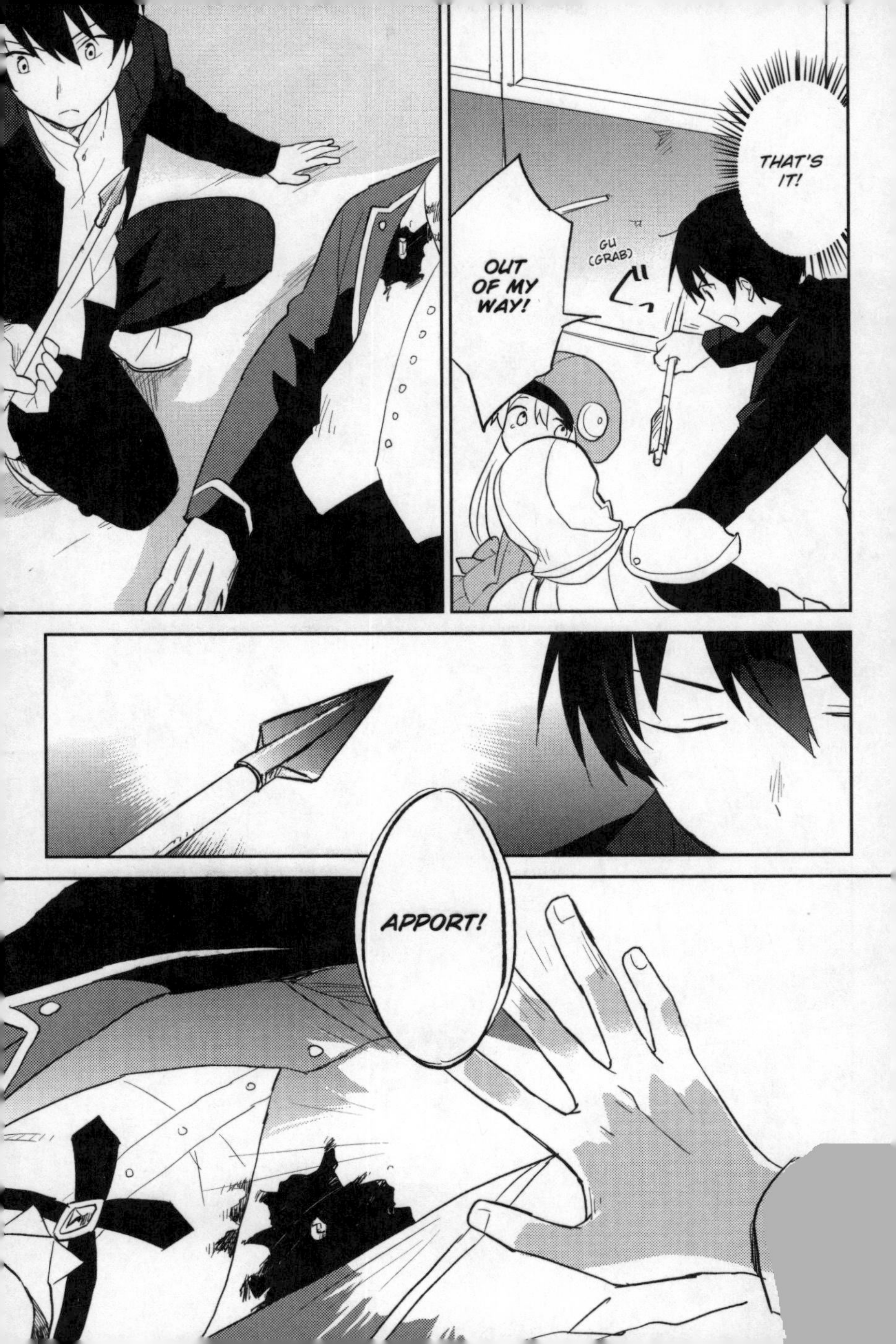
THAT'S IT!
GU (GRAB)
OUT OF MY WAY!
APPORT!

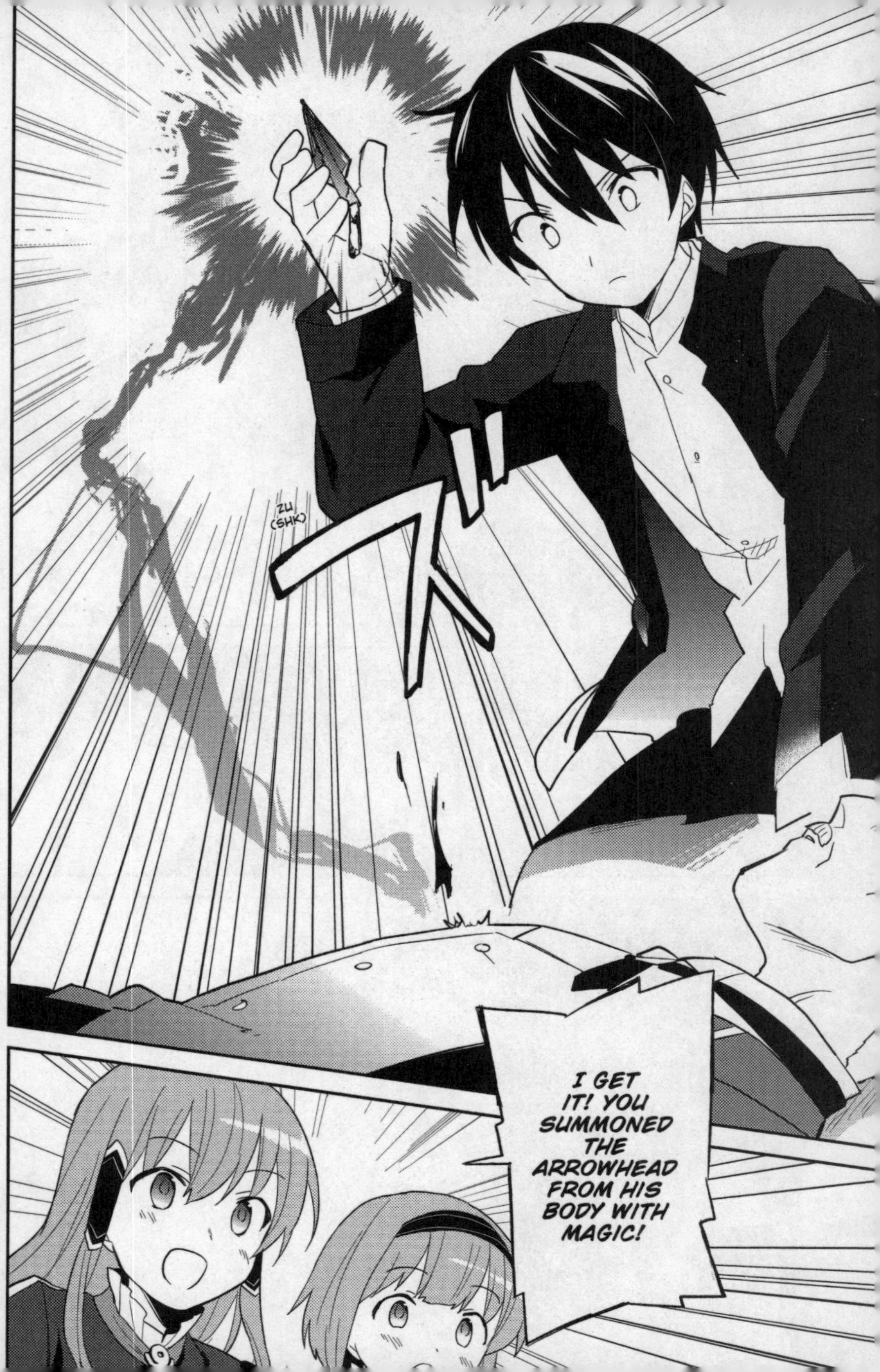
ZU (SHK)
I GET IT! YOU SUMMONED THE ARROWHEAD FROM HIS BODY WITH MAGIC!

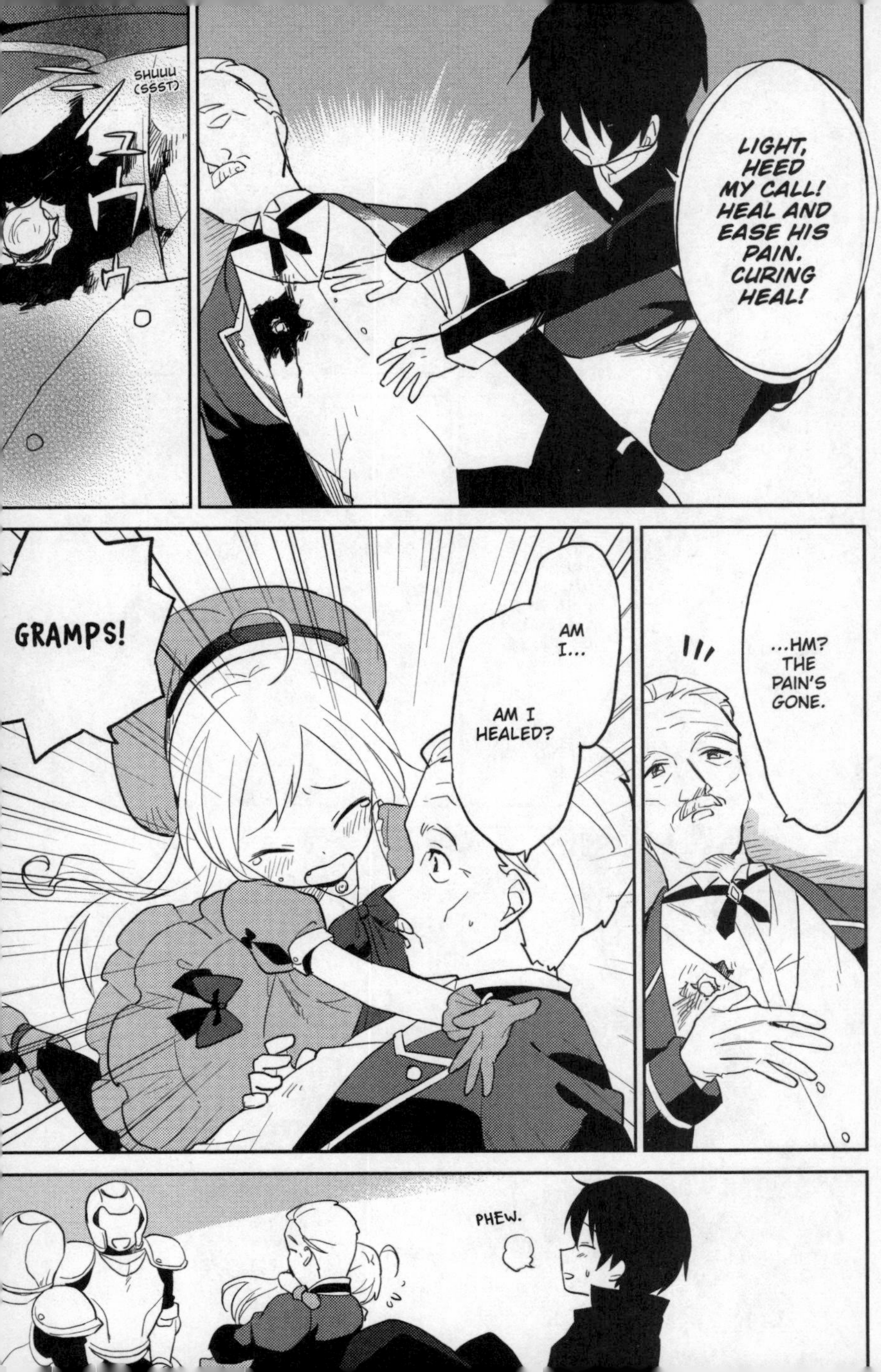
LIGHT, HEED MY CALL! HEAL AND EASE HIS PAIN. CURING HEAL!
SHUUU (SSST)
...HM? THE PAIN'S GONE.
AM I...
AM I HEALED?
GRAMPS!
PHEW.

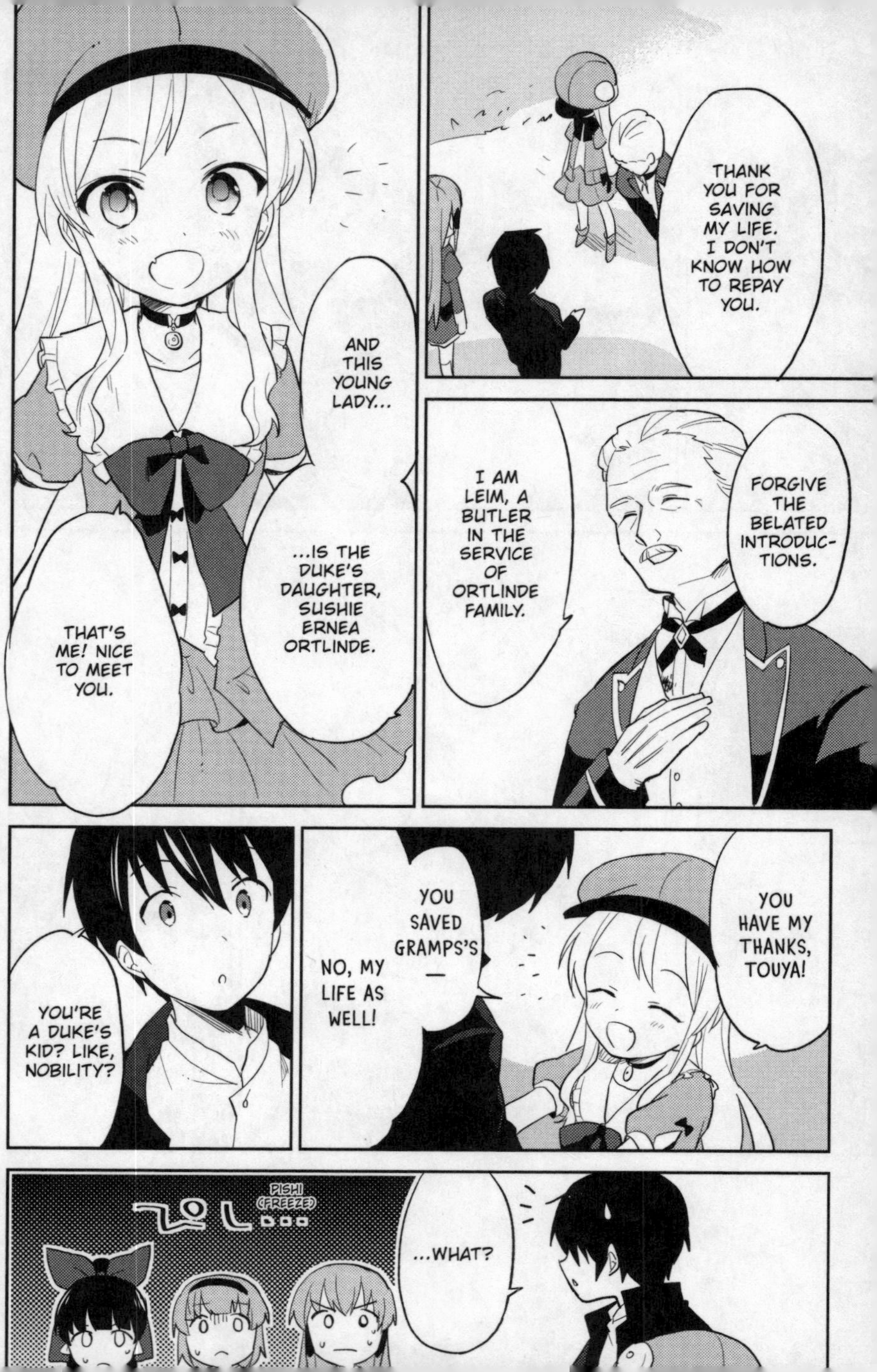
THANK YOU FOR SAVING MY LIFE. I DON'T KNOW HOW TO REPAY YOU.
FORGIVE THE BELATED INTRODUCTIONS.
I AM LEIM, A BUTLER IN THE SERVICE OF ORTLINDE FAMILY.
AND THIS YOUNG LADY...
...IS THE DUKE'S DAUGHTER, SUSHIE ERNEA ORTLINDE.
THAT'S ME! NICE TO MEET YOU.
YOU HAVE MY THANKS, TOUYA!
YOU SAVED GRAMPS'S—
NO, MY LIFE AS WELL!
YOU'RE A DUKE'S KID? LIKE, NOBILITY?
...WHAT?
PISHI (FREEZE)

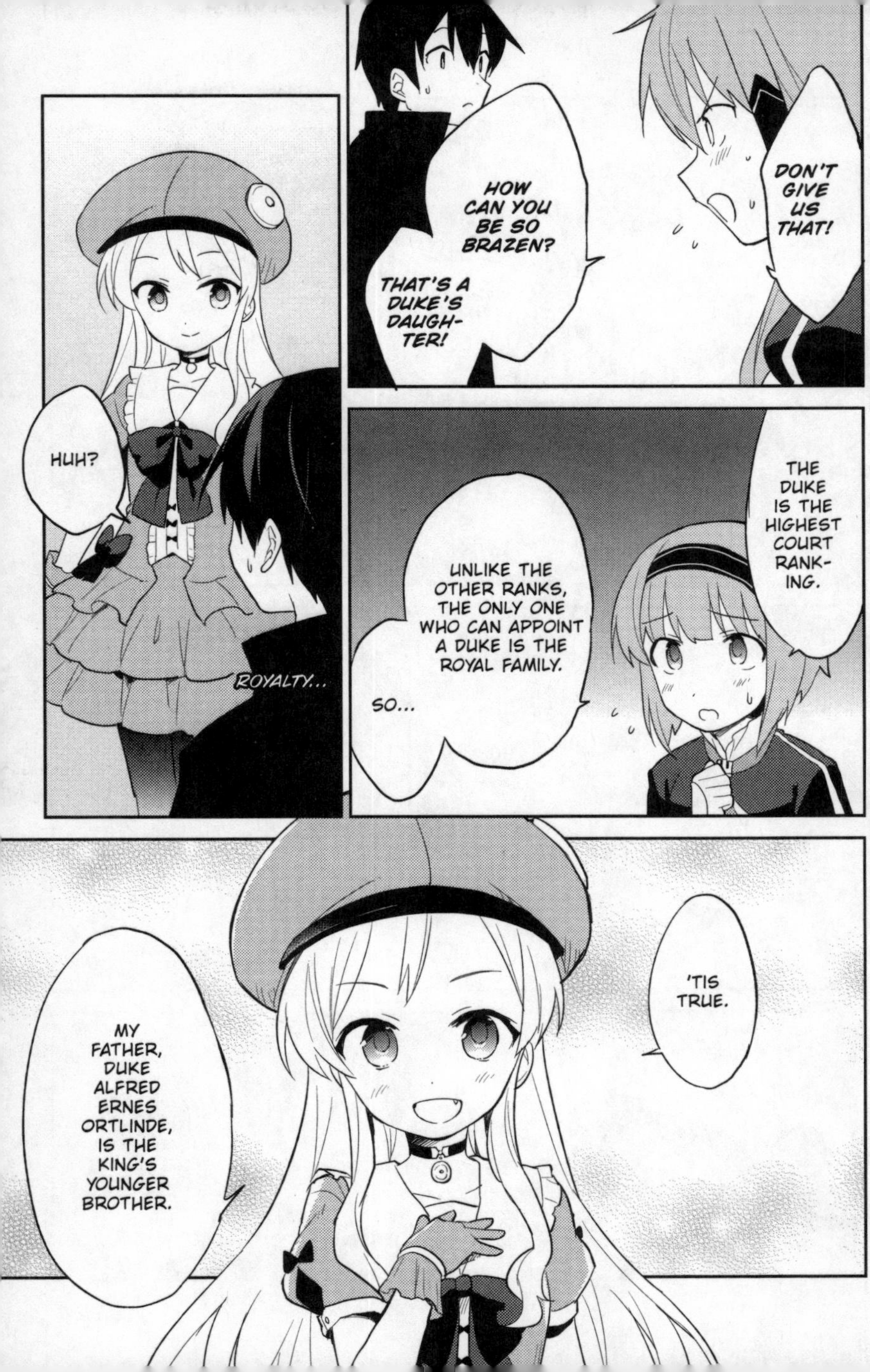
DON'T GIVE US THAT!
HOW CAN YOU BE SO BRAZEN?
THAT'S A DUKE'S DAUGHTER!
THE DUKE IS THE HIGHEST COURT RANKING.
UNLIKE THE OTHER RANKS, THE ONLY ONE WHO CAN APPOINT A DUKE IS THE ROYAL FAMILY.
SO...
HUH?
ROYALTY...
'TIS TRUE.
MY FATHER, DUKE ALFRED ERNES ORTLINDE, IS THE KING'S YOUNGER BROTHER.

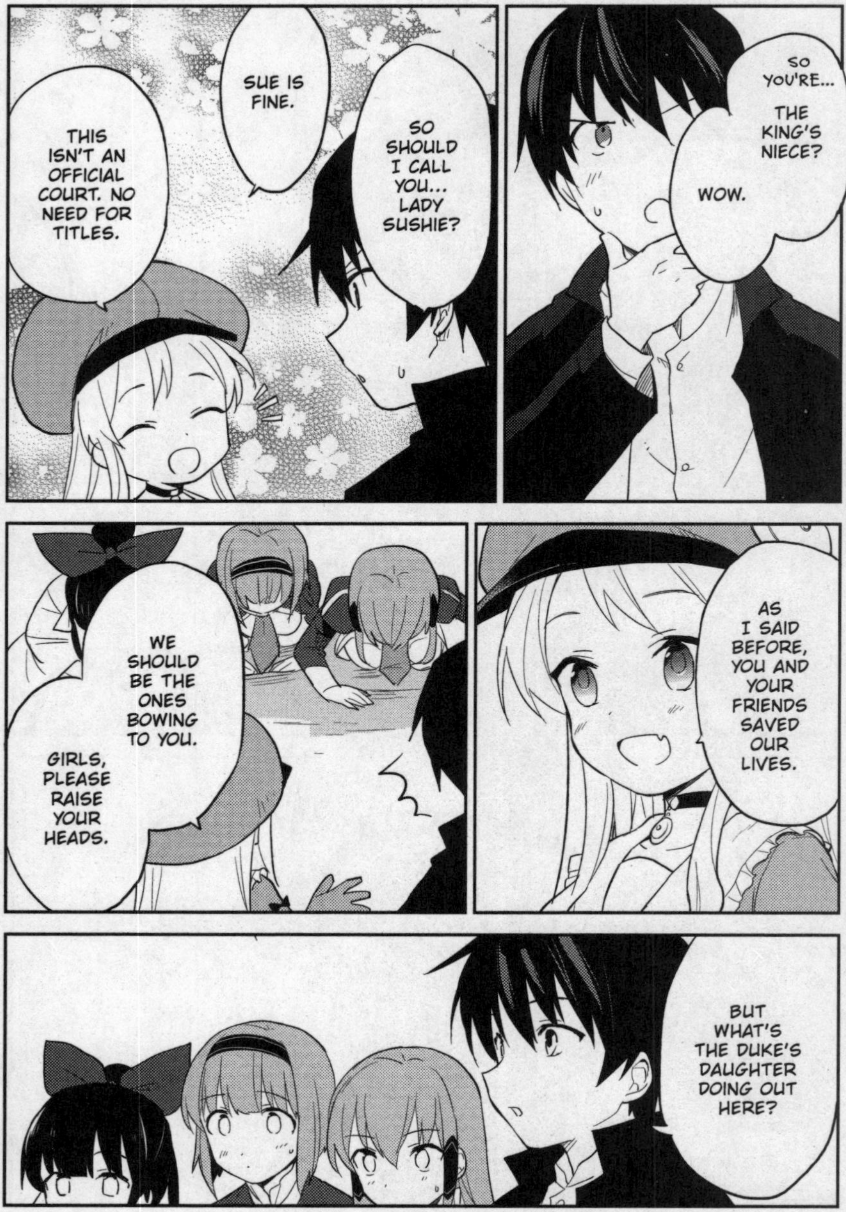
SO YOU'RE...
THE KING'S NIECE?
WOW.
SO SHOULD I CALL YOU... LADY SUSHIE?
SUE IS FINE.
THIS ISN'T AN OFFICIAL COURT. NO NEED FOR TITLES.
AS I SAID BEFORE, YOU AND YOUR FRIENDS SAVED OUR LIVES.
WE SHOULD BE THE ONES BOWING TO YOU.
GIRLS, PLEASE RAISE YOUR HEADS.
BUT WHAT'S THE DUKE'S DAUGHTER DOING OUT HERE?

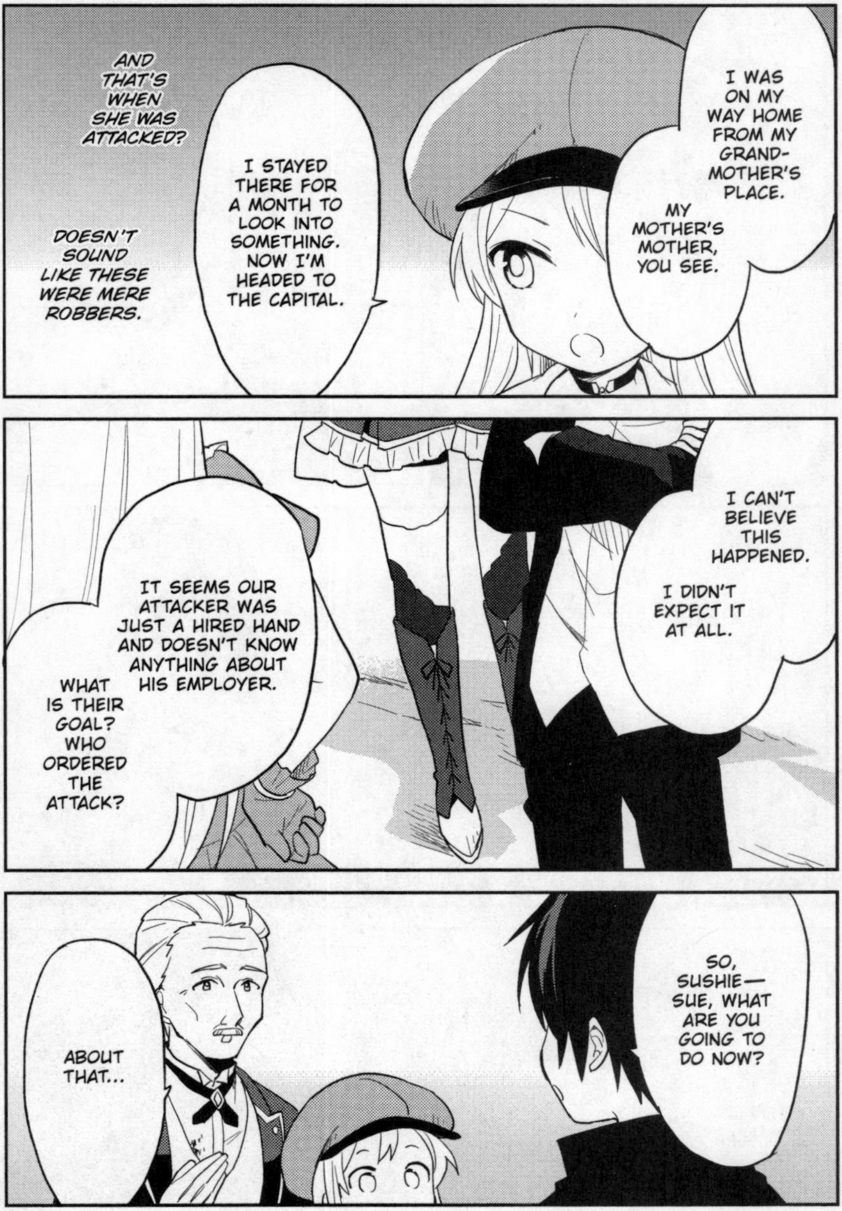
I WAS ON MY WAY HOME FROM MY GRAND-MOTHER'S PLACE.
MY MOTHER'S MOTHER, YOU SEE.
I STAYED THERE FOR A MONTH TO LOOK INTO SOMETHING. NOW I'M HEADED TO THE CAPITAL.
AND THAT'S WHEN SHE WAS ATTACKED?
DOESN'T SOUND LIKE THESE WERE MERE ROBBERS.
I CAN'T BELIEVE THIS HAPPENED.
I DIDN'T EXPECT IT AT ALL.
IT SEEMS OUR ATTACKER WAS JUST A HIRED HAND AND DOESN'T KNOW ANYTHING ABOUT HIS EMPLOYER.
WHAT IS THEIR GOAL? WHO ORDERED THE ATTACK?
SO, SUSHIE—SUE, WHAT ARE YOU GOING TO DO NOW?
ABOUT THAT...

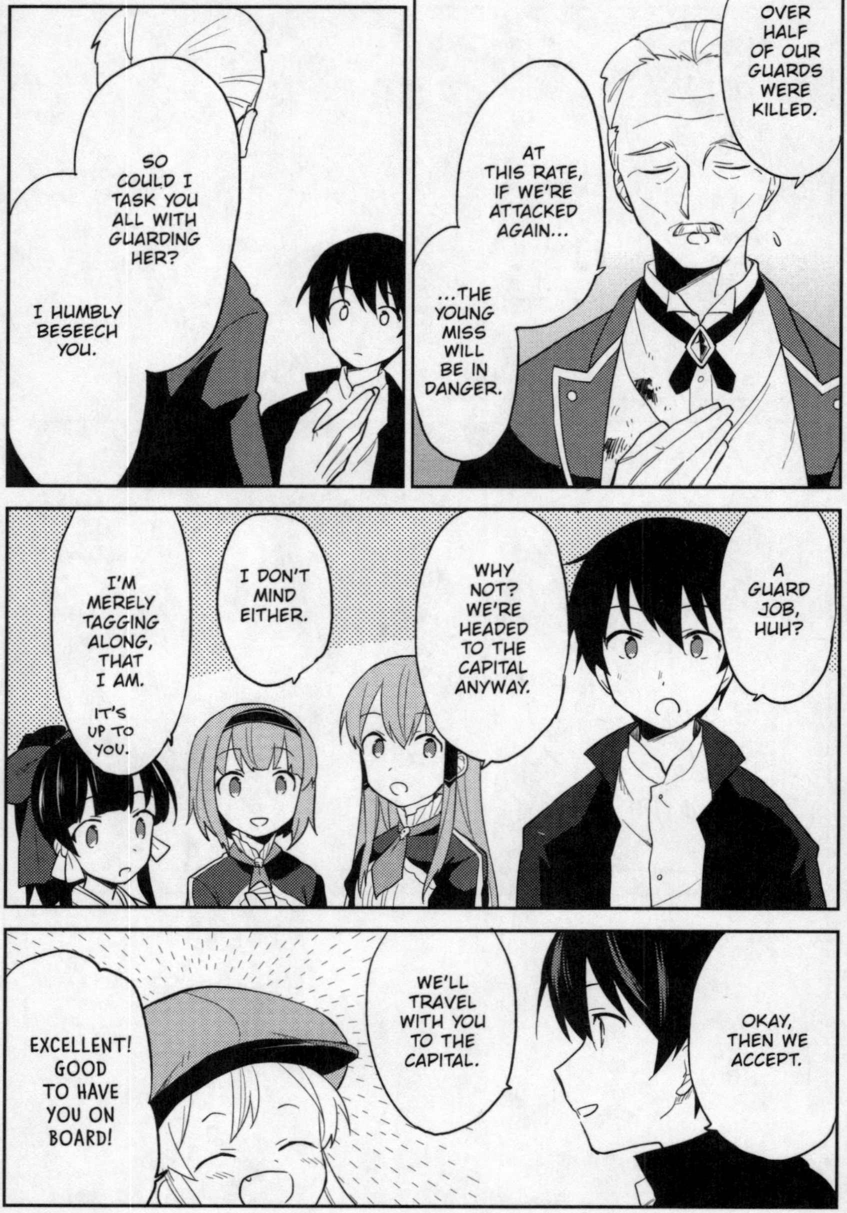
OVER HALF OF OUR GUARDS WERE KILLED.
AT THIS RATE, IF WE'RE ATTACKED AGAIN...
...THE YOUNG MISS WILL BE IN DANGER.
SO COULD I TASK YOU ALL WITH GUARDING HER?
I HUMBLY BESEECH YOU.
A GUARD JOB, HUH?
WHY NOT? WE'RE HEADED TO THE CAPITAL ANYWAY.
I DON'T MIND EITHER.
I'M MERELY TAGGING ALONG, THAT I AM.
IT'S UP TO YOU.
OKAY, THEN WE ACCEPT.
WE'LL TRAVEL WITH YOU TO THE CAPITAL.
EXCELLENT! GOOD TO HAVE YOU ON BOARD!

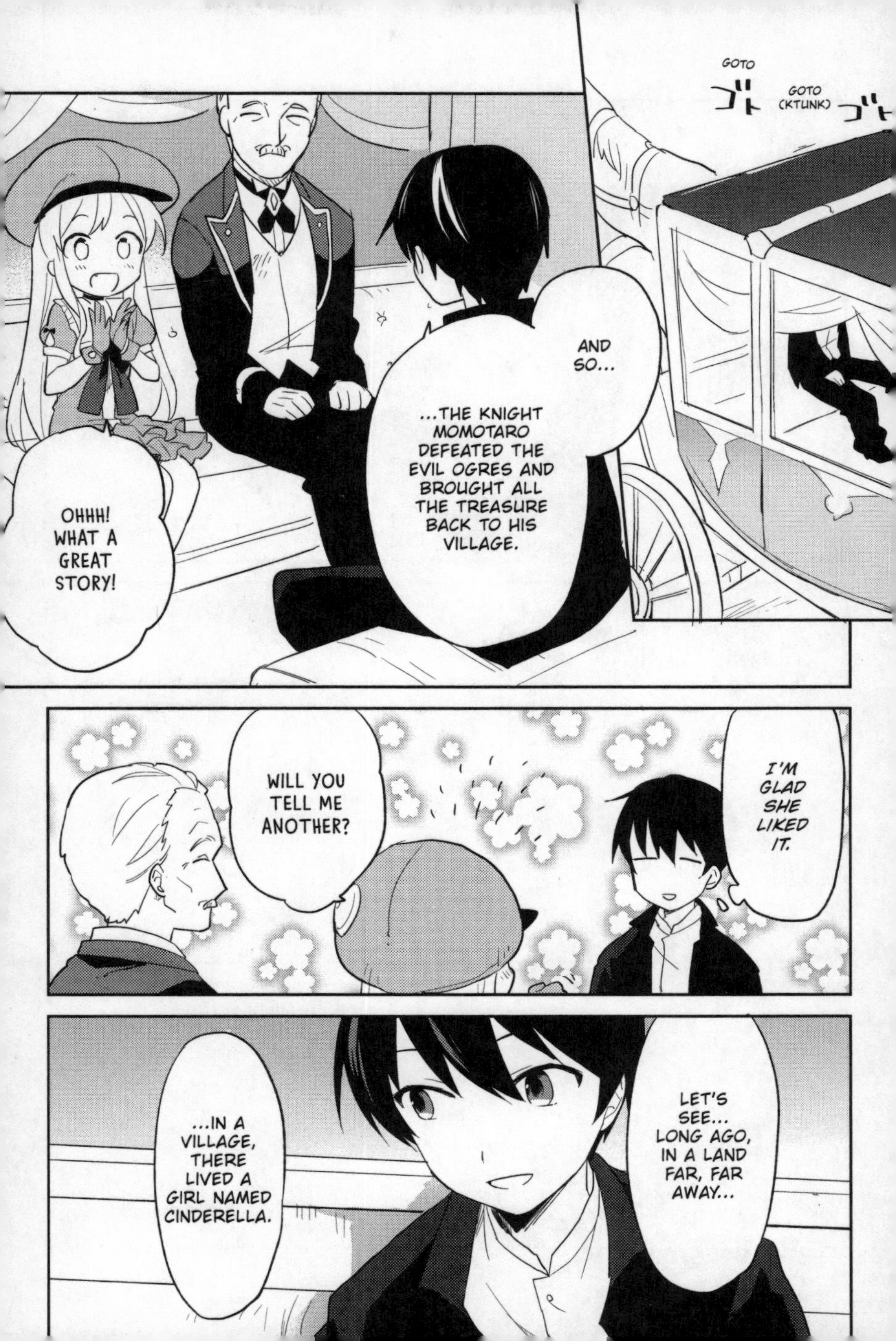
GOTO
GOTO (KTUNK)
ゴト ゴト
AND SO...
...THE KNIGHT MOMOTARO DEFEATED THE EVIL OGRES AND BROUGHT ALL THE TREASURE BACK TO HIS VILLAGE.
OHHH! WHAT A GREAT STORY!
I'M GLAD SHE LIKED IT.
WILL YOU TELL ME ANOTHER?
LET'S SEE... LONG AGO, IN A LAND FAR, FAR AWAY...
...IN A VILLAGE, THERE LIVED A GIRL NAMED CINDERELLA.

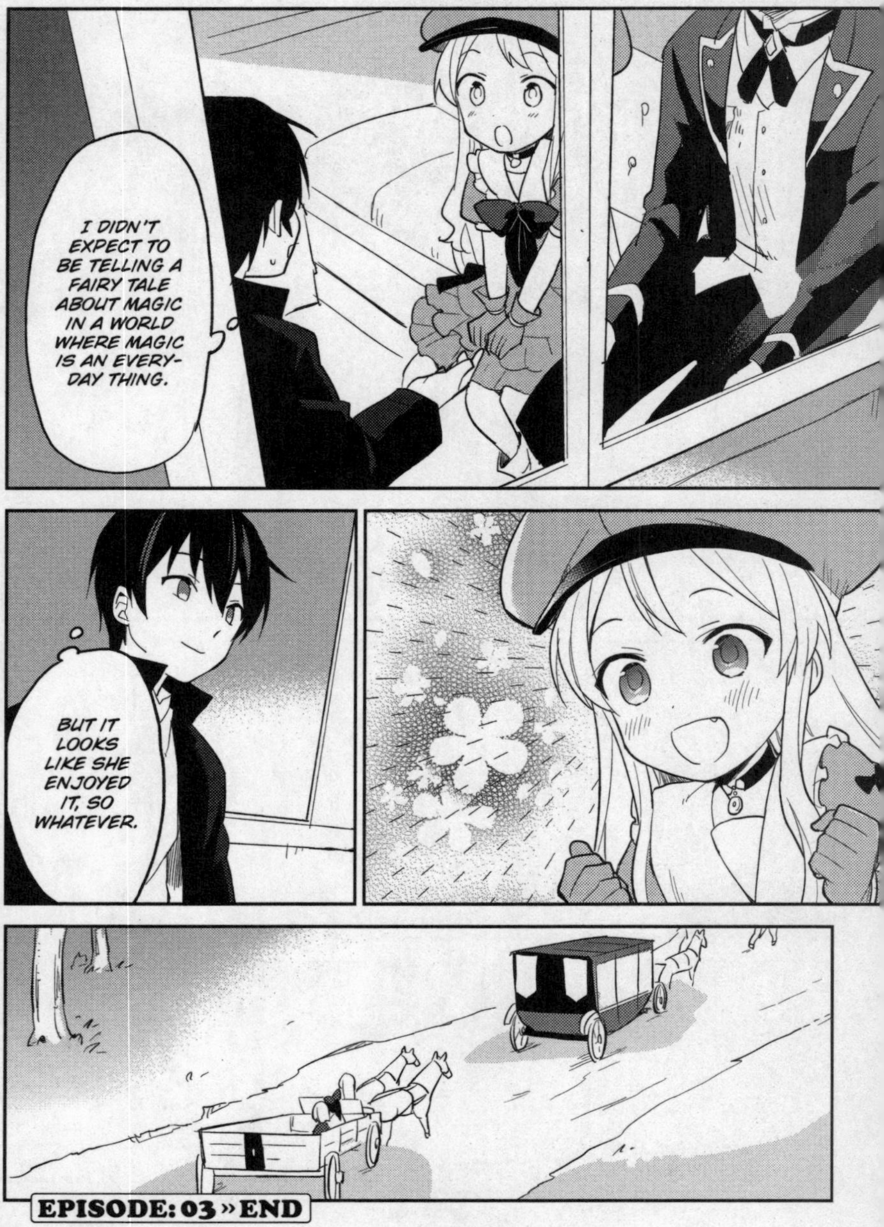
I DIDN'T EXPECT TO BE TELLING A FAIRY TALE ABOUT MAGIC IN A WORLD WHERE MAGIC IS AN EVERY-DAY THING.
BUT IT LOOKS LIKE SHE ENJOYED IT, SO WHATEVER.

EPISODE: 03 » END

In Another World With
My Smartphone

In Another World with My Smartphone

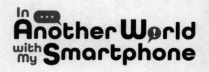

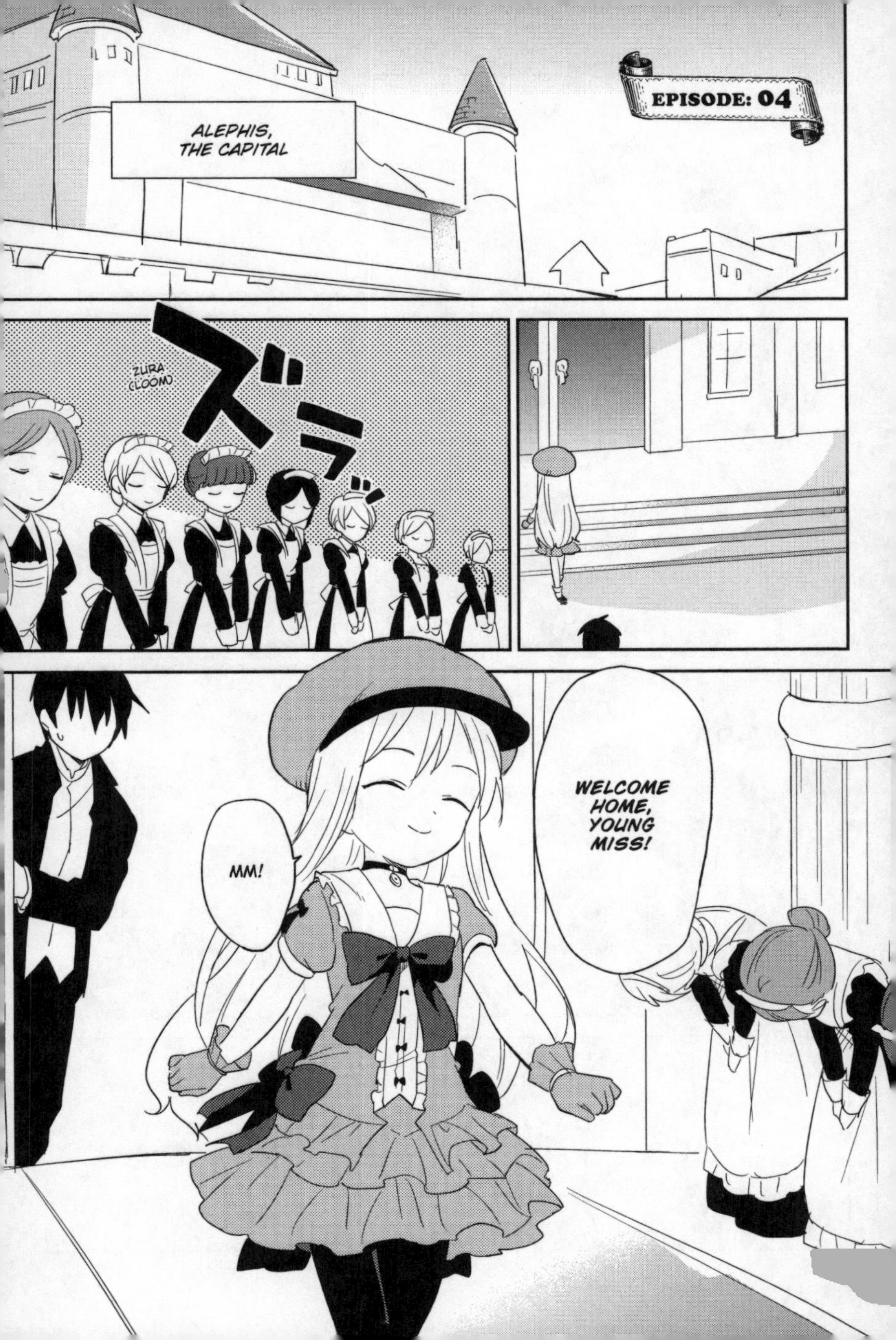
EPISODE: 04
ALEPHIS, THE CAPITAL
ズラ
ZURA (LOOM)
WELCOME HOME, YOUNG MISS!
MM!

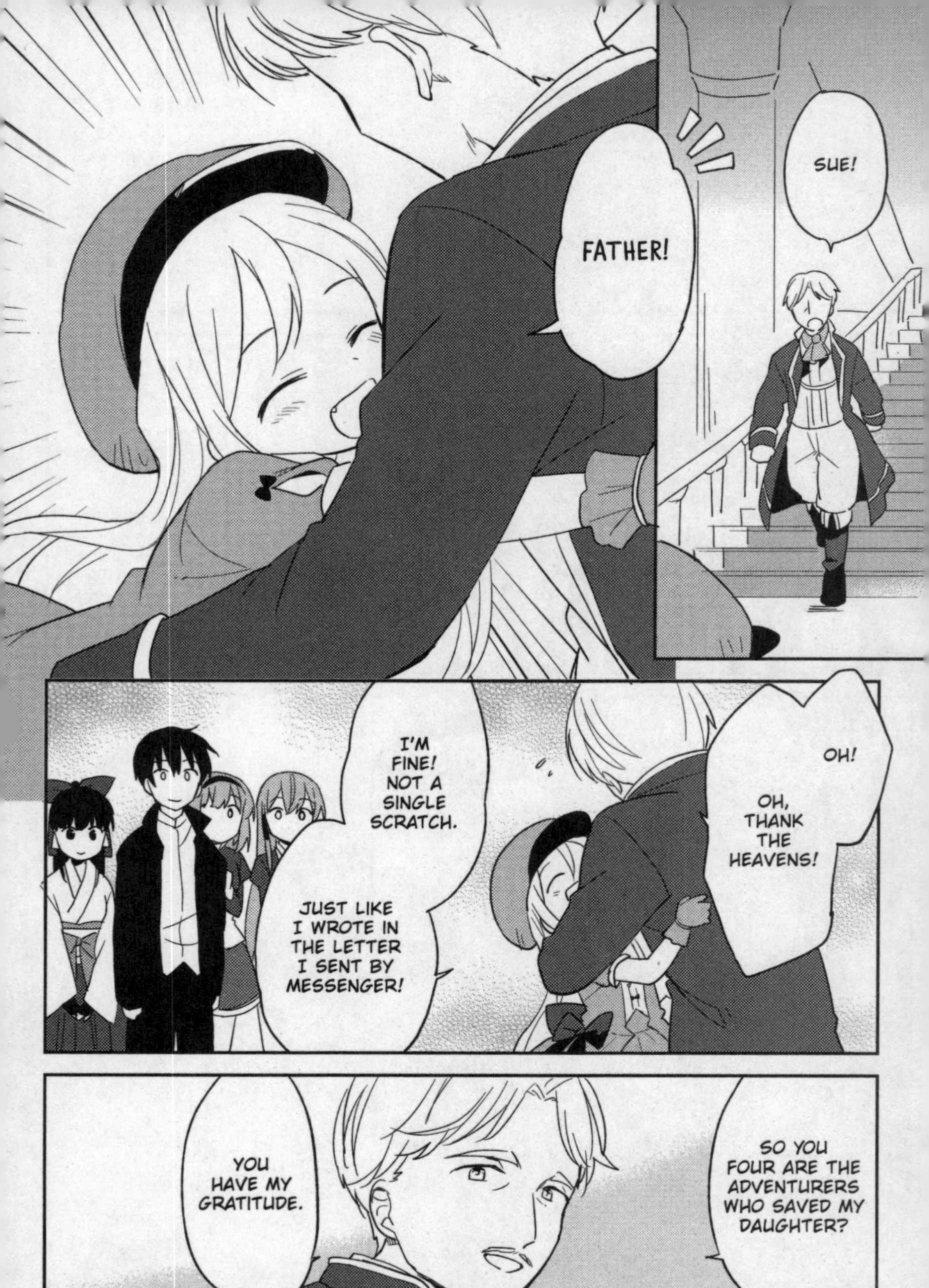
SUE!
FATHER!
OH!
OH, THANK THE HEAVENS!
I'M FINE! NOT A SINGLE SCRATCH.
JUST LIKE I WROTE IN THE LETTER I SENT BY MESSENGER!
SO YOU FOUR ARE THE ADVENTURERS WHO SAVED MY DAUGHTER?
YOU HAVE MY GRATITUDE.

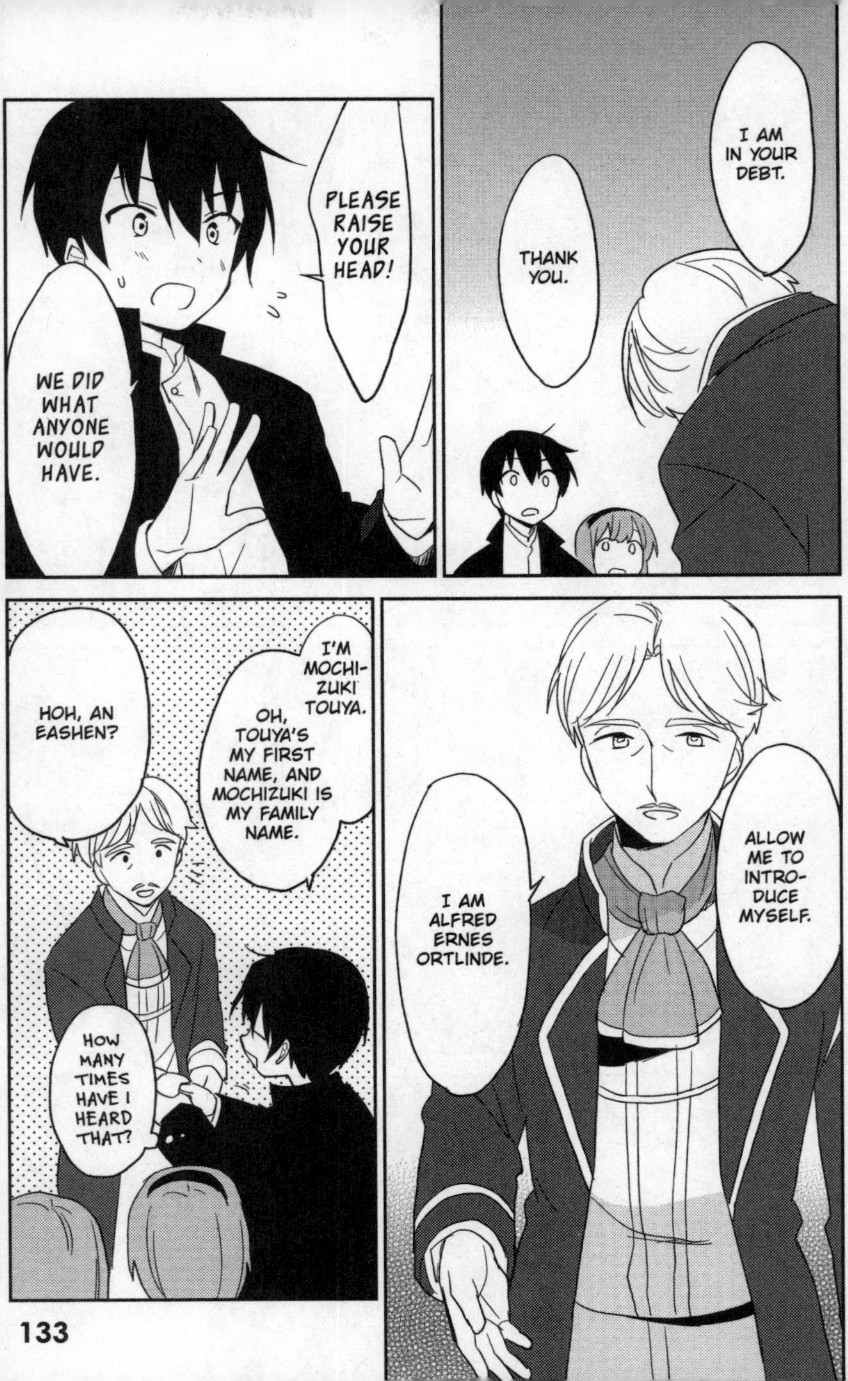
I AM IN YOUR DEBT.
THANK YOU.
PLEASE RAISE YOUR HEAD!
WE DID WHAT ANYONE WOULD HAVE.
ALLOW ME TO INTRODUCE MYSELF.
I AM ALFRED ERNES ORTLINDE.
I'M MOCHIZUKI TOUYA.
OH, TOUYA'S MY FIRST NAME, AND MOCHIZUKI IS MY FAMILY NAME.
HOH, AN EASHEN?
HOW MANY TIMES HAVE I HEARD THAT?

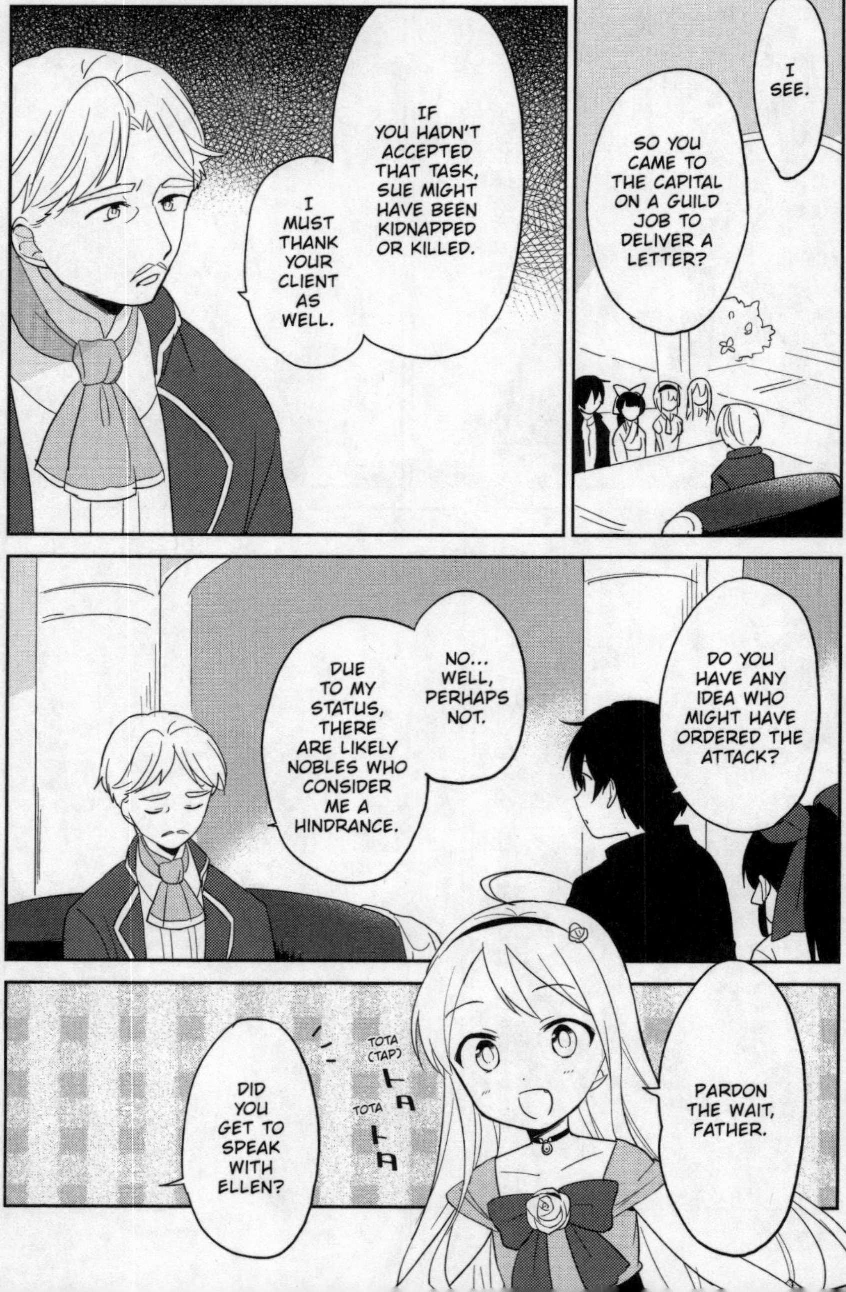
I SEE.
SO YOU CAME TO THE CAPITAL ON A GUILD JOB TO DELIVER A LETTER?
IF YOU HADN'T ACCEPTED THAT TASK, SUE MIGHT HAVE BEEN KIDNAPPED OR KILLED.
I MUST THANK YOUR CLIENT AS WELL.
DO YOU HAVE ANY IDEA WHO MIGHT HAVE ORDERED THE ATTACK?
NO... WELL, PERHAPS NOT.
DUE TO MY STATUS, THERE ARE LIKELY NOBLES WHO CONSIDER ME A HINDRANCE.
PARDON THE WAIT, FATHER.
TOTA (TAP) TOTA
DID YOU GET TO SPEAK WITH ELLEN?

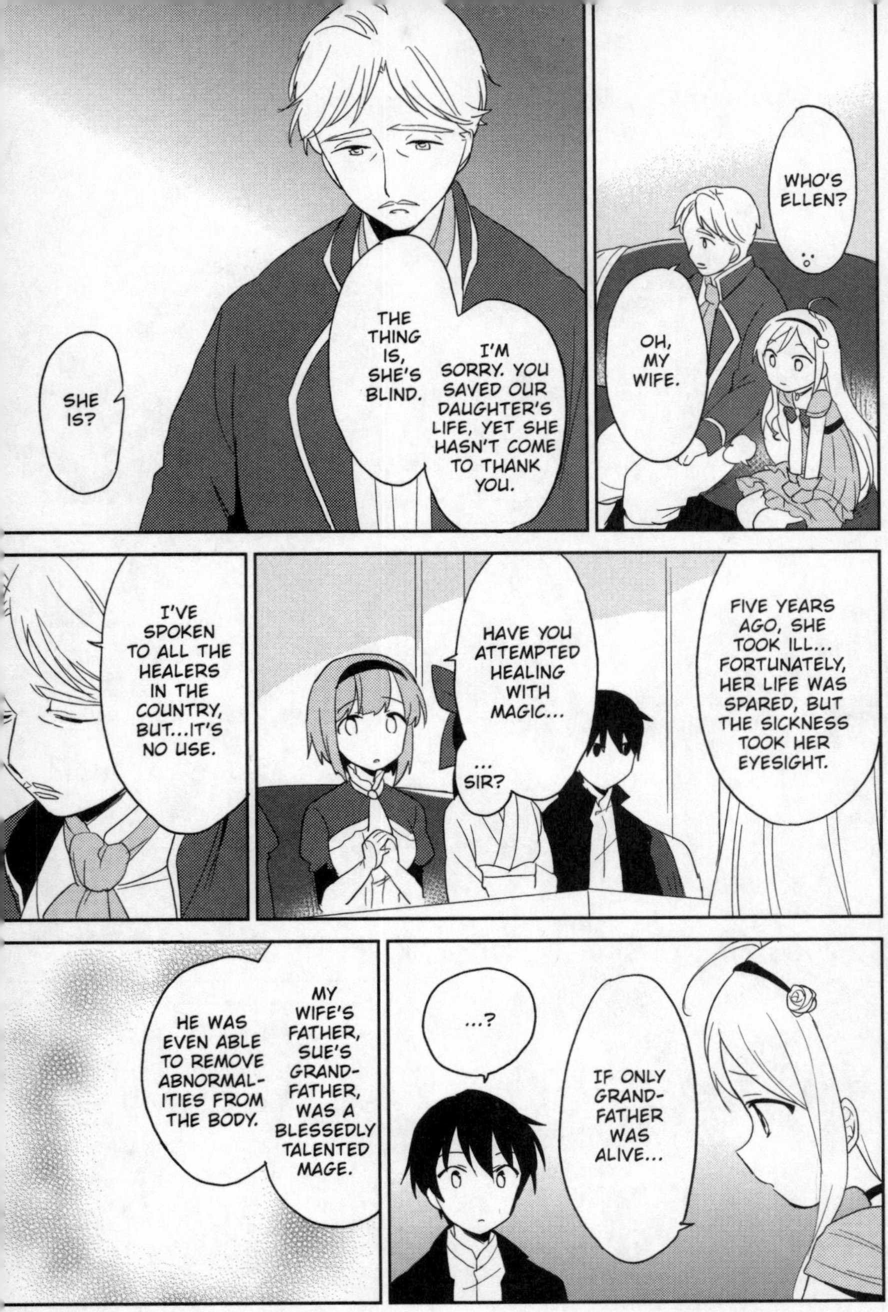
WHO'S ELLEN?
OH, MY WIFE.
I'M SORRY. YOU SAVED OUR DAUGHTER'S LIFE, YET SHE HASN'T COME TO THANK YOU.
THE THING IS, SHE'S BLIND.
SHE IS?
FIVE YEARS AGO, SHE TOOK ILL... FORTUNATELY, HER LIFE WAS SPARED, BUT THE SICKNESS TOOK HER EYESIGHT.
HAVE YOU ATTEMPTED HEALING WITH MAGIC...
...SIR?
I'VE SPOKEN TO ALL THE HEALERS IN THE COUNTRY, BUT...IT'S NO USE.
IF ONLY GRANDFATHER WAS ALIVE...
...?
MY WIFE'S FATHER, SUE'S GRANDFATHER, WAS A BLESSEDLY TALENTED MAGE.
HE WAS EVEN ABLE TO REMOVE ABNORMALITIES FROM THE BODY.

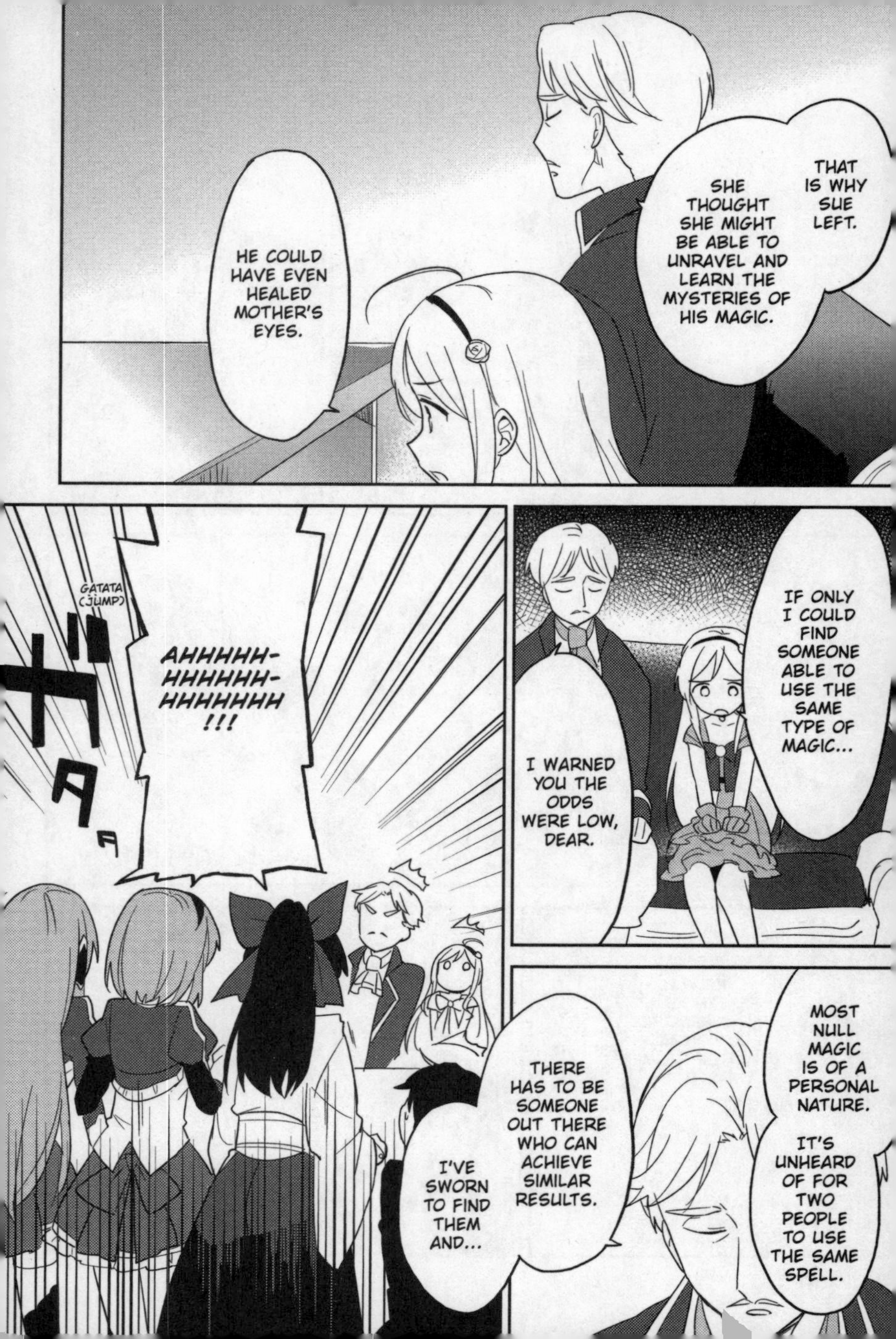
THAT IS WHY SUE LEFT.
SHE THOUGHT SHE MIGHT BE ABLE TO UNRAVEL AND LEARN THE MYSTERIES OF HIS MAGIC.
HE COULD HAVE EVEN HEALED MOTHER'S EYES.
IF ONLY I COULD FIND SOMEONE ABLE TO USE THE SAME TYPE OF MAGIC...
I WARNED YOU THE ODDS WERE LOW, DEAR.
MOST NULL MAGIC IS OF A PERSONAL NATURE.
IT'S UNHEARD OF FOR TWO PEOPLE TO USE THE SAME SPELL.
THERE HAS TO BE SOMEONE OUT THERE WHO CAN ACHIEVE SIMILAR RESULTS.
I'VE SWORN TO FIND THEM AND...
AHHHHH-HHHHHH-HHHHHHH!!!
ガタタ
GATATA (JUMP)

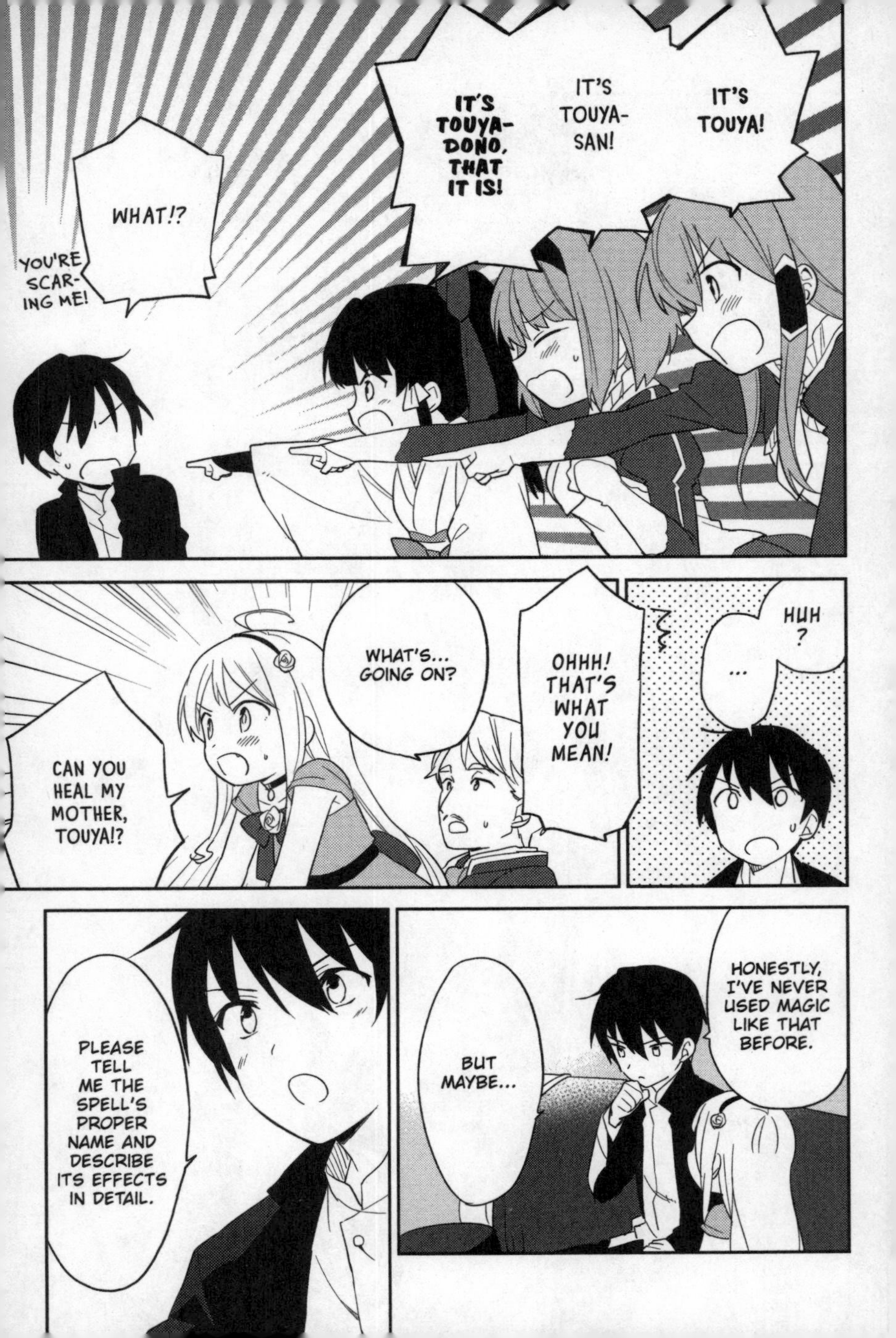
IT'S TOUYA!
IT'S TOUYA-SAN!
IT'S TOUYA-DONO, THAT IT IS!
WHAT!?
YOU'RE SCARING ME!
HUH? ...
OHHH! THAT'S WHAT YOU MEAN!
WHAT'S... GOING ON?
CAN YOU HEAL MY MOTHER, TOUYA!?
HONESTLY, I'VE NEVER USED MAGIC LIKE THAT BEFORE.
BUT MAYBE...
PLEASE TELL ME THE SPELL'S PROPER NAME AND DESCRIBE ITS EFFECTS IN DETAIL.

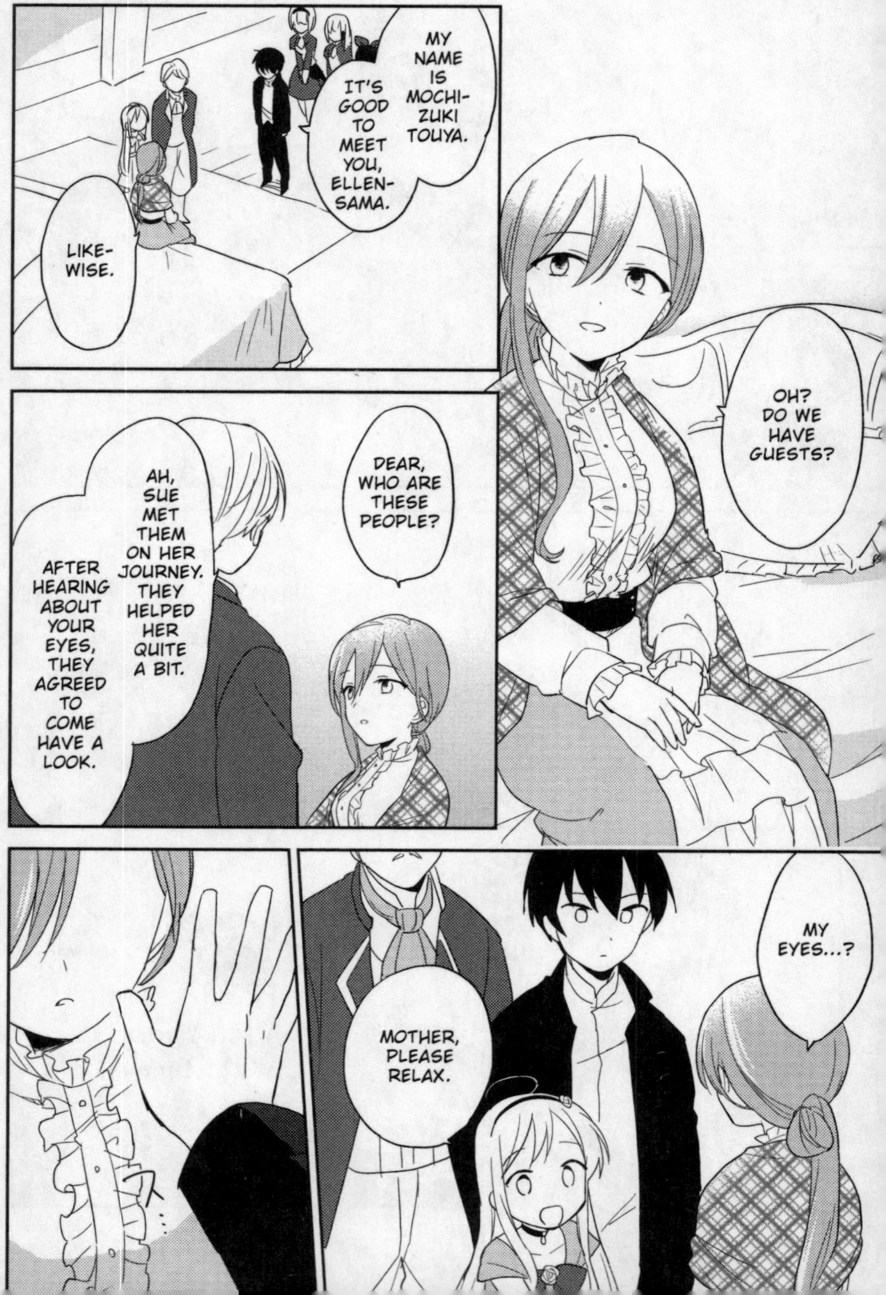
OH? DO WE HAVE GUESTS?
MY NAME IS MOCHI-ZUKI TOUYA.
IT'S GOOD TO MEET YOU, ELLEN-SAMA.
LIKE-WISE.
DEAR, WHO ARE THESE PEOPLE?
AH, SUE MET THEM ON HER JOURNEY. THEY HELPED HER QUITE A BIT.
AFTER HEARING ABOUT YOUR EYES, THEY AGREED TO COME HAVE A LOOK.
MY EYES...?
MOTHER, PLEASE RELAX.

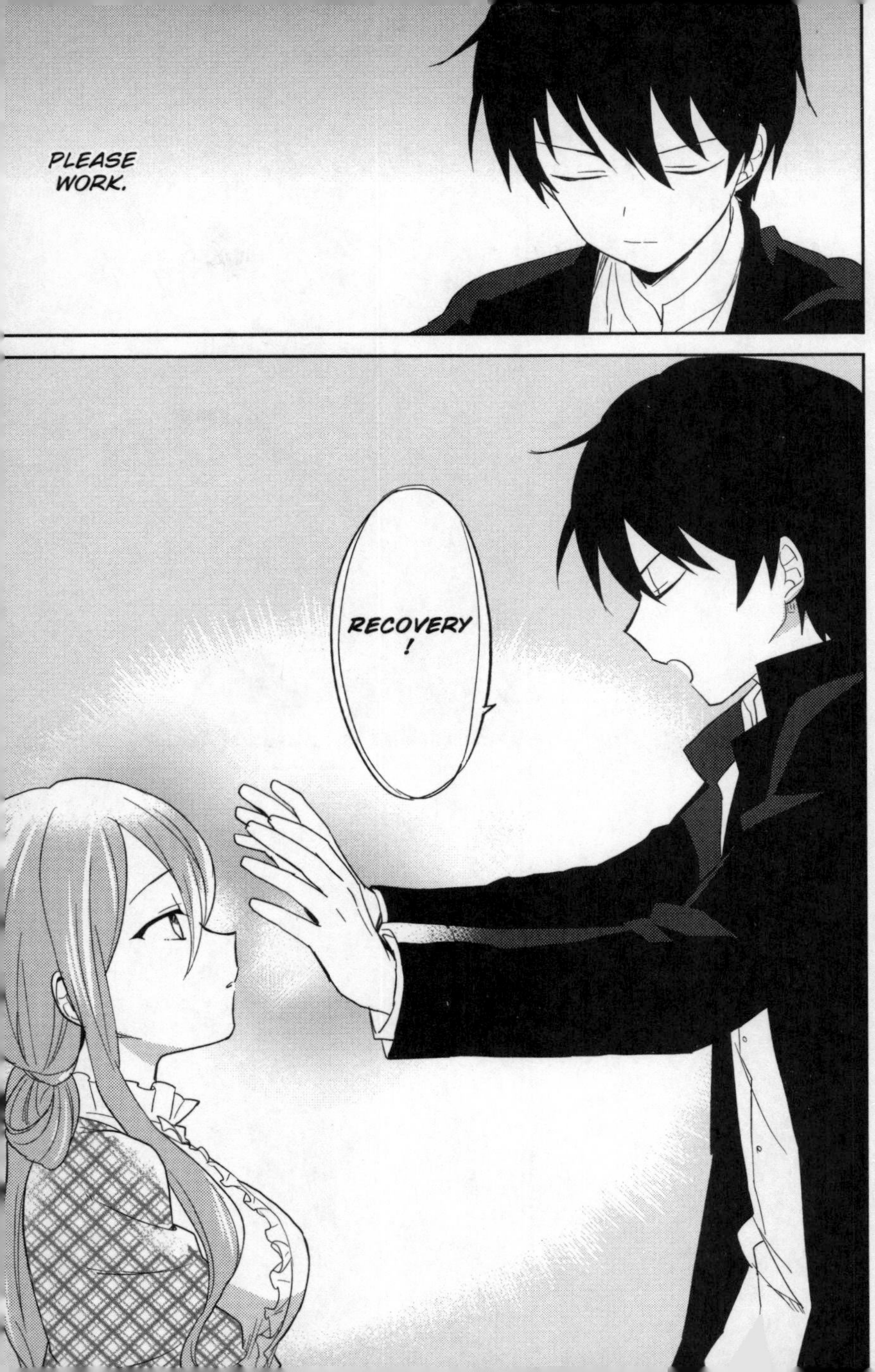
PLEASE WORK.
RECOVERY!

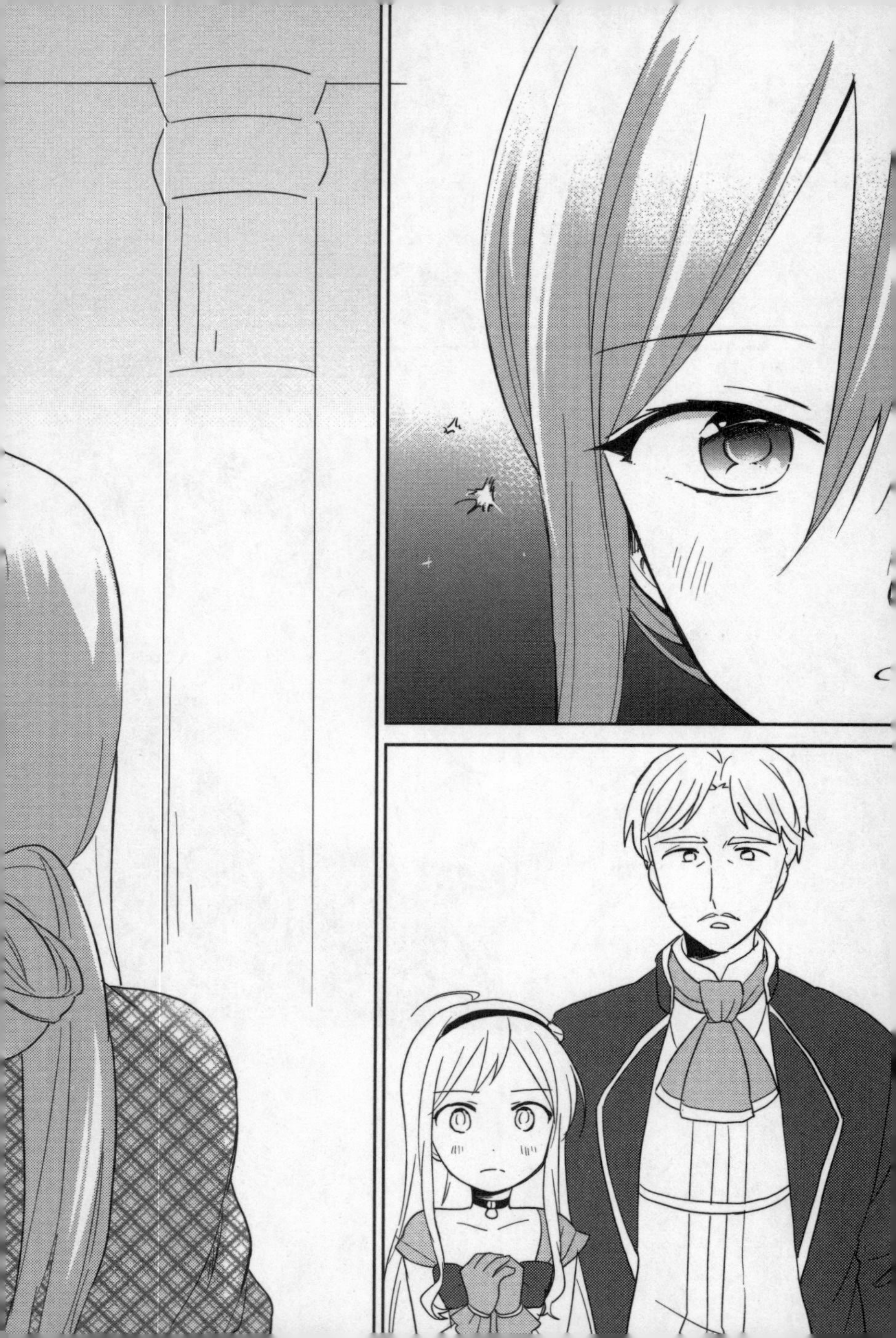

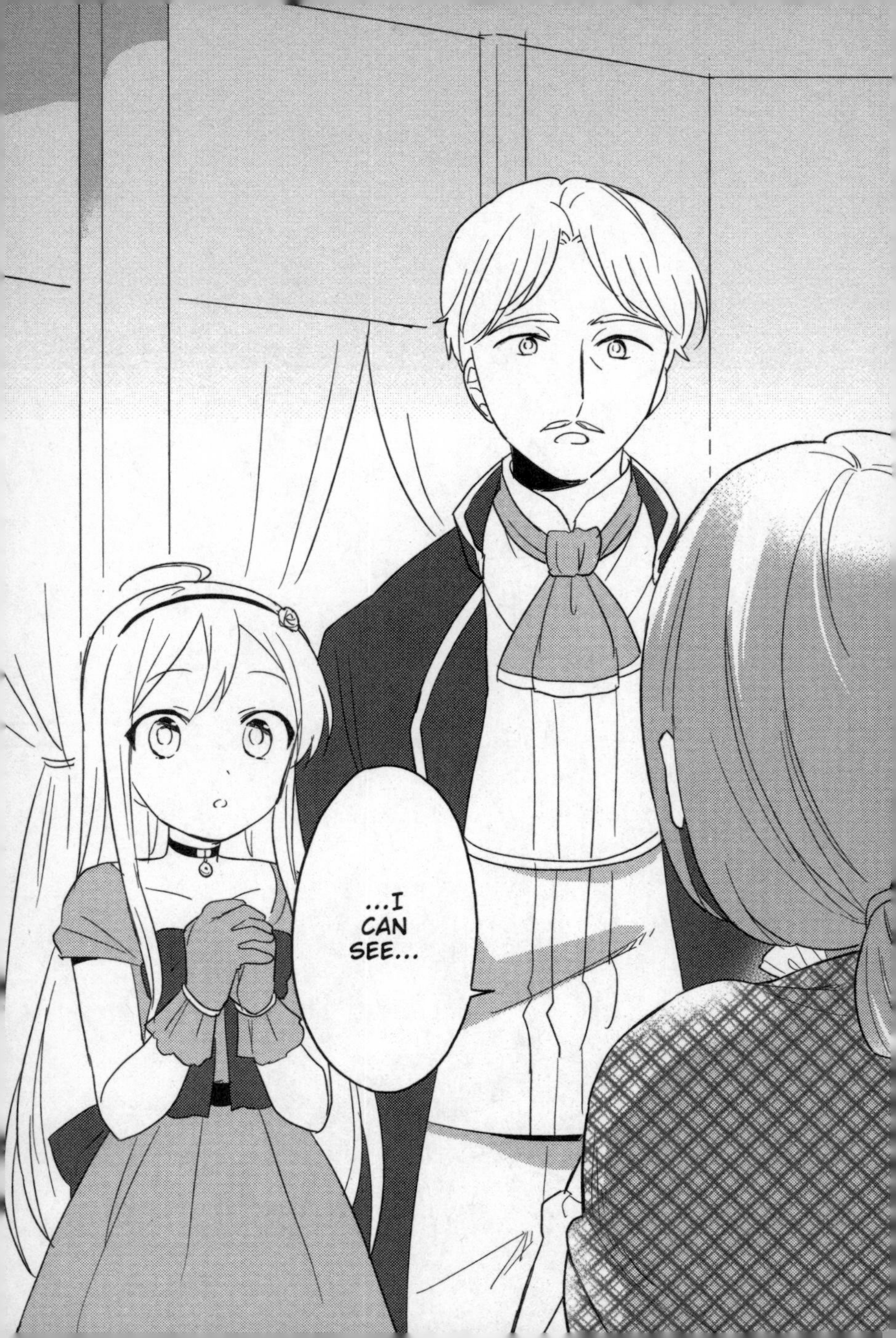
...I CAN SEE...

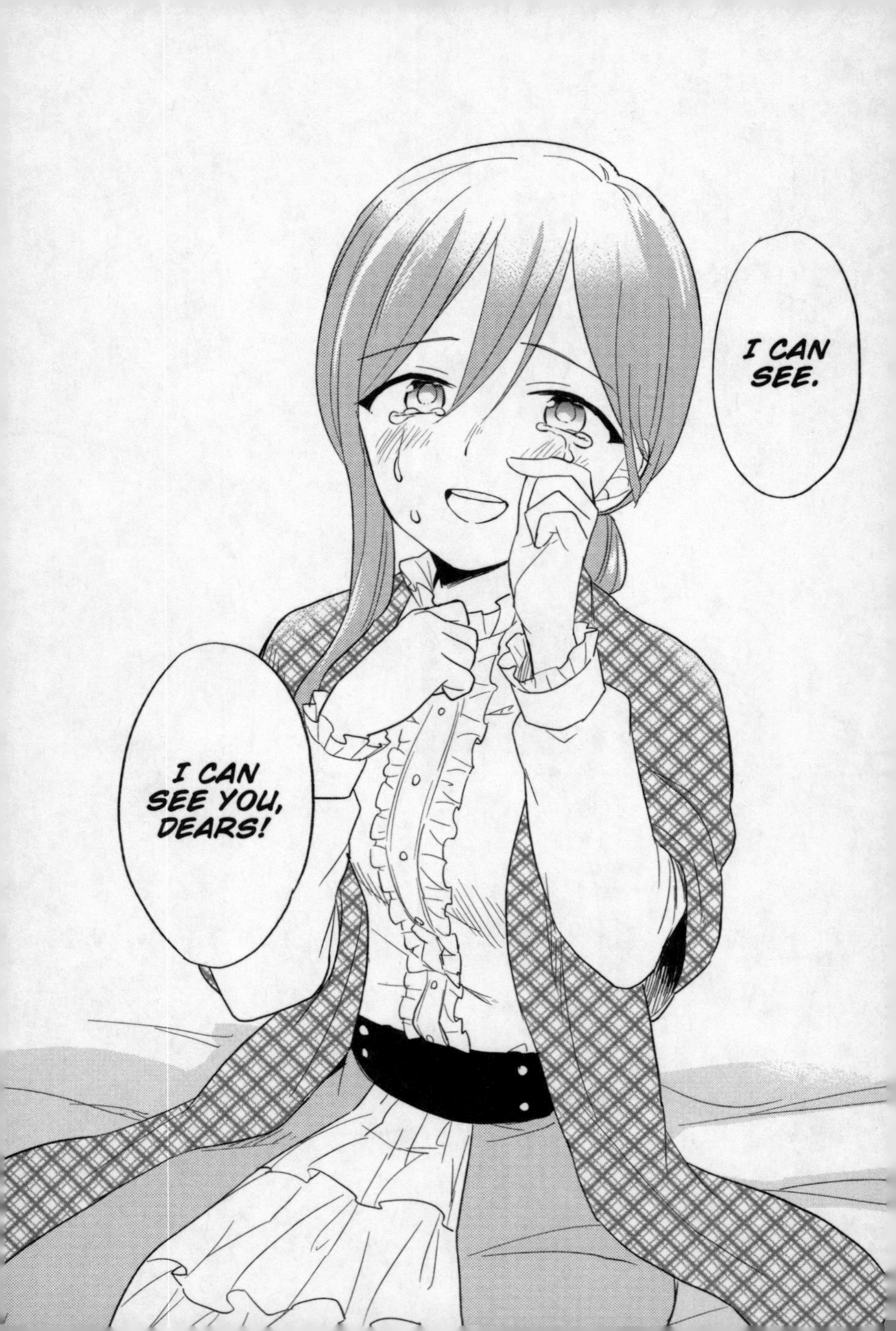
I CAN SEE.
I CAN SEE YOU, DEARS!

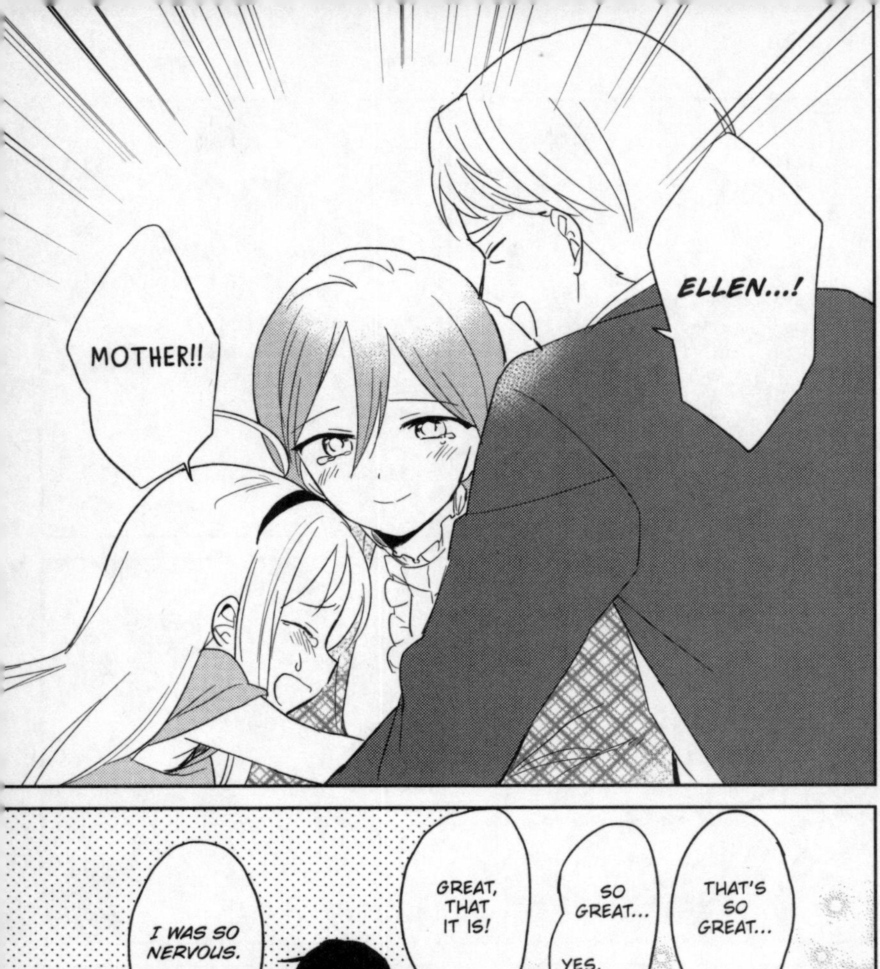
ELLEN...!
MOTHER!!
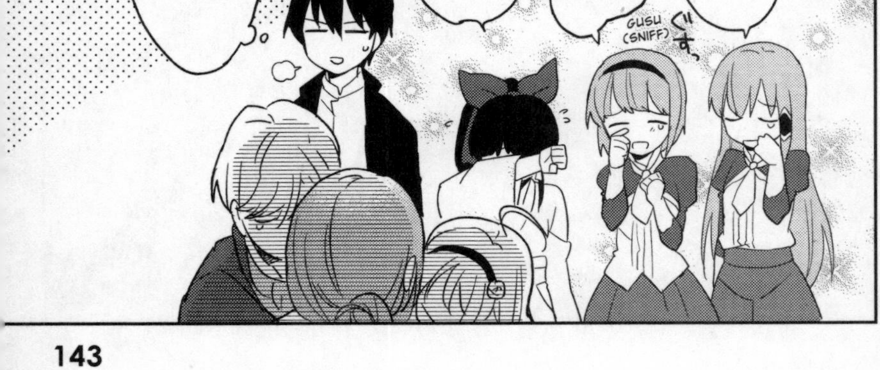
THAT'S SO GREAT...
GUSU (SNIFF)
SO GREAT... YES.
GREAT, THAT IT IS!
I WAS SO NERVOUS.

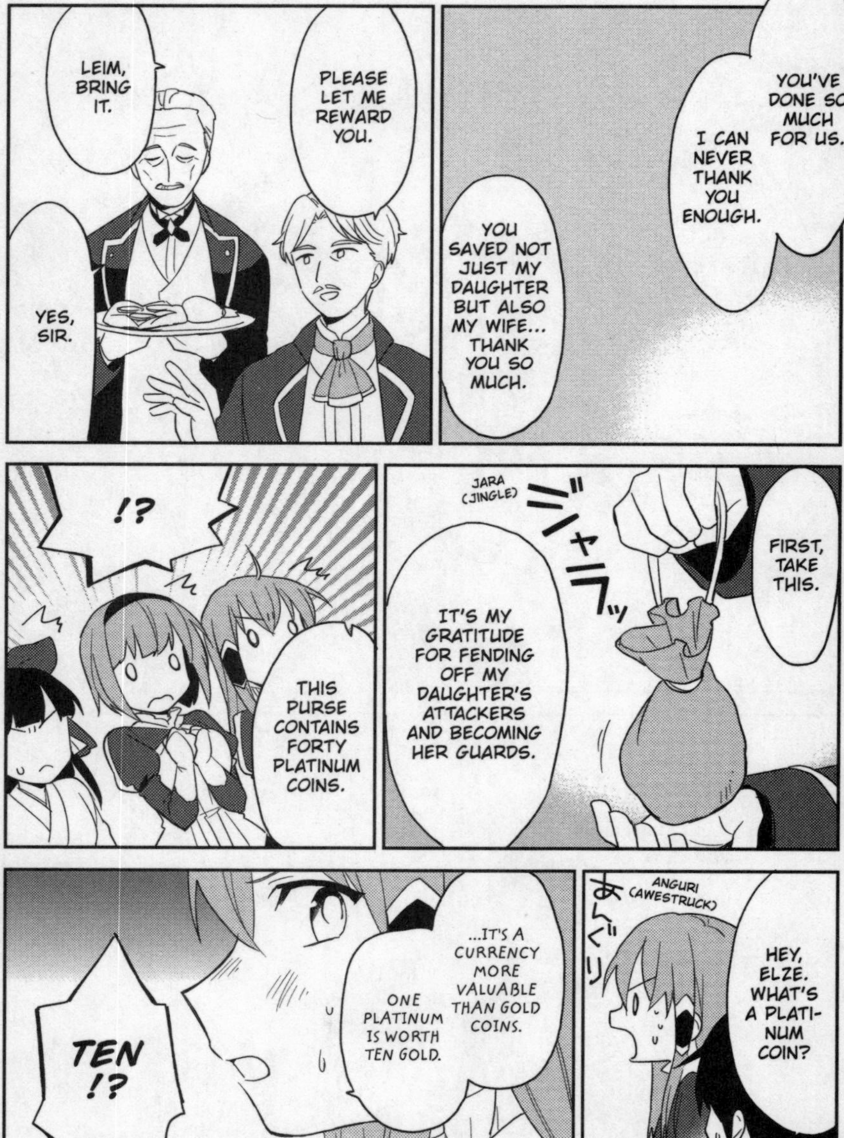
YOU'VE DONE SO MUCH FOR US.
I CAN NEVER THANK YOU ENOUGH.
YOU SAVED NOT JUST MY DAUGHTER BUT ALSO MY WIFE... THANK YOU SO MUCH.
PLEASE LET ME REWARD YOU.
LEIM, BRING IT.
YES, SIR.
FIRST, TAKE THIS.
ジャラッ
JARA (JINGLE)
IT'S MY GRATITUDE FOR FENDING OFF MY DAUGHTER'S ATTACKERS AND BECOMING HER GUARDS.
THIS PURSE CONTAINS FORTY PLATINUM COINS.
!?
HEY, ELZE. WHAT'S A PLATI-NUM COIN?
あんぐり
ANGURI (AWESTRUCK)
...IT'S A CURRENCY MORE VALUABLE THAN GOLD COINS.
ONE PLATINUM IS WORTH TEN GOLD.
TEN !?

In Another World with My Smartphone ①

Art • **Soto**   Original Story • **Patora Fuyuhara**

Character Design: Eiji Usatsuka

Translation: Alexander Keller-Nelson | Lettering: Chiho Christie

ISEKAI WA SMART PHONE TO TOMONI. Vol. 1
©Soto 2017
©Patora Fuyuhara
First published in Japan in 2017 by KADOKAWA CORPORATION, Tokyo. English translation rights arranged with KADOKAWA CORPORATION, Tokyo through Tuttle-Mori Agency, Inc., Tokyo.

English translation © 2021 by Yen Press, LLC

Yen Press
150 West 30th Street, 19th Floor
New York, NY 10001

Visit us!
yenpress.com • facebook.com/yenpress • twitter.com/yenpress
yenpress.tumblr.com • instagram.com/yenpress

First Yen Press Edition: March 2021

Yen Press is an imprint of Yen Press, LLC.
The Yen Press name and logo are trademarks of Yen Press, LLC.

Library of Congress Control Number: 2020951871

ISBNs: 978-1-9753-2103-1 (paperback)
978-1-9753-2104-8 (ebook)

10 9 8 7 6 5 4 3 2 1

WOR

Printed in the United States of America

In Another World with
My Smartphone

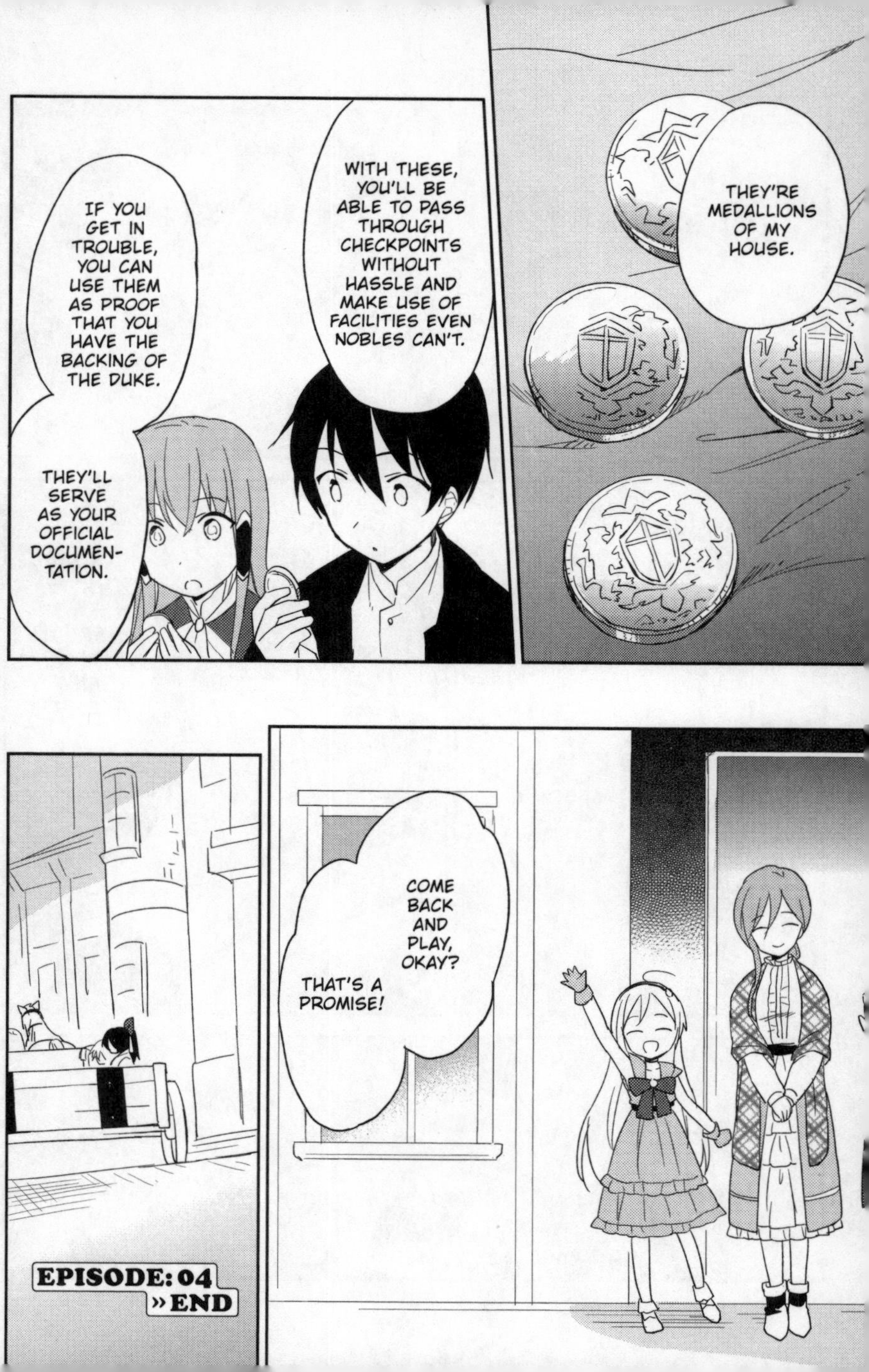
THEY'RE MEDALLIONS OF MY HOUSE.
WITH THESE, YOU'LL BE ABLE TO PASS THROUGH CHECKPOINTS WITHOUT HASSLE AND MAKE USE OF FACILITIES EVEN NOBLES CAN'T.
IF YOU GET IN TROUBLE, YOU CAN USE THEM AS PROOF THAT YOU HAVE THE BACKING OF THE DUKE.
THEY'LL SERVE AS YOUR OFFICIAL DOCUMENTATION.
COME BACK AND PLAY, OKAY?
THAT'S A PROMISE!
EPISODE: 04
» END

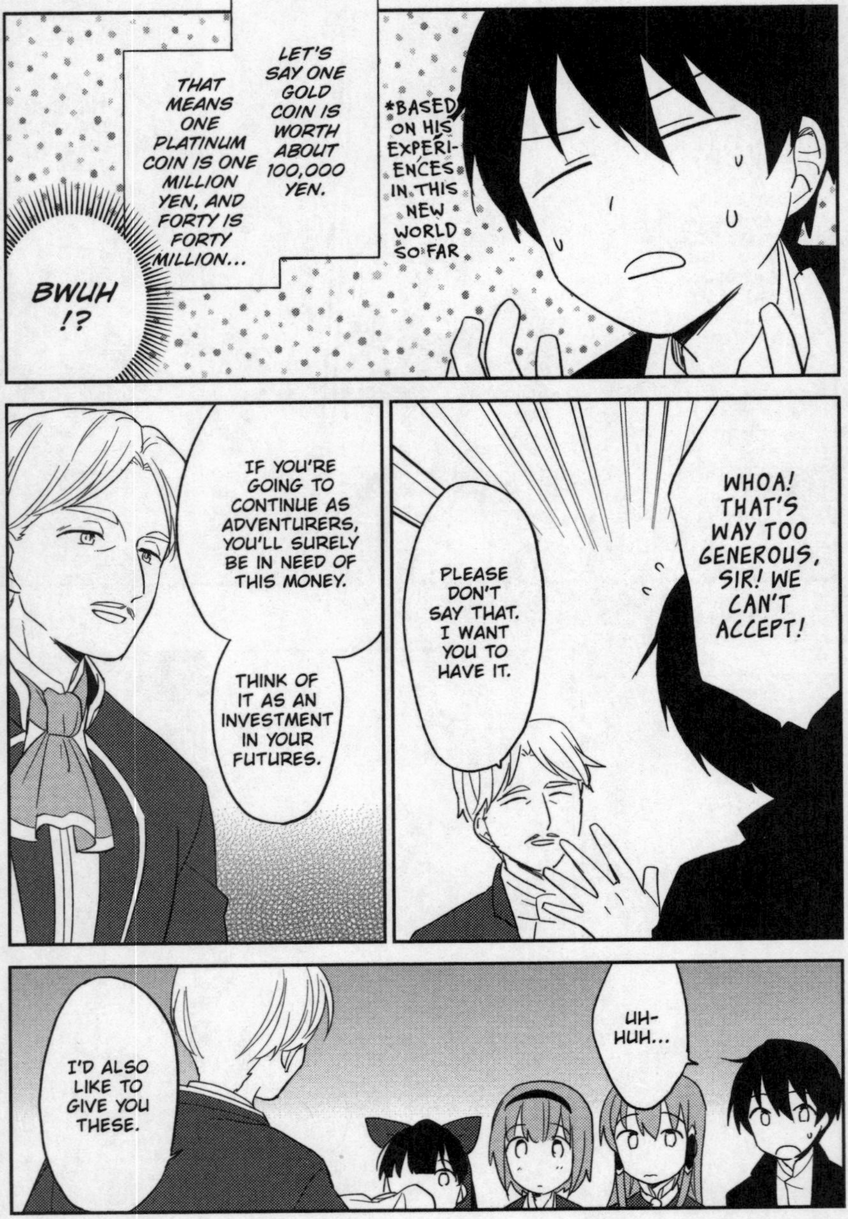
*BASED ON HIS EXPERIENCES IN THIS NEW WORLD SO FAR
LET'S SAY ONE GOLD COIN IS WORTH ABOUT 100,000 YEN.
THAT MEANS ONE PLATINUM COIN IS ONE MILLION YEN, AND FORTY IS FORTY MILLION...
BWUH !?
WHOA! THAT'S WAY TOO GENEROUS, SIR! WE CAN'T ACCEPT!
PLEASE DON'T SAY THAT. I WANT YOU TO HAVE IT.
IF YOU'RE GOING TO CONTINUE AS ADVENTURERS, YOU'LL SURELY BE IN NEED OF THIS MONEY.
THINK OF IT AS AN INVESTMENT IN YOUR FUTURES.
UH-HUH...
I'D ALSO LIKE TO GIVE YOU THESE.